THE ARMS CONTROL DELUSION

THE
ARMS CONTROL
DELUSION

Senator Malcolm Wallop
and
Angelo Codevilla

ICS PRESS

ICS

Institute for Contemporary Studies
San Francisco, California

Inquiries, book orders, and catalogue requests should be addressed to ICS Press, Institute for Contemporary Studies, 243 Kearny Street, San Francisco, California, 94108. (415) 981-5353.

Distributed to the trade by Kampmann & Co., New York.

Book design and production by Marian Hartsough.

Library of Congress Cataloging-in-Publication Data

Wallop, Malcolm
   The arms control delusion.

   Includes index.
   1. Arms control. 2. Nuclear arms control—United States. 3. Nuclear arms control—Soviet Union.
4. United States—National Security. I. Codevilla, Angelo M., 1943–　. II. Title.
JX1974.W238 1987　　327.1'74　　87-22562
ISBN 0-917616-91-X

Table of Contents

Acknowledgments   vii

Preface   ix

CHAPTER 1   Introduction   2

CHAPTER 2   Why Arms Control?   13

CHAPTER 3   Substituting for Reality   40

CHAPTER 4   What We Expected from the Treaties   87

CHAPTER 5   What We Got   110

CHAPTER 6   The Reagan Administration, Sincerity, and Arms Control   134

CHAPTER 7   Reykjavik and Beyond   174

CHAPTER 8   The Necessity for Choice   197

Notes   207

Index   213

Acknowledgments

The authors wish to thank Paul Weyrich of the Free Congress Foundation for insistently asking us the questions to which this book is an answer, and for help in the early stages of the research. The authors are also grateful to Glenn Campbell and the Hoover Institution for the intellectual and material support that made it possible to finish the book. We thank William Van Cleave, Mark Schneider, and Thomas Blau for reading the manuscript, and Betty Oates of the Hoover Institution for typing it. Of course we alone are responsible for the book's content.

Malcolm Wallop
Angelo Codevilla
September 1987

Preface

In the past ten years the Institute for Contemporary Studies has published several studies of defense and national security issues that have been at the forefront of public debate. In 1977, *Defending America* expressed alarm at the rapid Soviet military buildup during the post-Vietnam period. In 1980, *National Security in the 1980s: From Weakness to Strength* offered a blueprint for fundamental reconsideration of defense policy in the wake of the Iranian hostage fiasco and the Soviet invasion of Afghanistan. Edward Luttwak's *The Pentagon and the Art of War*, published by the Institute in 1985, is credited with being the single-greatest force in the bipartisan Pentagon reform movement.

But no issue of national security has engaged public concern as much as nuclear arms. In 1984 the Institute published *Nuclear Arms: Ethics, Strategy, Politics*, edited by R. James Woolsey, which clarified the moral and strategic issues the country faced with regard to nuclear weapons. Since that time debate has continued, particularly over arms control and the Strategic Defense Initiative, and it is clear that these issues will assume even greater importance in next few years.

For this reason, the Institute believes that even those who have great faith in arms control should read the work of Senator Malcolm Wallop and Angelo Codevilla, two of the nation's most incisive strategic analysts. Their critique of the "arms control process," which they argue is increasingly the product of American naiveté and Soviet improbity, is plain-spoken and provocative. *The Arms Control Delusion* asks crucial questions about national security that can no longer be ignored.

Works published by the Institute for Contemporary Studies have helped set the terms of debate over national security in the past ten years. *The Arms Control Delusion* is certain to promote deeper thought about this, the crucial issue of our time.

—Robert B. Hawkins, Jr.
President,
Institute for Contemporary Studies

September, 1987
San Francisco, California

THE ARMS CONTROL DELUSION

1

Introduction

How the arms control process, born out of fear, abstraction from reality, and demagogy, promised a safer world but produced precisely the reverse.

How, then, American arms controllers gave up any vestige of pretenses about being able to control Soviet behavior and convinced the Reagan administration — in the name of arms control — to transform their private dreams into American unilateral policy. This book is an attempt to understand how and why all this has happened.

This is not a conventional treatment of arms control. Most writings on arms control are by liberals. They try to show that without agreement between the U.S. and the Soviet Union to reduce, freeze, or even slow down the growth of strategic arsenals, life on this planet will become too dangerous, or at any rate, intolerable. Paradoxically, those writings try to show that the Soviet Union does not pose so much of a threat to us as many believe, and that this giant military power is really quite willing to reduce that threat if only we will bring the appropriate inducements to the negotiating table. A few writings on arms control are by conservatives. They argue that we have brought too many concessions to the negotiating table, that we have struck bad bargains with the Soviets, that the Soviets have cheated, that the Soviet threat is worse than many believe, that we must insist on compliance, and that our negotiating positions must be "tougher and more realistic." Liberal and conservative tracts alike argue about the ceilings and subceilings on missiles, launchers, and warheads in agreements and proposals, as though the figures reliably represent either side's war-fighting forces and as though they reflect, on their face, an agreement by both sides that such forces shall be sufficient. We believe that all such treatments of arms control are as meaningless as they are boring.

Our treatment flows from neither liberalism nor conservatism. We believe that it flows from common sense. Since we have dealt with the intelligence systems and procedures by which the U.S. government arrives at tentative counts and evaluations of Soviet weaponry, and since we are painfully aware of the limits of the U.S. government's knowledge of these matters, we eschew numerology. Having observed the changes that the application of modern tech-

nology has wrought on weaponry, we cannot treat such weapons
as anything but the dreadfully real military tools they are. We note
that during the quarter century during which arms control has been
in the forefront of our national agenda, a massive change in the balance of power between the U.S. and Soviet arsenals has taken place
in favor of the Soviet Union, and that, by all measures, the danger
of war is greater now than when the arms control process began.

idiots

More important, because so many Americans have been preoc-
cupied with the notion of arms control, the U.S. has built an arsenal
peculiarly suited not to defending itself, but, rather, to senseless
destruction. Hence we set out to explain how it has come to be that
talk of arms control, the so-called "arms control process," more than
arms control agreements themselves, has produced very nearly the
opposite of what the American advocates of arms control have said
they meant to accomplish. We will show that those Americans who
support arms control do so regardless of what it has accomplished,
and regardless of what it can realistically be expected to accomplish
in the future. Marx once called religion "the opiate of the people."
His modern Soviet heirs have far more reason to observe that talk
of arms control is an opiate that some Americans administer unto
others. When American politicians ask, "Do you believe in arms
control?" it becomes clear that the whole matter has taken on theo-
logical trappings.

We mean to show that the "arms control process" between the
U.S. and the Soviet Union is a delusion foisted by some Americans
upon other Americans, and perhaps on themselves. This book is
an account of how the arms control process arose out of a combination of a little fear, a generous sprinkling of utopian ideology, and
apparently inexpensive demagogy and arrogance. It shows how the
process matured by magically transforming fundamental military
problems and political conflicts into the technicalities of monitoring trivialities through exotic technology.

The book follows the "process" as America's leading public
figures invested their political fortunes in it by concluding treaties
that, they claimed, solved America's strategic problems and en-
meshed the Soviet Union in a web of cooperation. Then we briefly

turn to reality, showing that the military forces the Soviet Union has built—by a few violations, much evasion, but mostly within the treaties, if loosely interpreted—have become precisely the ones we had sought to avoid by entering into the arms control process in the first place. This realization helped to elect the Reagan administration and placed before it the tasks of repairing the harm that a decade of arms control had done to our defenses and of dispelling the illusion.

Perhaps the primary element of this delusion is that arms control agreements can influence Soviet behavior. But in fact, since no one can propose any means of making the Soviet Union comply more faithfully with future agreements than it has with past ones, the Reagan administration has found it difficult to state precisely how arms control agreements would constrain a Soviet Union bent on military superiority. Thus the administration now skirts this topic entirely and has made arms control an integral part of its domestic policy and of its policy toward America's European allies. So, despite an early flood of dollars, and of words about reversing the ideology upon which arms control had been based, the Reagan administration is allowing the United States' strategic situation vis-à-vis the Soviet Union to worsen indefinitely. Moreover, it does so while rebuilding the notion, legitimately and badly battered in public opinion in the late 1970s, that arms control is essential to peace.

We then examine the Reagan administration's efforts to prove its sincerity toward arms control—by not telling the truth about it, even by its own lights. These efforts, meant to deflect criticism from the administration's military program, have in fact reduced that program's potentially most consequential element, SDI, to mere research. We also show that in its attempts to display "sincerity," the Reagan administration has declared itself in favor of arrangements that neither it nor any American administration would ever carry out—e.g., the abolition of nuclear weapons—and thereby has made itself vulnerable to the Soviet Union's arms control proposals of 1986. The administration dares not accept them, but cannot reject them without impeaching its own record in arms control.

Thus, the administration is reduced to quibbling with the pro-

posals while continuing to grant to the Soviet leaders the credentials of men of goodwill interested in a good agreement, credentials
that the Soviets use to point up the contradictions in the Reagan
administration. The result is a continued ratcheting down of
America's strategic forces relative to the threat facing them, and the
consignment of SDI to never-never land. Thus the book concludes
that arms control, while shorn of any realistic hopes of constraining the Soviet Union to solve our strategic problems for us, has
become neither more nor less than a fact of our domestic political life.

In 1985 there was a controversy in the U.S. over whether to live
by the "restrictive" interpretation of the ABM Treaty, which American arms controllers favor but which the Soviets never agreed to,
or by a "permissive" interpretation, which accounts for many Soviet
activities. The administration acknowledged that the restrictive
interpretation was not legally legitimate, that there was no chance
at all of inducing the Soviets to live by it, and that the permissive
one was the "legally correct" interpretation. But nevertheless, the
administration decided not to live by the permissive one, and it
specifically decided not to deploy anti-missile defenses while the
Soviets actually built anti-missile defenses. Arms controllers thus
shed their last pretense: the arms control process is really about
the unilateral shaping of American military forces by the American foreign policy establishment. Any effect arms control might have
on the Soviet Union is of secondary importance.

This book is not primarily about Soviet treachery. It is about
American solipsism: the arms control process is something we do
to ourselves, largely by ourselves. Recently, a conference of arms
control proponents at Stanford University was called to develop reasons why the arms control process should continue despite the
Soviet Union's violations. Asked why he thought the Soviets had
violated the treaties, Henry Rowen, former chairman of the National
Intelligence Council, gave the conferees as straight a dose of reality as they could assimilate. Arms control, he said, does not have
much "salience" in the Soviet Union. Observing the agreements
is simply not important to the Soviet leadership. Unlike our government, the Soviet Union does not station arms control monitors
throughout its defense bureaucracy to make sure that it adheres

to the letter, never mind the spirit, of the agreement.[1]

Professor Rowen's analysis is true. Arms control is not "salient" within the Soviet government. But, together with its obverse, it is even more biting. The "process" is our process, in which some among us restrain others among us, citing the necessity of dealing with the Soviets as yet one more reason for doing so. The Soviets hardly have to say or do anything for this process to proceed among us. The treaties are *our* treaties—"salient" for *us*, not for them. It is up to us to explain to ourselves both the Soviets' activities and our own in terms of the treaties. Most of the time, without any help, we do a good job of shaping our own strategic forces and the information we collect about Soviet strategic forces in the image of our arms controllers' dreams, all because we value the process.

The Soviet Union is there to help. In the Soviet armed forces, arms control affairs are handled by the same organization that is in charge of *Maskirovka*, the strategic and tactical concealment and deception program. The Soviet Union has massively increased its *Maskirovka* activities since the beginning of the arms control process. Thus, U.S. intelligence is shown fleeting glimpses of flagrant but relatively inconsequential violations—e.g., the SS-16—which focus controversy away from massive military realities such as the SS-20 launchers' ability to launch ICBMs. These are not violations, but they wholly undo the ostensible purpose for which the U.S. entered into the arms control process. Thus, also, the Soviet Union sends scientists to the West—for example, Y. P. Velikhov—scientists who are principal figures in their own programs to build anti-missile defenses. Yet these same scientists happily explain to Western audiences that they have deemed that anti-missile defenses are both impossible and dangerous. When, very rarely, they are timidly asked about their own role in Soviet programs, some even suggest publicly (in the West—not, of course, in *Pravda*) that they believe their own programs to be foolish, and that they fight against them, even as Western scientists should fight against Western programs. The success of such ploys should not be credited to any devilish cleverness on the Soviets' part, but to some Americans' solipsistic will to believe.

This book is not about particular schemes to reduce arms or

to establish particular symmetries. The closer one looks at the arms control process, the more one is compelled to conclude that there are no real schemes—no plans for defining and knowing about the arms to be limited so that, in fact, after a time, each side would have no more and no less than certain military capabilities. The incredible fact is that our arms controllers chose not to have the treaties deal with arms themselves, but with visible, insubstantial symbols of arms—launchers instead of missiles, "release maneuvers" instead of warheads, etc. They did this consciously, and just as consciously abstracted in their own minds from any political purpose or military strategy that either side might attach to its weapons. Tragically, therefore, they did not formulate treaty regimens reasonably designed to bring about a correlation of forces that, if employed, would produce results at least as tolerable for ourselves as for the Soviets. Moreover, there have never been plans for enforcing *any* controlling regimen in case the Soviets were found to have somehow circumvented any provision. In other words, the U.S. government has made no attempts, even half serious, to answer the question Fred Iklé posed in 1961: "After detection, what?"[2]

The more one looks at the several agreements and proposals that make up the arms control process, the more one is driven to the realization that the medium is the message. The argument in favor of the arms control process is that it *may* lead to useful agreements. The chief argument in favor of any given agreement has been that it will further the process. This argument is especially useful for covering insufficiencies in proposed agreements, as well as counterproductive results of past agreements. Advocates of arms control are much more favorable to the idea of arms control than to any specific instance of it. After all, if they committed themselves to any instance of it, they would have to commit themselves to trying to enforce it or, somehow, to making the agreement bear the fruits they claimed for it. Instead, from Eisenhower to Reagan, they have only made easy, nonresponsible commitments to hope: the arms control process is exploratory. We will see if there is safety to be gained, honorably, at the negotiating table.

Who could object? Meanwhile those who speak this way build their stock as peacemakers, men with faith in a bright and easy future—bold men willing to "take chances for peace." But not too many. And, as they build a taste among the public for illusory safety, politicians feel obliged to feed that appetite with ever more illusions. The more arms control has failed to deliver the benefits promised for it, the more politicians have redoubled their "acts of faith" in it—and the more extravagant their promises have become. This is less like faith, which St. Paul called the substance of things hoped for and the proof of things unseen, and more like drug addiction.

This book is not about Soviet violations. It is about how Americans framed treaties that are arguably verifiable, at the cost of defining the arms to be limited in ways far removed from reality. It is about how the reality of Soviet military programs has been essentially not affected by our delusion. The Soviets' gains came only partially through violations. Mostly they came within the letter of the treaties' definitions of what was to be limited. Of course, the Soviets' gains were wholly outside the spirit of what U.S. negotiators intended to accomplish through the treaties. Yet who would deny that these gains were wholly consistent with the spirit of what the Soviet negotiators sought to achieve. The Soviet gains also came about because American policymakers were bound not so much by the letter of the agreements as by the spirit of those agreements as defined by American arms controllers. Had we followed the letter, American and Soviet arsenals would be very much more alike than they are. Hence the book is about how the agenda of American arms controllers, which, in the treaties, was abstracted into elliptical metaphors, became a hard, concrete discipline within the United States.

The Department of Defense's proposals for procuring American strategic forces have not deviated significantly from the dogmas of American arms controllers in the 1970s. When President Reagan issued his first report on the Soviet Union's violation of arms control agreements, the Department of Defense's lobbyists on Capitol Hill rushed to convey one message: Soviet violations could not be allowed to become a basis for questioning, much less reshaping, the U.S. defense budget. That budget is set according to elaborate internal debates about doctrines, requirements, and the roles and missions of the several services that, by definition, already take into account everything that might happen in the world.

The Department of Defense's lobbyists bolstered their case for military-bureaucratic inertia by pointing to the relative military insignificance of the individual violations. In so doing, they showed that they had sublimated military realities into legal artifices. The famous radar at Krasnoyarsk, for example, violates the ABM Treaty because of its location. Taken by itself, its military significance is relatively small. But taken in the context of eight other radars that are identical to it but do not violate the treaty, its significance is enormous. Thus, this book, unlike Secretary of Defense Weinberger and many conservatives, does not make a big thing of Soviet violations *qua* violations. Rather, it focuses on the military predicament in which the U.S. has placed itself by following the arms controllers' unrealistic view of the world.

Much to the authors' regret, this book is about how the Reagan administration has reinforced the hold of arms controllers and their ideas on American military policy even while sometimes eloquently elaborating facts and arguments that contradict them. By the early 1980s, responsible observers, regardless of their orientation, recognized that the prevalence of arms control thinking in U.S. policymaking circles had allowed the Soviet Union to be the only country that had taken advantage of available technology to build for itself a usable force of offensive anti-missile missiles, known as counterforce missiles. The Reagan administration never considered trying to catch up with the Soviets in this category of weaponry. But, realizing the implications of a perpetual Soviet monopoly on the capacity for decapitating strikes, it sought a way out. There was only one: to make Soviet missiles obsolete by building good defenses against them.

On March 23, 1983, President Reagan told the American people he had chosen that way. But no sooner had he spoken than the arms control priorities that had dug the hole began to gnaw at the only ladder leading out of it. The President had already been convinced that at least ritual bows in favor of arms control were necessary to "cover" the administration's military spending against charges of militarism. Then he was pressed to show his "sincerity" for arms control.

The turn toward strategic defense came at about the time when the President was considering Soviet violations of arms control agreements. He was convinced to wrap "sincerity," "toughness on violations," and strategic defense into the same bundle. Thus, he would insist that they, the Soviets, "stop the erosion of the ABM Treaty" (an interesting euphemism for violations) and revive the "integrity" of the treaty—at least until his Strategic Defense Initiative's research phase was completed and we were ready to roll. All of this was too clever by half. Of course, one could not sincerely demand "integrity" without practicing it. But practicing it meant enforcing the American arms controllers' integral views of the ABM Treaty on the Strategic Defense Initiative. After all, nothing would so erode the ABM Treaty as the United States' building a massive strategic defense. Never mind the fact that the Soviet Union has been doing precisely that since 1972. This contradiction in turn has given to SDI what one might call the "MX disease," a congenital, deforming illness that attacks strategic programs soon after conception, delays birth, and yields only cripples.

The President's simultaneous pursuit of SDI and arms control has proved once again that any attempt to espouse mutually contradictory propositions must end by discrediting both.

The book concludes by examining the controversy that occurred when the State Department's legal adviser ruled between two contending interpretations of the ABM Treaty (and, he might have added, of other agreements as well): a restrictive one (by which Americans must live) and a permissive one (by which the Soviets live—so far as it suits them). But arms controllers legitimately feared lest the administration recognize that there are two legitimate treaties and two legitimate spirits in the treaty, and openly choose among two contending spirits in the field of national security policy. They need not have worried, because the President at first declared that the U.S. would continue to abide, unilaterally, by the "restrictive" interpretation. Then he declared that, regardless of any acceptance of the "permissive" interpretation, he would not decide to deploy defenses in excess of the ABM Treaty for the remainder of his presidency. This incident shows that the arms control process is not about international law or the Soviet Union at all. The idiom of arms control has been a tool by which some Americans

have sought to protect policy preferences that the American people would surely reject if they were presented on their own merits.

Today the arms control process stands shorn of the pretense
that through it we can influence Soviet behavior. Hence we can see
more clearly the choices we face with regard to our national security. Above all, the demystification of arms control makes it possible to see our pressing need for a defense against Soviet missiles.
The U.S. must choose between seeking an illusory safety in a continuation of the arms control process, or providing for that safety
through anti-missile weaponry made in the U.S.A.

2

Why Arms Control?

How, after the first atomic bomb, a wave of millennialist hopes and fears almost submerged the lessons that the tragic events leading up to World War II had taught about arms control.

How, nevertheless, until the end of the 1950s American proponents of arms control continued to insist that any arms control agreement with the Soviet Union be based on international ownership or, at least, thorough knowledge of the field to be controlled.

How the second Eisenhower administration's attitudes toward arms control led to the crucial congressional debate in 1961, in which desire for arms control—without reference to the advantages and drawbacks of specific concepts, and without the responsibility of planning for possible failures—narrowly overcame sober talk.

How the advent of national technical means of intelligence (space-based photo reconnaissance and collection of telemetry signals) so dazzled U.S. government officials who heretofore had known next to nothing about Soviet strategic forces that they then became convinced they knew next to everything.

How this hubris, together with the doctrine of Mutual Assured Destruction that Robert McNamara, McGeorge Bundy, and Henry Kissinger implanted in Washington, proved to be a powerful catalyst in the formation of a new attitude toward arms control.

Those Americans who first proposed that the U.S. government negotiate with the Soviet Union about controlling arms were moved neither by pressing military problems—for the U.S. really did not have any until the late 1960s—nor by any pressure on the part of public opinion to reduce American military power. Indeed, virtually every congressman and senator who spoke in favor of the Arms Control and Disarmament Act of 1961 expressed concern lest their constituents construe their support of arms control as a sign of less than wholehearted commitment to American military supremacy.

Rather, it seems that those who placed arms control on the public agenda in this country did so either because they themselves believed it possible to establish our security vis-à-vis the Soviet Union on a nonmilitary basis, or because they felt the need to look good to people who actually believed in security-by-treaty. The would-be arms controllers theorized about the effect of an "arms race" between the U.S. and the Soviet Union. Since they referred not to the actual U.S. and USSR but to abstract models of the two, they were able to focus the discussion on scenarios either excessively pessimistic or excessively optimistic. Remarkably, those who placed arms control on the public agenda did not, for the most part, espouse particular plans for controlling arms. In no instance whatever did they examine, let alone explain, what should be done if an unwise plan were adopted or if the Soviets cheated on a wise plan. In short, arms control was espoused and sold not so much for the sake of any specific benefits it might bring, but for its own sake.

Advocates of arms control typically believe in the idea itself. To believe in arms control is to accept that a nation possessed of serious reasons, and weapons, for fighting another can and will set aside those reasons long enough to deprive itself of the weapons. Little by little, so goes the creed, as the means disappear from their hands and as they become accustomed to feeling less and less threatened, that nation's leaders will also discard the reasons why they armed in the first place. But even if the leaders retain their bellicose ambitions and language, arms control will have deprived them of the ability to translate them into deadly deeds.

Thus they must assume either that these foreign leaders are not truly serious about what they say they want to accomplish in the world or that they are willing to be less than rational in their military preparations for supporting their policies. In other words, to believe in arms control one must be willing to abstract from normal political and military considerations—and one must believe that others are doing likewise. This is not easy. However, in order to accept that nations would deprive themselves of the means to translate their intentions into deeds, one must suppose that the existence of "the bomb" has submerged all of their other concerns.

The belief that the advent of nuclear weapons had made nonsense of normal political reasoning gave license to many Americans to ignore concrete political and military problems. They did this by discussing anything having to do with nuclear weapons in what amounted to a new language, which abstracted from reality, and assumed that no one could want anything badly enough to fight for it with nukes. Still, at its inception, this abstraction was limited to ends. While the original arms controllers made wild assumptions about the Soviet Union's willingness to agree to world government, they were meticulous about the means by which utopia would be created. The first generation of American arms controllers envisioned not just agreements about, but actual controls on, nuclear weapons. For the logic of arms control to have a chance of working, sovereign nations must actually surrender their sovereign perogatives over certain weapons. Whether they surrender them to "third" parties, supranational entities, or one another is of secondary importance. But arms control, at least as understood in the postwar years, required that nation-states actually give up to others the power to decide how they shall be armed. *Agreements* about arms control can be the legal signs of arms control. But they should not be confused with *controls* themselves.

The real controllers of a nation's armaments are the people who have the power to decide what weapons and how many the nation's factories shall build. The President and the Congress of the U.S. and the Politburo of the USSR control their respective countries' armaments. International arms control traditionally implied the existence of teams of international controllers in the participant nations' arms factories who, at least theoretically, would be empowered to "pull the plug," and to order that this or that item should not be produced. If their recommendations were disregarded, the controllers would warn higher authorities to apply sanctions.

The Americans who became interested in arms control after World War II were very much aware of the distinction between controls and agreements—and they initially sought the latter, not for their own sake but for the sake of controls. These, however, were difficult to conceive and even more difficult to implement. Let us look in some detail at why, and then at how, the intensity of their commitment came to translate their interest in controls into pursuit of agreements for their own sake.

After World War II, arms control could not have attracted converts had not the existence of nuclear weapons cast doubt on history's verdict on international arms control agreements. World War II had etched that verdict into the minds of Western statesmen. Germany and Japan had prepared their assault on the democracies under the "constraints" of arms control and disarmament agreements. Indeed, during the 1920s, international teams roamed German factories. The democracies had lacked neither information about what Germany and Japan were doing, nor the power to stop them. But the arms control process helped to confuse the meaning of the facts available to the democracies and, above all, to confound the democracies' decision making. The architects of arms control in those days did not mean for these things to happen. The Treaty of Versailles, the Washington Naval Agreements, and the other lesser agreements and protocols added legal right to the self-interest the democracies had in stopping the German and Japanese buildups. But the arms control process proved to have its own inner logic, or to be more precise, seductive illogic.

These agreements added solemn obligations to the democracies' earnest desire to restrain their own armament. They made it easier for the democracies to do what they wanted to do anyway. The agreements legitimized the most irresponsible elements within democracies by framing discussion of the military problems posed by Germany and Japan not in military terms, but in terms of the agreements and of the international law that underlay them. Thus, the democracies saw the German and Japanese buildup as stretching the terms of the agreements, or as mere "violations," and tended to think of reactions to those violations as the responsibility of the League of Nations rather than their own. They did not react, in part because unilateral reactions would have undermined the very system of collective security they were trying to establish. The Allied Control Commissions that had unimpeded access to all of Germany after 1919 were substantially slowed in their understanding of German rearmament by the German authorities' deception. Nevertheless, by 1923, they had concluded that Germany was in violation of the Versailles Treaty.[1]

But the perceived necessity to avoid another war, and to keep the process "moving," led the Allied governments to deny their publics the information that the treaty had, in fact, collapsed. To the contrary, they took a heroic chance for peace by leading public opinion in absolutely the opposite direction: the Locarno Pact welcomed Germany back into the family of nations, violations and all. Germany's subsequent rearmament, under the Weimar Republic as well as under the Third Reich, was carried out under the protective political and legal cover of subsequent arms control agreements. Because of these agreements, Allied governments could not denounce what Germany was doing without denouncing their own judgment in entering into them. Thus the agreements themselves provided the framework for refusing to think that what the Germans were doing was actually threatening.

Thus, in legal terms, the Germans' construction of the "battle cruisers" Scharnhorst and Gneisenau was a clever packing into the London Naval Agreement's definition of "cruisers" the two most powerful battleships of the day. At least the Germans had shown deference to the form of the treaty. The fact that they had violated its purpose was certainly an unwelcome development, but no reason to scrap arms control—only to do a better job next time. Alas, the next agreement had to reflect the new balance of power. When that agreement allowed the Germans two 35,000-ton battleships, the Germans interpreted it as allowing the ships, unarmed, to displace that weight. Armed and at 45,000 tons, the Bismarck and Tirpitz were the most powerful surface ships ever built.[2]

The Germans acquired a military capability as if there had been no treaty. But the democracies acted so passively largely because they were able to cast into legal terms information that, in the absence of treaties, would have been clear signals of danger. They acted as they did also because of the domestic political implications of charging the Germans with treaty violations. Such news was too disturbing to comfortable democracies.

Similarly, in the field of aviation, Westerners debated whether the whole number of German aircraft should be considered, or only that portion thereof arbitrarily designated as assigned to "front-line" units. Such distinctions, of course, were meaningful only in their own terms. But, precisely because such distinctions were abstracted from the political intentions and the military capabilities of enemies, they helped democratic politicians, publicists, and military men to avoid thinking thoughts they did not want to think about whether the German and Japanese governments would fight. They thus escaped contemplating the onerous military steps that would have to be taken to actually fight against the military machines that were arising before their very eyes.

Finally, when Winston Churchill and a few like him tried to focus the public's attention on the looming danger, these agreements and their legal abstractions proved to be an irresistible temptation for other politicians to portray themselves on the side of law, on the side of peace, and on the side of responsible assessment of foreign developments, while alarmists and warmongers like Churchill were on the other side.

In the depths of World War II, however, Walter Lippmann, faithful mirror of "the best and the brightest" of his day, summed up "the disarmament movement" as having been "tragically successful in disarming the nations that believed in disarmament." Like those he mirrored, he confessed to having been "too weak-minded," to "following the fashion," to having "celebrated the disaster as a triumph," and to "having had no excuse for not knowing better." American leaders could say no less to their constituents, who were paying in blood for their utopianism.

The explosions over Hiroshima and Nagasaki, however, ushered in a new fashion, according to which "everything" now was, or could be, different. In a little book written within weeks of Hiroshima and published in 1946, Bernard Brodie et al. developed the thesis that nuclear weapons had forever made major war a nonpaying proposition.[3] Although most Americans, and even a large proportion of today's policymakers, have never heard of this little book, the conceptual tools it developed have shaped the thoughts of two generations of our American foreign policy establishment. Countless thoughtless utterances by our contemporaries make sense only in the framework Brodie laid out.

The book did not try to show that it would be impossible for one nation's nuclear-armed bombers to destroy another nation's nuclear-armed bombers and then hold the disarmed nation hostage. It did not try to show that anti-bomber defenses would be unable to reduce threats from nuclear bombers to militarily irrational levels. It could not, and did not, attempt to show that if ballistic missiles were ever fitted with nuclear weapons, nations could not profitably use a combination of strikes against other nations' missiles on the ground and devices to destroy the remainder in flight. But though the book did not directly try to refute common sense, it built a structure of fantasy alongside reality, and invited the reader in. The book hardly noticed that nuclear weapons would be most likely directed against one another and instead assumed that cities would be the targets—as they had been for the Allies, but not for the Soviets, in World War II. Having found that mutual destruction of cities is indeed irrational, the book concluded that major war in the modern world had become irrational and would remain so forever. This conclusion abstracted from the facts as they were— and from any that might arise in the future—in favor of an equal mixture of utopian hope and millennialist fear. Since 1946, this conclusion has proved a serviceable argument against reality. After all, if weapons are ultimately both meaningless and the engines of Armageddon, why quibble about kinds, numbers, and, above all, strategies for employing them?

The irrational hopes and fears reflected in the premises of "the absolute weapon" made it possible once again to discuss arms control, a subject that had so recently and so completely been discredited. The Baruch-Lilienthal plan to place all the world's nuclear affairs—including the only stocks of atom bombs to enforce this monopoly—into the hands of the United Nations was at once utopian and very practical. The utopian element was that the dominant weapon of the age could be safely turned over to people who would mechanically obey the U.N. Security Council's decisions. Had the plan been implemented, it would have led either to a kind of world empire by—or in the name of—the U.N., or to the diffusion of nuclear weapons (or of control over them) to all the U.N.'s member "states", or to the effective removal of nuclear weapons from the world scene, i.e., to making the world safe for conventional wars in which Americans would be hugely outnumbered by the Soviets. None of the alternatives would have been nice. The plan's hard-nosed practicality, however, lay in the nature of the controls it proposed. The U.N., much less the U.S., would not have to monitor each nation's nuclear program, or to decide whether any act was a violation, or then to decide on sanctions. That is because no country would have had a nuclear program of its own. The only nuclear facilities in each country would have been literally controlled by U.N. personnel. So, although on the wholesale level the plan was subject to criticism for utopianism, its details, if implemented, would actually have shifted control of important things from both Soviet and American hands to the U.N. At any rate, the Baruch Plan was the first and the last American arms control plan in which the means were proportionate to the ends, however ill-conceived those ends might have been.

The Soviets rejected the plan's concrete instruments, but demanded immediate pledges of nuclear disarmament. The U.S. refusal of this counteroffer was a refusal to actually give up nuclear weapons in exchange for the right to complain about inadequate assurances that the Soviets were doing likewise. For over a decade thereafter, American discussions of arms control were framed by rock-hard insistence on verification, the typical instance of which was Harry Truman's in 1950:

> The safeguards must be adequate to give immediate warning of any threatened violation. Disarmament must be policed continuously and thoroughly. It must be founded upon free and open interchange of information across national borders.

Obviously, no deal with the Soviet Union could meet such conditions. The Baruch Plan had proved that. Truman's formulation, however, was silent on what the U.S. would do in case it received the warning it sought. Go to war? Thus, while being most demanding as regards verification, Truman was already shifting away from the notion of control in arms control.

Also, while giving disarmament short shrift in practice, Harry Truman spoke appealingly of it. He told the American people that there was "nothing inconsistent" about "the buildup of the defenses of the free world" and cutting them down, along with other nations, in a way "that would be fair to all." This would be "another way to security and peace—a way we would much prefer to take."[4] He implied that the Soviets, not ourselves, would determine whether we, the U.S., would build up or cut down our armed forces.

Nevertheless, as he examined the Soviet threat, President Truman discovered that unless the U.S. armed forces relied on nuclear weapons even more than they wanted to, he could not meet U.S. military responsibilities around the world without grossly unbalancing the budget and militarizing American society. So, while talking about the potential benefits of nuclear disarmament, he seized the concrete benefits of nuclear buildup. Thus, his assessment of Soviet intentions and of the military power required to thwart Soviet forces clearly put that "preference" for arms control outside the realm of possibility. But, why would such a clearheaded leader who did not believe there was any prospect of the lion lying peacefully with the lamb, legitimize—even as a remote possibility—a course of action that, if pursued, would ruin his country? Perhaps he found it inexpensive to associate himself with a natural longing for times with out stress, trusting that reality would always inform and discipline that longing.

Surely, throughout the 1950s it was difficult to find responsible Americans who would say that it would be good for American soldiers to confront the Soviet and Chinese hordes in a world without nuclear weapons. This has not changed. Indeed, the balance of conventional forces has continued to shift against the U.S. Nevertheless, much has happened to push this sobering bit of reality into the background. Thus, the history of arms control between the Soviet rejection of the Baruch Plan in 1946 and the formal beginning of SALT in 1969 is that of the emasculation of the arms controllers' understanding of "control," and of increasing detachment from reality of discussions about arms control. It is an account of how arms control became a placebo, and of how national policy came to be built on hope-against-hope.

*   *   *

The fundamental axiom of political discourse in the U.S. for nearly a generation after World War II was that the Soviet Union means the American people harm—that it seeks to make Americans poorer, and to take away Americans' basic religious and civil liberties. To accomplish this, the Soviet Union is building a military machine out of proportion with defensive needs, and is conquering whatever pieces of the world it can as political-military bases. Given, then, that the Soviets could be expected to foster the very opposite of what might make the lives of Americans safer and more confident, Americans did not spend much effort trying to find whether there might be "out there" awaiting discovery, a potential set of arrangements and procedures on which both sides might agree to their mutual benefit. Besides, the U.S. was doing very well in the early and mid-1950s. The American people's security was being assured by the U.S. armed forces—including an air defense system that, at its peak in 1962, employed 250,000 people, 122 fighter-interceptor squadrons, 280 batteries of surface-to-air missiles, and overlapping radar coverage of the North American continent. Thus, all discussions of disarmament by responsible Americans through the 1950s were unhurried and had a ritual character about them. Of course we would be ready, willing, and able to disarm "if and when" the Soviets showed that they were ready to stop threatening free peoples with war and enslavement, and to prove it by opening themselves to us Americans even as our society is open to them. In other words, if and when arms were no longer needed, we would dispense with them.

Nevertheless, the new drive for arms control began in the 1950s. Its father, President Dwight Eisenhower, was the very opposite of a radical. Yet President Eisenhower, who was even more concerned about balanced budgets than Truman, pushed the U.S. military to rely on nuclear weapons yet more heavily than had his predecessor. Still, his foremost concern as President was to return the country to normalcy. He saw the military's highly popular demand for bigger budgets as perhaps the foremost threat to that normalcy. By forcing the U.S. military to adopt a nuclear "new look," Ike was able to reduce manpower and budgets by 30 percent. But he could not in good conscience cut the U.S. military further, given how worried most Americans were about the Soviet threat. If only the Soviets would agree to be less threatening, the budget could really be cut! A treaty would not really be needed. Perhaps it would be enough, the Eisenhower administration thought, if, in the course of negotiations, we were to learn enough about how weak the Soviet Union really is to prove to the Congress how oversized the U.S. military really was.

Especially prior to the launch of Sputnik in October 1957, the Eisenhower administration took American military supremacy axiomatically—as this country's inalienable birthright. From the top down, the administration really believed that an unbalanced budget and excessive devotion of national resources to the military posed a far greater threat than the Soviet armed forces. Hence, Eisenhower often spoke of how the money spent for individual weapons could pay for a variety of civilian items. Prior to the Geneva summit conference of 1955, he appointed Harold Stassen as his Special Assistant for Disarmament, and charged him with exploring any possibilities for arms control—a charge he shared with his successor under Kennedy, John McCone, and thereafter with every director and employee of the U.S. Arms Control and Disarmament Agency (ACDA). Such men became *de facto* (and under the Arms Control Act of 1961, also *de jure*) advocates of arms control within the U.S. government. But neither Harold Stassen nor his successors until the end of the 1960s had a clear vision of the arms control regime they wanted to advocate, and of how the U.S. would go about maintaining it.

Meanwhile, the Eisenhower administration pursued the other goal of arms control: information. The U-2 reconnaisance plane began secret operations in June 1956. While it was being built, Eisenhower had proposed that both the U.S. and the Soviet Union have "open skies," that is, that they allow each other to transit each other's airspace at will.

On the eve of the missile age, in January 1957, President Eisenhower proposed that both the Soviet Union and the United States essentially give up their budding space and missile programs to "international inspection and participation"—a kind of Baruch Plan for space. The U.S. would have given up the option of building spy satellites, for which arms control advocates were clamoring quite as much as were nuclear targeters. But, as in the Baruch Plan, this renunciation was premised on the Soviets' placing rocketry, an important aspect of their military power, outside the system of secrecy in which all of Soviet society is enveloped. But this is something the Soviets have never even considered. In a Soviet society, where even telephone directories are state secrets, a wholly open space program was simply out of the question. The U.S., then, spurred by Sputnik and by news of Soviet tests of intercontinental missiles, had to build both its own missiles and spy satellites for looking at Soviet missiles.

By their refusal to open up their space progam and to allow free access to their airspace—much less to their society—the Soviets were making impossible one kind of arms control. At the same time, by so doing, they forced Americans to decide whether they wanted to give up the pleasure and profits from talk about arms control, or engage in another kind of arms control—agreements that would be mere mutual pledges backed only by the United States' ability to play the "cops" to the Soviet Union's "robbers." The Soviets counted on the Americans' desire for arms control to erase the distinction between the two kinds. The Soviets turned out to be correct. This is how it happened.

In January 1958, Eisenhower proposed that the U.S. and the Soviet Union stop testing all missiles and agree to a system of mutual inspection to make sure that the only rockets that each side fired, or—and this was the sticking point—prepared to fire, into outer space would be for peaceful purposes. Once again, the Soviets refused the kind of permanent presence in their society that would have made it possible for the U.S. to know well before any launching the nature and purpose of the launch. President Eisenhower's proposal was stillborn.

Nevertheless, American advocates of arms control would not take *nyet* for an answer. Almost two years later, Jerome Wiesner, then one of Eisenhower's science advisers, proposed an arms control plan for space that abstracted from the need to discriminate between rockets. Wiesner proposed a complete ban on the testing of all big rockets. This would have prevented not just a new generation of weapons from arising; he said that it "would also get the U.S. out of the space race, which otherwise will continue to be a serious source of embarrassment and frustration."[5] So draconian an agreement had the advantage of not requiring Soviet acquiescence for its verification. No one would be allowed to launch anything into space for any reason. Any and all uses of space would have been foreclosed to all. This regimen would have allowed both sides to keep the few highly inaccurate, first-generation missiles they had built—good for threats of retaliation and perhaps for threatening air bases, but not yet serious military weapons. This proposal was the first of its kind—vaguely aiming not at disarming, but at stopping technical advances so as to maintain vulnerability to senseless destruction. But in 1959, this proposal did not stir interest in the Soviets or among most Americans, who very much wanted a U.S. missile force just as soon as it could be made.

The most lively arms control issue of the late 1950s was restrictions on nuclear testing. In 1958, spurred by tall tales about the impending destruction of humanity and about the absorption of a by-product of nuclear tests—Strontium 90—into milk, the Eisen-

hower administration entered into an agreed-upon, but uninspected, moratorium on atmospheric testing. The administration
did not expect the moratorium to have great practical effect. A total
ban on nuclear tests, including ones underground, would have
made impossible the development of newer, smaller, counterforce
warheads and would have made it very difficult to gauge the effect
of nuclear explosions on nuclear warheads, i.e., to develop an ABM.
Indeed, if such a ban were to endure for a decade, it would destroy
both nations' confidence in the reliability of its stockpile of nuclear
weapons. A test ban in the atmosphere alone, though, would not
lead to nuclear disarmament. It would only raise the cost of testing and reduce knowledge of weapons effects. This in turn would
make more difficult the use of nuclear weapons for defense. Moreover, since the moratorium was uninspected, the Soviets could use
it to prepare for a big series of tests and steal a march on us. Hence,
the main attraction of the atmospheric test ban for the U.S., other
than relieving the pressure from the "Ban the Bomb" campaign,
was as a "first step." But surely the primary reason for agreeing to
the moratorium was unwillingness on the part of the Eisenhower
administration to appear insensitive before the spectacle of world
catastrophe painted by the "Ban the Bomb" campaign.

Nevertheless, the moratorium was justified as a "first step." Having made that first step, so the proponents' arguments went, we
could negotiate a system of inspection to prevent the preparation
of a major series of atmospheric tests. Once that was secured—but
responsible officials seldom followed the thread of their argument
so far—we could use the goodwill and mutual confidence thus built
up to move to a system of inspection sufficiently strict to ban underground tests as well, and thus move to real nuclear disarmament.

Had the administration gotten that far in its reasoning, it might
have asked seriously whether it really meant to place all nuclear
armament on the road to obsolescence, and whether such a course
of action was consistent with its goal of reducing the military
budget—never mind whether it was consistent with national
defense. At any rate, because the Soviets would not seriously discuss inspection, President Eisenhower declared in 1960 that the U.S.
did not feel bound by the moratorium. Why he said this without

ordering new U.S. tests is not clear. Perhaps he thought his words would put pressure on the Soviets that might lead them to concessions on inspection, whereas real U.S. actions to resume testing would preclude such progress. At any rate, if any such Soviet reasoning occurred, it was too subtle. A generation later, though, Jerome Wiesner mustered sufficient gullibility to argue that this declaration wiped out the moratorium and hence that the U.S. had no right to be upset when in 1961 the Soviets broke that moratorium with a series of tests so prolonged and complex that obviously it had to have been long-planned.[6] (A generation later, President Ronald Reagan declared that the U.S. would no longer be bound by the terms of the SALT II Treaty. But he too did not accompany his words with actions that departed from the logic of the treaty.)

At any rate, as the 1960s began, Americans who yearned for arms control had failed to convince the Soviets to agree to place any part of its military establishment under international control, or even under international inspection. With the moratorium, they had tried arms control for the sake of building a climate of trust—and it had backfired. Just as important, they had not explained—possibly even to themselves—why the U.S. would be better off in a world without nuclear weapons, or long-range missiles, or satellites, than in a world in which it had at least as many and as capable nuclear weapons as did the Soviet Union. Indeed, in those years anyone who might have wanted to argue for any concrete arms control regime would have had to have shown an American public that was overwhelmingly committed to America's overwhelming military superiority why the scheme they proposed would be better than our superiority. Not surprisingly, no one tried. Nevertheless, an undercurrent in the public debate, pushed by the novel and movie *On the Beach*—never forcefully contradicted by U.S. officials—was that nuclear weapons themselves, not the Soviet Union, are to be feared.

As the 1960s began and President Kennedy was inaugurated, there was more sentiment for arms control in Washington than ever. The "Ban the Bomb" campaigns of the late 1950s had sought to give the public the impression that in the nuclear age, armaments—of any kind—produce peril, not safety. On the surface, the "peaceniks" failed. The U.S. undertook the procurement of 1,000 Minuteman missiles and 41 Polaris-Poseidon submarines. But on a deeper level, they had succeeded beyond their dreams. American political leaders, while denouncing the "peaceniks" and voting for big military appropriations, also led the public to conclude that strategic weapons were useless, and that if "the balloon ever goes up" or if "the button ever gets pushed," we would all be dead. Politicians came to conclude that it is necessary to speak such patent untruths to convince voters that they, the people's elected representatives, loved peace. While publicly justifying the purchase of weapons, American leaders typically qualified their actions by saying that in the event of their use, the United States would already have suffered a defeat. The chief purpose in arming was to maintain the peace. That rhetoric had a core of common sense: all agree that war is tragically costly, and everyone much prefers peace. But because the common sense was lost in the rhetoric, the public received the same message from its leaders as it did from the "peaceniks": Abandon hope in our weaponry. There must, there just *must*, be a better way.

Inability to describe that earnestly desired, much talked about, nebulous "better way" did not prevent countless politicians, especially liberals, from associating their names and reputations with that "way." Indeed, the more nebulous the "way," the easier it became to speak well of it. At the same time, the politicians of the early 1960s, without exception, made clear that they supported American military superiority, were eager to speak the harshest words about the Soviet Union, and were quick to say that in present circumstances, arms control was impossible. Inevitably, they then would utter apocalyptic words about there being no alternative to the end of the world except hastening the day when perpetual peace would dawn on the earth, and each would leave no doubt that he was firmly and unalterably opposed to ending the world.

Each politician also sought to leave no doubt that "if and when" the world was ready, he personally would be the very first to beat swords into plowshares. Indeed, speakers would typically say: The fact that we do not now see a way to that more peaceful world means only that we should look harder. If we really try, we may discover the way to a world in which we and the Soviets would agree not to do each other grievous harm – and we just can't afford not to find it. Indeed, the speaker would emphasize that he was confident the world would come to its senses, especially if it listened to the likes of him. Having thus defined a favorable image for himself, the politician would challenge anyone who might oppose him to take the side of Armageddon. Naturally no one would, and just about all utterances by public figures on the subject of strategic armament in those years followed this line of argument. This was most clearly evident in the first major debate the U.S. Congress held on arms control. That was in 1961, on President Kennedy's proposal to establish an Arms Control and Disarmament Agency.

This debate is well worth reviewing because it shows that, from the outset, political support for arms control was based on the postponement of hard questions and on the willingness to live with the logical inconsistency of two sets of views about the Soviet Union and two sets of views about the function of military force.

Senator Hubert Humphrey marshaled virtually all the forces of American liberalism in support of the bill. Pages 17541 through 17551 of the *Congressional Record* (Senate) for September 8, 1961, are filled with testimonial letters on arms control from every major liberal figure in American politics at that time – e.g., Theodore Hesburgh, president of Notre Dame; Herbert Lehman, former governor of New York; Henry Luce, publisher of *Time* magazine; Henry Ford; and representatives from every major liberal newspaper: the *New York Times, Atlanta Constitution, Washington Post, San Francisco Chronicle, Minneapolis Star, Boston Globe,* and even minor ones like the *Champaign-Urbana* (Ill.) *Courier.* A generation later, their arguments, as well as those of the arms control bill's proponents, are even more fascinating than when they were first made.

President Kennedy's letter transmitting the administration's proposed test for the arms control bill foreshadowed the entire campaign on its own behalf. By establishing ACDA, said Kennedy, the U.S. would "make an intensified effort to develop acceptable political and technical alternatives to the present arms race." Kennedy called the threat of war "primitive" and called for the application of ingenuity to the "development of a system of control" for nuclear weapons, to "strengthen international institutions and the rule of law," to "drive toward the creation of a peaceful world society in which disarmament, except for the forces needed to apply international sanctions, is the accepted condition of international life."[7] Kennedy did not mention any concrete scheme for controlling arms. He did not even say that such a scheme existed; indeed, he implied that it did not. Nor did he mention the problem at hand: a Soviet Union firmly controlled by men whose very understanding of what they are about is in terms of enmity to our freedom, and who fervently desire military superiority in order to extinguish that freedom. But President Kennedy implied that just as no one could hazard a guess as to what scheme might bring the Soviet regime to shed its self-understanding and its weapons, no one could prove, *a priori*, that such a scheme would be impossible. Who could be so mean-spirited as to object to putting the nation's invincible brainpower to this grand hope, be it ever so farfetched?

Proponents of the bill depicted objections to the proposal to establish ACDA as objections to putting hope and effort into arms control. Opponents of the bill, for their part, objected to the assumptions of American liberals that underlay arms control.

Barry Goldwater, for example, argued that the very notion of an arms control process by which we could bring "the Castros and the Khrushchevs" to "bow meekly to our wisdom, maturity, and purpose of process" was a kind of self-delusion that would enervate our country and shift the balance of power toward the Soviet Union.[8] While the Soviets are out to increase their power and force their system on other nations—in other words, to win—said Goldwater, we cannot afford to give up the realistic and honorable goal of victory for freedom for the sake of a "process" that exists only in our own minds.

But Hubert Humphrey countered that Goldwater's point of view was outdated. Humphrey's argument deserves to be remembered for its clarity:

> Once it was said that arms themselves were no cause of war, not even a cause of rising tension among nations. The arms were not considered a cause, but merely a symptom of the

basic disputes which prevented nations from living together in relative calm and peace. But the splitting of the atom, the penetration into outer space, and the other recent discoveries of science and technology have shattered this principle, which heretofore had been accepted as a governing factor in international relations. The weapons now being devised, built, and stored throughout many parts of the world have such destructive power, and in a sense are so uncontrollable by the men who must use them, that they, themselves, have become a source of tension. They are now a potential cause of war, not just a by-product of the political disputes among nations. We must not, therefore, ignore the weapons as being unimportant. The weapons themselves, as well as the disputes, have now become a great source of concern to us all.[9]

Here was the pure doctrine of arms control. Arms control makes sense only if on both sides the fear of the weapons themselves overcomes all desires and calculations. Clearly, fear of the bomb had had this effect on American arms controllers. Nevertheless, few said they knew for a fact that the Soviets felt likewise. Nor could they.

Like Humphrey, Senator Wiley (D-Wisconsin) did not hesitate to point out that "the outlook for progress is not too bright at the present time" because the Soviets appeared more interested in building weapons than in limiting them. However, his colleague from Wisconsin, William Proxmire, spoke for many when he said that only by pursuing the arms control process could we determine "how feasible, how effective, how workable, an arms control program will be." Thus, the arms controllers' argument was that if we did not pursue the process, we would be rejecting the prospects for peace out of sheer prejudice. On the most fundamental level, this position was that of the anti-nuclear marchers: "All we are saying, is give peace a chance."[10] Congressman Broomfield (R-Michigan) used these very words. What decent person could object to that?

Besides, as the proponents noted, even if we did not achieve the arms control regime of our dreams, our espousal of it would, in Senator Wiley's words, "give us a stronger, clearer voice in presenting U.S. policies to the world."[11] Not incidentally, it would give those who espoused it the chance to look like peacemakers. The proponents showed that they were willing to give the "peace" issue a hard edge—at least in domestic politics. They did not mince words. Proxmire: "There is no question that unless we can begin to have arms control we shall have nuclear destruction."[12] Humphrey: "We will either go to the conference table with Mr. Khrushchev or World War III is only hours away. I think it might be well for the nation to ponder what World War III would mean."[13] The nation did indeed ponder this in the 1964 presidential campaign, when the Johnson-Humphrey team depicted Barry Goldwater as a war-monger willing to blow up little girls walking in daisy fields for his opposition to arms control.

Goldwater, for his part, asked, "What are we engaged in, anyway, a popularity contest or a struggle to the death between freedom and slavery?"[14] Senator Sparkman (D-Alabama) answered with an article of faith, which weighed even more heavily because it had once been expressed by George C. Marshall, former Armed Forces Chief of Staff: "I say to you people that the greatest single force among men in this world is the force of public opinion—world public opinion. . . . Some day, it will influence Russia."[15] Meanwhile, of course, it would influence America—to Senators Sparkman's and Proxmire's personal benefit.

Senator Richard Russell (D-Georgia) was skeptical of "world public opinion." He mentioned that the Soviets, during the Belgrade Conference of Nonaligned Nations, had just resumed nuclear testing in defiance of a mutually agreed moratorium. "These are the very people we are told daily we must undertake to attract." Yet, he noted, "that Conference condemned the United States more than it condemned Russia."[16] He concluded that perhaps Khrushchev understood better than American liberals what the wellspring of the nonaligned nations' allegiance is—namely, fear.

In the House of Representatives, the liberal Congressman Silvio Conte (R-Massachusetts) noted the very phenomenon that had vexed Senator Russell. But Conte made it into an argument in favor of arms control:

> It is certainly disappointing that at the Belgrade Conference the nonaligned countries did not take a more forthright stand against the atmospheric testing by the Soviet Union. Perhaps the answer lies in the weakness of our foreign policy.[17]

The world's nonaligned nations were not well informed enough, and the U.S. was not sufficiently committed to arms control. Both these impediments would be removed if we initiated "serious and practical efforts to insure a more peaceful world." This was also the opinion of Congressman Johnson (D-Maryland), who said that "America has failed to give the leadership that is expected of a great country as ours." We simply had to go out and "convince the world that we are a peaceful nation."[18] Congressman Ashbrook (R-Ohio) replied that we did not have to prove any such thing to anyone. Only those who are irreversibly predisposed to be our enemies "could envision America as the aggressor, the warmonger, the threat to peace." He implied that only those who lacked confidence in our country and what we stood for would think it necessary to make such an effort, and that the effort would wind up strengthening the hand of those "who think that no sacrifice of sovereignty, honor, or principle is too great to make in pursuit of the illusive goal of peace."[19] But to no avail. The majority wanted to prove its purity.

Nevertheless, the majority went out of its way to hide such sentiments. Most pleas for arms control were sandwiched between ringing ritual affirmations of commitment to American military power. In view of the voting record these speakers have compiled, they were clearly making a record of verbal toughness to which they could point when attacked for their support of disarmament. Here, then, is William Proxmire:

> I feel very strongly that this is a time when we must be strong and firm, and a time when we must increase, not decrease our armaments. This is a time when we must do all we can to strengthen our nuclear ability. . . . I feel we must do all we possibly can to establish the greatest nuclear deterrent, the greatest Air Force, the most powerful Army, and the most powerful Navy in the world today.[20]

Senator Jacob Javits (R-New York), one of the more perceptive people ever to have served in the Senate, and a lifelong supporter of arms control, explained the necessity of such talk:

> The people of the United States are deeply disquieted about what disarmament would mean. They are deeply disquieted

> to think that the wily Russian opponent, whom we may find
> working against us in terms of disarmament, may work out
> a deal in which we will find ourselves at a disadvantage before
> we wake up to what is going on around us.[21]

In the same vein, Congressman Ross Adair of Indiana said: "We
wanted to make it entirely clear that those who vote for this legis-
lation are not voting, for an instant, for any weakening of our defense
posture."[22] Hence, Javits argued that proponents of arms control
should stress that they would gladly vote to spend a huge chunk
of the GNP for military purposes, and that they are unalterably committed to foolproof verification.

Advocate after arms control advocate followed this advice then
and has followed it since. It is essential to note that arms controllers
did not feel pressure from the voters to enter into agreements with
the Soviet Union. Rather, they feared the voters' retribution for seeking such agreements and protected themselves in two ways: first,
they made loud public commitments to a military superiority that
they did not believe in—at least if such belief is to be judged by their
voting record. Second, they pointed to "verification" as the ultimate
safety net in arms control and thereby obscured from themselves
as well as from others the fundamental question: "After detection,
what?"

The reader may search the pronouncements of arms controllers
in this and other debates in the 1960s, 1970s, and 1980s without ever
finding a discussion of what the U.S. should do if it found that the
Soviet Union had behaved fraudulently or that an arms control
agreement had proved counterproductive. Arms controllers have
considered discussions of enforcement simply to be in bad taste—
somewhat as a hypnotist might consider a ringing telephone.

Senator Russell was perhaps the most eloquent of those who
pointed out the inherent incongruity of an arms control process
alongside a commitment to a worldwide struggle against the Soviet
Union:

> I submit that it would be absolutely impossible to explain to
> all the peoples of the world—those associated with us and
> those who call themselves neutralists—that we are serious

in our determination to defend liberty and the institutions
of our government and the rights of free men everywhere with
a vast arms program, while at the same time we are creating
a disarmament agency. We may be able to explain it to most
of our own people, but I do not think even all the American
people will understand. It looks very much as if we are going
in both directions at the same time.[23]

Senator Russell's point was equally substantive and political.
It began from the premise to which everyone, then and even nowa-
days, pays lip service: that there is a fundamental incompatibility
between our purposes and those of the Soviet Union, and that both
countries arm in order to serve those irreconcilable political purposes. Hence, he asked, on what basis does the U.S. decide what
arms it ought to have? *We cannot have both too much and too little at
the same time.* What about our own political orientation? We cannot, at the same time, think of the Soviets as plausible partners in
an enterprise the purpose of which is to make us both less able to
achieve our ends, and as plausible enemies intent on undoing us,
against whom we must sacrifice much.

That set of contradictions has not been resolved either substan-
tively or politically on the level of public opinion. Rather, it has been
fought out on another level of politics. Senator John Sparkman
(D-Alabama) took up the challenge:

How can the Senate consistently support increased budgets
for defense and during the same session support the creation of a disarmament agency?[24]

He answered by quoting Eisenhower's Secretary of Defense,
Thomas Gates, at the end of a long line of liberal military figures:

I think it is a good time . . . to assert our moral responsibilities *and to stand up for our long-term principles for peace, and world
law, and justice.*[25] (Emphasis added.)

The same statement was also quoted by Congresswoman Bolton
in the House.[26]

The answer, then, it seems, is that there are politicians who
want to arm while disarming, or to disarm while arming, or to give

the impression that they are doing the first while doing the second, or to give the impression that they are doing the second while doing the first, or to speak well of both arming and disarming—in an effort to be all things to all men. The answer also seems to be that some Americans felt an inner need to "stand up" for peace, whatever that meant.

So, without specifying the gains to be made and the risks to be incurred, arms control got an emotional send-off—best summed up by John McCormack (D-Massachusetts), Speaker of the House of Representatives:

> The cause of peace will likely be lost unless we marshal the nation's energies, unless we mobilize our national talents and devote them to a creative quest for the modern Grail, the cup of peace. Unless the world drinks deeply, thinks deeply of peace, the dry dust of nuclear fall-out will envelop us all.[27]

All in all, not sober talk.

Those who had argued that the Arms Control and Disarmament Agency—the now-institutionalized arms control movement in the U.S.—would be powerless because it could not change the reality of these fundamental contradictions to which Richard Russell had pointed, proved half right. The arms control movement in fact ceased trying to tinker with something so stubborn as reality. Instead, it seized on the development of intelligence satellites and of second-generation ballistic missiles—wondrous things, the significance of which was not self-evident—to lay the foundations for a massive delusion that would serve, at least for domestic political purposes, as a working substitute for reality.

These foundations of our establishment's delusion about arms control have two main, interconnected parts. First is the impression that, with our satellites, we could see everything of military significance in the Soviet Union. This is an exaggeration so gross as to turn the little light shed by the satellites on Soviet reality into a cause of greater darkness. Nevertheless, this exaggeration helped to transmogrify the early notion that arms control had to involve the ability to make the Soviet Union *comply* with its undertakings into the very different notion that arms control depended on our ability to *observe and listen* to the Soviet Union. Exaggerated expectations of U.S. satellites proved to be a convenient excuse for American arms controllers to shift definitively away from the relatively hard-nosed approach of the postwar period to the total delusion of contemporary arms control.

Indeed, Ambassador Gerard Smith put it bluntly in testimony to Congress: "We did not work out the limitations and then check to see if the National Technical means were adequate to verify them. We tailored the limitations to fit the capabilities of National Technical means verification."[28] This, of course, is circular reasoning. One does not need sophistication to understand that things that exist outside the national technical means of verification can and do pose severe peril to national survival. Yet because of our inability to verify them, Ambassador Smith and his negotiators preferred to overlook these perils. They impeded their goal of achieving a treaty. Thus the terms of the treaty satisfied the process without even feigning to address the real security balance. Security was never the goal. The goal was political—to achieve agreement.

It is difficult to overestimate the impact of the technical revolution in U.S. intelligence on the incoming Kennedy administration. In a word, it accentuated the New Frontiersmen's hubris. Within months, intelligence officers and policymakers went from working with the sketchiest inferences about Soviet sites to looking at good-quality overhead photography and reading missile telemetry. At the new CIA headquarters, wallpaper appeared in the lobby showing a facsimile close-up of downtown Moscow, implying that the U.S. could now know what was going on in each of those streets and buildings. Of course, no serious person would have argued that we could. Still, we were seeing so many interesting things, and the mood was so upbeat, that intellectual caution went to the winds. People who had known next-to-nothing started to believe that what they were seeing amounted to next-to-everything.

In a nutshell, policymakers concluded that we could see "everything we had to," and that the Soviet Union, under this scrutiny, "wouldn't dare" violate any agreement we might make. It did not occur to anyone to argue that seeing is not knowing, so they comfortably embraced agreements that they dreamed would be self-enforcing. This was less a considered conclusion than a powerful, widely shared *feeling*. The policymakers did not, however, consider the implications of this feeling until later in the decade, when they were already deeply involved in negotiations. But by then, other assumptions and commitments had been laid on this unexamined foundation.

The second foundation is the impression that the only things we were concerned about in the Soviet Union boiled down to missiles, that these had taken on something like their ultimate forms, and that these forms left no one on either side any choice about how they might be used. American arms controllers hence formulated an item of unchallengeable dogma: The inherent, unalterable characteristics of these *observable* weapons made it more sensible for both sides to have a relatively low, equal, number than to go through the expense of trying to achieve superiority. This is the belief, so willful on the part of technology managers who knew better, that the U.S. and the Soviet Union had climbed onto a technological plateau that stretched out forever. As we shall see, this was a wish that arms controllers tried to make into reality by writing legal language with which they intended to restrict and encompass forever human inventiveness—a task as inherently futile as whipping the ocean's waves.

In the 1960s, there emerged a third part to this foundation—the belief that the U.S. had become militarily "so strong" that it could afford to "take chances for peace." This idea has had a strange relationship to arms control. In the early 1970s, Henry Kissinger reversed it and argued that the U.S. should accept the terms of SALT I that it might otherwise have deemed unsatisfactory because a deteriorating military balance had put us in "not the world's most brilliant bargaining position." This was also one of the Carter administration's arguments for SALT II. At the close of the 1980s, this argument continues to be the basis of the Joint Chiefs of Staff's support for arms control before President Reagan and the Congress. Of course this argument leaves unanswered what kind of deal can be expected from negotiating from a bad position. More important, no one who has ever used it has proposed military options that, even by his lights, would restore U.S. military superiority so that future deals could be negotiated from a strengthened position.

The Reagan administration, while privately placing great stock in the Joint Chiefs' argument, has publicly returned to the contrary argument of the 1960s: We can resume "taking chances" in negotiations because we are now "so much stronger." There is a twist, however. The Reagan administration does not say we are stronger than the Soviet Union in absolute terms, or even that we are in a better relative position than we were during the Carter administration — both of which propositions are demonstrably untrue. Rather, the Reagan administration argues only that the U.S. military is in better shape in absolute terms than it had been during the Carter administration. This is both true and irrelevant. But our point here is that both strength and weakness have been made to argue for arms control — sometimes simultaneously.

Let us now look in some detail at how, under the impact of the desire to "find a way," American policymakers built on these psychological foundations the edifice of an arms control process that, while doing precisely nothing to reduce the Soviet Union's military power, corrupted both our own military forces and, even more significantly, the way influential Americans think about our foremost military problem: the Soviet Union.

3

Substituting for Reality

How the essence of the arms control negotiations has been to translate political and military problems, which if confronted would make arms control impossible, into technical terms that the two sides can discuss and resolve.

How, whereas standard diplomatic practice requires that the other side's political intentions be ascertained as a prerequisite for negotiations, the arms control process is premised on shaping the other side's intentions through negotiations.

How American arms controllers decided that any question of the Soviets' planning to use their forces in a militarily reasonable way could not, indeed must not, be allowed to intrude into the negotiations.

How American arms controllers built, as the intellectual basis of the treaties, a tautological world in which Soviet strategic weaponry was defined as being whatever U.S. intelligence could see, and whatever U.S. intelligence could not manage to see was to be ignored. Thus was the stage set for negotiations exclusively among Americans about whether any given Soviet activity met or did not meet one of the treaties' standards, and about whether the level of information available would or would not permit judgments.

How this sterile exercise has diverted American eyes from reality.

American liberals, either unaware of or ignoring the historical experience of democracies with arms control, pressed ahead. They did not recall how the German aero sport clubs of the 1930s became the Luftwaffe. They did not recall that with on-site inspection in the shipyards, the Scharnhorst and Gneisenau materialized from arms control cruisers into the largest battleships of their era. They did not recall that their European liberal counterparts of the 1930s had Mussolini dead to rights when in 1936 the new cruiser Gorizia was actually weighed and measured 10 percent in excess of the cruiser weight limits. The British Committee of the Interior under Chamberlain's government overlooked the breach because they were trying to seduce the Italian government into a rapprochement with the 1936 London Naval Treaty. Violations then, as violations now, were no diversion to the pursuit of the process.

With history comfortably out of mind, American liberals had been telling the country that there just *had* to be a better way to provide for our security than to earn it, precariously, by never-ending vigilance, toil, and even the commitment of blood. In 1961 they had established an agency to spend millions of dollars to pay a lot of bright people to search for such a way. Without doubt, these people would come up with ideas. Their contracts called for papers and conferences. They surely would propose schemes. But it was up to high officials, both elected and appointed, to sift these ideas and to tell the difference between schemes that would make arms control serve the cause of peace—something that had proved impossible in the interwar and postwar periods—and schemes that simply made it *look* as if we were achieving security, at the price of actual insecurity.

Yet, the liberals who dominated American government and

opinion in the 1960s and 1970s made themselves unfit to make this distinction. True, they justified the arms control process as merely an impartial investigation into *whether* "good" arms control was possible. Nevertheless, they had already convinced themselves that such an arrangement just *had* to be possible. Indeed, those who wrote and passed the Arms Control and Disarmament Act formally gave to ACDA the task of *advocating* arms control within the U.S. political process. The hundreds of millions of dollars that ACDA expended bought no hardware. But they did create a new, well-heeled class with a newly respectable occupation—selling arms control to the American people. It is not unfair to assume that the new class of people who had become prominent through advocacy of the possibility of arms control were under real pressure to advocate *something*. Hardly an impartial jury, they were disposed, at the very least, to look uncritically at the proposals that would come their way.

Well before advancing specific schemes, advocates of arms control set about shaping the discourse in terms of which the schemes would be judged. Unable or unwilling to deal with the world as it was, the foreign policy establishment of the 1960s and 1970s constructed a model of the world—more pleasing to itself, but wholly fictitious. On the basis of that model, arms control made sense. On the basis of that model, American foreign policy, American strategic forces, and American politics itself were altered.

Let us see how they built this model by abstracting from political, military, and technological reality.

Abstracting from Political Reality

The premise of arms control is that weapons are not tools dearly bought to accomplish ends for the sake of which foreign leaders are willing to kill and die, but rather, that they are expensive burdens that these leaders would prefer to shed[1]—if only we would do likewise. Americans can apply this premise to the Soviet Union only by misinterpreting the Soviet Union and what it is after, or by a mental process that, while acknowledging the Soviet Union's antagonism, discounts it. In fact, the arms control process is based both on misinterpretation and on the discounting of Soviet policy.

Why does the Soviet Union arm itself so heavily? Is it because of a kind of quaint paranoia, an excessive concern lest it be invaded yet once more? Does the Soviet government merely want to ensure, as it repeatedly stated in Stalin's early days, "socialism in one country," or does it want to cast a shadow beyond its own borders — a shadow that would foster kindred regimes and cause uncongenial ones to wither? How long a shadow does it wish to cast? Is the casting of a shadow optional for the Soviet regime, or is it something it feels compelled to do to the extent it can? Are the quantity and quality of its current armament programs consistent with the Soviets' acceptance of "socialism in one country," or with the desire to cast the longest and most effective shadow possible?

In the early 1960s, American advocates of arms control provided answers to these questions very different from the consensus of the 1950s. The Soviet Union no longer armed itself heavily because it was bent on bringing the world under socialism. It was suddenly seeking only a minimum of power to deter an attack from the U.S. Had the Soviets ever sought world socialism, they abandoned it when the Kennedy administration embarked on a program to build 1,000 Minuteman ICBMs and over 600 submarine-launched missiles. "Conventional wisdom" has it that in the Cuban missile crisis, Soviet leaders facing hundreds of American missiles with 14 ICBMs of their own forever learned that they could never win a war against the U.S. on the highest level of violence, let alone a contest in technology and industry. Hence, though the Soviets could be expected to improve their strategic forces to make them respectable, the Soviet threat would manifest itself primarily through support of "wars of national liberation" in the "underdeveloped nations." Political competition would continue and would include violence, but it would take place in the back alleys of the world, unaffected by American and Soviet possession of big bombs and rockets.

This convenient misinterpretation occurred despite the Soviet leaders' continued reference — whenever they discussed support of wars of national liberation, or anything else for that matter — to the "correlation of forces." According to this concept, any given instance of the conflict between the imperialist camp and their own cannot help but be affected by all the forces at the disposal of either camp — be they nuclear, conventional, unconventional, economic, social, political, etc. How, then, could anyone believe that the Soviets would try to encircle and squeeze the West through the underdeveloped world without at some point gaining the ability to fight and win a war against the U.S. on the highest and most sophisticated level of violence of which the two sides are capable? Arms controllers conveniently ignored the fact that, since the 1940s, American policymakers had realized that our own nuclear superiority could "cover" the nonnuclear and even the nonmilitary operations of even distant allies. In the jargon of the 1960s, "extended deterrence" could be secured by "strategic nuclear superiority," because "strategic nuclear superiority" would supply "escalation dominance." Not surprisingly, the Soviets, for their part, saw the "covering" role of strategic superiority in precisely the same way. This had nothing to do with Marxism. It was and still is common sense. Khrushchev's doctrine of "peaceful coexistence" explicitly stated that growing Soviet power would somehow cover movements of national liberation. The regular pronouncements of such movements have long pointed to the overall power of the Soviet Union as the indispensable foundation of their own success. From where, then, did a generation of "strategists" arise who were unable, or refused, to see that the Soviets, in order to support their version of "extended deterrence," had at any cost to achieve "escalation dominance"?

The answer lies in the tendency of so many Western analysts to project their own priorities upon the Soviets, to see the Soviets as mirror images of themselves. During the Cuban missile crisis, liberal American policymakers went to the brink of war and saw no reason — none at all — why they might ever want to go there again. They learned something about themselves. They would not have used nuclear weapons. They wanted to believe that the Soviets had been similarly impressed, and that for them, too, nuclear-armed missiles and bombers had lost all usefulness for casting shadows on the world. The lesson of the Cuban missile crisis, which our "best and brightest" decided was universal, was that such weapons would be useful only for deterring nuclear attack on the homeland of those possessing them. For this purpose, only a few such weapons are needed; any number beyond that would be literally useless and expendable.

Thus in the aftermath of the 1962 Cuban missile crisis, our own "best and brightest" regretted that they had placed orders for as many missiles and bombers as they had and so cut back those orders to the maximum extent they could. They decided that the Soviets, having reached the same conclusions, and unencumbered by having endured as big an arsenal as we, would scale down any plans they might have had. This foolishness continued when, in the late 1960s, as the Soviets' missile numbers approached ours, the CIA decided that those numbers would not exceed ours substantially. Then, in the early 1970s, when they did exceed ours substantially, the CIA judged that nonetheless, the Soviets would not pursue the ability to fight and win a war. Why should they? We had decided that the task was futile, and surely they must have too, or soon would.

Since we were willing to fight in the world's alleys and jungles (above all, in Vietnam) without thought of using our nuclear superiority even politically, and since they were obviously willing to fight us in Vietnam (they were fighting, weren't they?) despite their nuclear inferiority, it seemed to follow that the Soviets did not think nuclear superiority relevant to the kind of warfare in which they were engaging. Of course it did not follow that because the Soviets fought with what they had, they would not seek more with which to win.

Grave as it was, this misestimation was not as significant as the failure to take seriously important questions about the Soviet Union's intentions. Since the dawn of time, successful diplomats have lived by the rule that ascertaining the other party's intentions is the indispensable prerequisite for any negotiation. What is the other side after? What does it want from us in these negotiations? Wise diplomats have realized that they cannot change the other side's intentions, and that it would be self-deceptive to think otherwise. Indeed, wise diplomats must assume that the other side is entering into negotiations in order to facilitate its achievement of some purpose—to remove obstacles from its own path rather than put them there. Hence the irreducible need to find out what the other side wishes to accomplish.

No responsible American claimed to *know* why the Soviets were talking to us about arms control. After all, U.S. intelligence does not have access to Soviet leaders' deliberations. So the easy acceptance of the most soporific explanations of Soviet motives cannot be counted as misinterpretations. They were noninterpretations —castles of imagination built on imagination—that stood only because those who built them dismissed *a priori* the need to test their own assumptions.

Here, then, are the cards with which American arms controllers built their *a priori* explanation of Soviet intentions. The Soviet Union was having economic difficulties. Despite the fact that it had placed a satellite in orbit before the U.S. and had beaten the U.S. in missilery, the Soviet Union was technologically backward and knew it could not afford unrestrained military competition with the U.S. The Soviet Union, it is true, had once been highly dangerous. But Soviet leaders had matured. They desired only the benefits of ordinary international intercourse. They realized that the world had become interdependent, and the future of all nations' prosperity lay in the peaceful arts of technology, trade, and finance—not in military confrontation. The arms control process would allow the Soviet leaders to do something they wanted to do anyhow, but they needed international support in order to restrain the appetites of their own military-industrial complex.

The temptation to build this castle of imagination seems perennial. On March 5, 1987, President Reagan said that, while he personally realized the Soviets had not given up on their plans of world domination, it was also true that Gorbachev had many economic problems and even worse trouble with the Soviet bureaucracy. It was, therefore, urgent for Gorbachev to have an arms control agreement so that he could get on with modernizing his country. It would seem logical, however, that such circumstances would more ideally suit U.S. pressures on the Soviets to return to compliance with old agreements rather than a rush toward new ones. Yet to demand proof of Soviet intentions seems to be outside the rules of the game.

But these cards would not stand examination—much less could

they be built into an edifice that could withstand pressure. Of course the Soviet Union has been having terrible economic woes since 1918! The Soviet Communist Party considers most of its people's privations as the foundation of its own power. None of these economic shortcomings have stopped or even slowed the Soviet Union from building the world's most powerful military force. Yes, the Soviet leaders know they cannot afford unrestrained competition with the U.S. That is why *they* seek to restrain the U.S. But by what logic does this imply that the Soviet leaders are willing to restrain themselves, especially since Americans have exacted no price whatever for the Soviet Union's lack of reciprocal restraint? The Soviets know as well as anyone what the difference is between guns and butter. But they realize better than American arms controllers that superiority in guns can persuade those who own the butter to make a peace offering of it. The arms control process would indeed give to the supreme authorities of the U.S. and the USSR the ability to curb their military forces. But what might occur if Soviet political and military leaders made common cause with American arms controllers to restrain the U.S. military without any intention of restraining their own?

Even today the Joint Chiefs use a strange twist on the verification versus intentions issue. Though the Soviets are clearly in violation of major provisions of the ABM Treaty, we should not opt out of it, they counsel the President, for the Soviets are in far better position to exploit their advantages gained through noncompliance than are we starting from our compliance. But the Joint Chiefs fail to be persuasive in their next step of reasoning. How, if the Soviets have achieved that superior position under the agreement that controls us but not them, do we enhance our safety by remaining bound to it?

Whenever such questions were asked about their premises, American arms controllers would fend them off by saying that the arms control process itself is the only way of finding the answers. Indeed, they saw the process not so much as a means of inquiry, but as the only means of *manufacturing* the right answer, because the process would teach the Soviet leaders sophistication—the table manners of nuclear weapons. So, American arms controllers turned

on its head the tradition that dedicates the opening round of diplomatic negotiations to finding out the other party's intentions. This
is because to question Soviet motives would be to underscore that
the arms control process itself is based on premises about Soviet
intentions that are either demonstrably false, or at best, undemon-
strable. Instead, they focused the arms control process, including
the preliminary negotiating rounds, on lecturing the Soviets about
what their intentions ought to be and surely must be.

We chose to focus on the technicalities of verification to comfort ourselves about Soviet intentions. But "verification" means
something only in the context of very specific treaty provisions.
Whenever one speaks of it, one is compelled to do so in narrow,
technical terms precisely related to the provisions. Hence, insofar
as American arms control negotiators have pursued preliminary
explorations of Soviet intentions, they have done so by probing what
kinds of verification provisions and/or treaty provisions the Soviets would accept. This effectively moves the question of intentions
from *prerequisite* to *afterthought*.

In fact, when American arms controllers are asked in public
about the Soviet Union's intentions regarding arms control, they
often profess agnosticism, and state that intentions cannot be determined *a priori*. Only through verification of the Soviet Union's compliance with concrete agreements will we be able to ascertain what
their intentions had been in entering into those agreements.[2]

The very process of negotiations, which normally would be
premised on the existence of the proper set of intentions on the other
side, becomes the means for creating those appropriate intentions.
Thus, Secretary of State William Rogers, in a speech delivered to
set the scene for the formal opening of the SALT I negotiations,
recalled that preliminary talks had been going on for years "to
improve U.S.-Soviet understanding by establishing a continuing process of discussion of issues arising from the strategic situation." He
added that "what counts at this point," more than any concrete
agreement, is a continuation of the "dialogue" about the "management of the strategic relations of two superpowers."[3]

Thus, by the wondrous substitution of procedure for substance
— by an application of methodical doubt and suspension of judg-

ment about Soviet intentions that would have made Descartes proud – and without need for demonstrating anything – American arms controllers transformed in their own minds a mortal enemy into a partner with an equal interest in the management of a great enterprise. This line of thought does not axiomatically deny that one day we might have to deal with a Soviet Union intent on actually using its weapons to its own advantage. But it pushes that day out of the mind's practical reach.

Abstracting from Military Reality

Are Soviet strategic weapons meant to fight and win wars, or not? Essential questions thrown out through the front door often climb back in through the window. Those who would banish such questions must shutter the windows as well. Thus anyone who is led to suspend judgment about whether the Soviet Union means its strategic weaponry to serve a rational political purpose might well reconsider once he looks closely at that weaponry itself. After all, possession of certain numbers and kinds of missiles inherently gives the Soviets, or anyone else, certain options. Even one who believes that the era of interdependence has arrived, and that the Soviets do not mean to make life precarious for any but regimes under their discipline, might well bridle at the prospect of the Soviets' having the means to fight and win wars. He might ask "what if," for whatever reason, the Soviets sought to put their war-winning potential to good use? If they have the means, common sense says they might just catch the intentions on the spur of some moment. And if they developed such impressively well-tailored means laboriously, year after year, who would be so foolish as to deny the possibility that they had done it with a view to using them? That is why advocates of arms control have worked hard to banish questions of how the Soviets could use their strategic weapons to fight and win wars.

The arms control process served to delegitimize, to remove from discourse, the questions that would delegitimize *it*. Raymond Garthoff, one of America's best known and most persistent advocates of arms control, thus desribed the SALT I negotiations:

Matters . . . not directly precipitated by the process of negotiations tended to get short shrift or no attention at all. Another limitation was the Soviet stance, evidently established prior to SALT by the cautious and suspicious military leadership in Moscow, that military doctrine and operational concepts were not a necessary or proper subject for discussion in the negotiations.[4]

According to Mr. Garthoff, American arms controllers were no less eager than the Soviets to limit discussion to the technical parameters of possible points of agreement. Garthoff recounts strong disagreement with some Americans'

continual stress on possible incentives to preemptive initiation of war if one or another element of strategic forces (primarily fixed, land-based ICBM launchers) of one or the other side were to become vulnerable. Such situations should, of course, be avoided or minimized; but the actual likelihood of Soviet or American leaders being "attracted" to start a war by any such "incentives" is in my judgment exceedingly low, and should not have been seen or depicted as in a range of serious consideration.[5]

Hence, while Gerard Smith, Garthoff, Nitze, and others on the "eager" side of the U.S. delegation would regularly lecture the Soviets about the benefits of strategic stability, plus-sum games, etc., they successfully curtailed the authority of William Van Cleave and others from the Department of Defense to talk to the Soviets about how unfavorably the U.S. would view the Soviet Union's replacement of "light" ICBMs with "heavy" ones.

That Mr. Garthoff's position won out within the American delegation in 1969–72 is a remarkable example of the power of abstraction achieved by restricting the scope of discussion. It is remarkable because by that time, the U.S. government already possessed enough intelligence information to lead a reasonable person to conclude that the Soviet Union was building its missiles to be militarily useful in fighting, surviving, and winning a war against the U.S. What would have happened to the negotiations if these "illegitimate" questions about the military usefulness of certain systems had managed to sneak into the discussion with the Soviet negotiators, and, more important, into the headlines?

Mr. Garthoff's position that nuclear weapons are militarily useless had reigned unchallenged in Washington between circa 1965 and 1967. In 1963, Secretary of Defense Robert McNamara had begun revising the outlook upon which American military planning was based. The U.S. had ordered 1,000 Minuteman missiles, and at least 40 submarines to carry the Polaris-Poseidon missiles. Prior to 1961, tentative plans existed to purchase many more. Initially, McNamara thought that having large numbers of such weapons was good because, like his immediate Republican predecessor, Thomas Gates, he believed that nuclear weapons should be used as better means in the service of the traditionally primordial military purpose: protection of one's own population through destruction of the enemy's military forces. But as McNamara and his "Whiz Kids" looked at the Soviet Union's expanding missile force, as well as at its emplacement in blast-resistant silos and submarines, they realized that, to meet their own criteria, they would have to continually improve American offensive forces in quality as well as in size. Furthermore, they would have to spend much to develop anti-missile defenses. No one could say where the cycle of countermeasures and counter-counter-measures would stop. For a variety of reasons, Robert McNamara was unwilling to undertake such an open-ended commitment.

Hence, in 1963–64, McNamara froze the numbers and, to a certain extent, the quality of U.S. strategic forces, and sought a way of using them that would make these static forces sufficient against a changing threat. This new way consisted of shifting the focus of U.S. targeting toward the Soviet population and industry. *That*, by golly, would remain fairly constant. This targeting by the U.S. would make war perpetually irrational, and therefore well-nigh impossible, *regardless of what the Soviets did* with their own military forces. This last cannot be overemphasized. U.S. planners, discomfited by the prospect of dealing militarily—and in terms of the budget— with an open-ended Soviet military challenge, decided to abstract from that challenge, not to deal with it on its own terms. We would find terms that would give us the assurance of peace at relatively low cost *regardless of what the Soviets did*.

So, whereas by late 1967, according to McNamara's standards of 1961–62, the U.S. was now under-armed (that is, unable to ensure its own protection by destroying Soviet missiles and warheads), according to his new standards the U.S. was quite well enough armed. We could indeed deliver well over 400-megaton equivalents on Soviet cities and, with that, presumably kill at least 25 percent of the Soviet population. Naturally, since actually doing this would result in no good at all for the American people, the U.S. did not have the slightest incentive to carry out such an attack—before, during, or after a Soviet strike on the U.S. So, and this is the point, by the mid-1960s, U.S. military planners had stopped thinking in terms of rational objectives for nuclear war. Indeed, there were now no objectives at all for war. If the Soviets were to start the war, our self-renunciation with regard to strategic weaponry would preclude our having the objective to win.

From Secretary McNamara's day forward, there have been sporadic attempts to embrace the concept of victory in a war started by others, but media opinion coupled with a lack of articulate response from the executive branch of the government has always turned them back. It is certain, however, that if one side does not pursue victory, as we now do not, and the other side does, as the Soviets do, the latter side will shape the outcome of war to its purposes. Having never planned to win, we have foregone the ability and the choice to determine when to stop short of victory.

As the U.S. military planners, who totally shared McNamara's orientation, looked at the Soviet Union during those years, they saw grounds for hoping that the Soviets might think the same way as they did. True, they saw the Soviets starting the construction of missile silos and submarines at a frightening rate. But, since they counted Soviet forces only when they became operational, they were able, at any given time, to discount the acceleration of the Soviet program and therefore delay for about two years facing the implications of truly big figures for Soviet missiles. Like McNamara, they indulged the illusion that the Soviets were not trying to build as large a missile force as ours.

Marshal V. D. Sokolovskii's book, *Soviet Military Strategy*, had explained that the Soviet Union would have to achieve superiority in missile strike forces for purposes of deciding the war during its opening phase.[6] The rate of commencement of Soviet silo construction certainly was consistent with Soviet military thought. Nevertheless, our "best and brightest" figured that the Soviets just had to look at nuclear war as a mutually annihilating spasm. Thus, our "best and brightest" saw arms control negotiations as an essential means of confirming the Soviet military in their own outlook. Besides, they argued, given the kinds of missiles the Soviets then had, the SS-7s and SS-8s, the Soviets could not reasonably try to destroy our missile silos. They concluded that the Soviets were not even technically able to choose for or against rationally waging nuclear war, and that therefore they had not done so. It was necessary for our "best and brightest's" peace of mind to suppose that the Soviets were technically backward and would remain so, and that the Soviets would wait for a technical capability before even deciding whether they wanted it! Hence for a brief moment in the mid-1960s, by a powerful effort at solipsism, McNamara's dreams seemed to correspond to reality.

By 1967, however, fact came to trouble some of our arms controllers' dreams. The Soviets were testing a missile—that we called the SS-9—large enough to carry a 25-megaton bomb. Such a bomb, even given the SS-9's relative inaccuracy, was enough to destroy blast-resistant American silos. For most of American arms controllers, however, the SS-9 was easily explained away. McNamara and arms controllers rejected the notion that the SS-9's combination of huge yield with somewhat mitigated inaccuracy might be the Soviet Union's way of achieving the capability to fight and win a war. Instead, they called it an anti-city terror weapon. McNamara and his cohorts had to admit, however, that such concentrated high yield was a peculiarly inefficient way of destroying cities. Arrogantly, they resorted to the explanation that the Soviets had built such inefficient city-killers because they were technically unable to build efficient ones like the U.S. Poseidon. Nevertheless, beginning in the late 1960s, as the number of SS-9s grew and grew, even these Americans could not deny at least the possibility that the Soviet SS-9 missile—at least in two- or three-on-one attacks—could be used to destroy American Minuteman silos. Sadly, only after McNamara had left office, when the number of SS-9s passed the number of Minuteman launch control centers (100), did the argument about the SS-9's role change. Everyone agreed that great numbers of SS-9s *could* be a threat to the Minuteman force itself, and it became a national priority somehow to avoid their actually becoming one. Since roughly 1968–69, avoiding, and later fixing, "Minuteman vulnerability" became America's number one strategic obsession. Among the many options for dealing with this problem that the Soviets now posed was to ask the Soviets to limit it and solve our problem for us.

So, by the time the SALT I talks formally began in late 1969, a totally new reason had arisen for seeking an arms control agreement. The U.S. now, for the first time, had a serious military problem on its hands. The number of SS-9s might approach, and even surpass, the number of Minutemen. In that case, the Minutemen would be vulnerable. If the Soviets could destroy most of them, as well as a few dozen air bases and submarine ports in a first strike, they could drastically reduce our ability to retaliate. Indeed, in 1969 the Department of Defense judged that the existence of 400 SS-9s, equipped with three 5-megaton MRV warheads, would pose an unacceptable threat to Minuteman. If those MRVs became independently guided, the threat would be total. The Soviets could, in effect, win the war by reducing the U.S. retaliatory force to the unusable option of doing relatively little senseless damage to the Soviet Union. Relatively little, that is, by comparison with what the Soviets could do to the U.S. thereafter.

This very prospect was simultaneously terribly unsettling to advocates of arms control, and terribly attractive. It was attractive because it represented, for the very first time, concrete pressure for the U.S. to enter into an arms control agreement. It was unsettling because if it were the case that the Soviet Union was actually trying to acquire the ability to fight and win a nuclear war and was succeeding, its objectives in entering an arms control agreement had to be unacceptable to the U.S. After all, if the Soviets were working to achieve a war-winning capability, it would be literally nonsense, or deception, for them to enter into a treaty that would deny that to them.

What could be their purpose in entering such a treaty? Prudence would counsel going no further until we were sure that the Soviet Union's objectives were compatible with our own. Moreover, this whole discussion was upsetting because if the Soviets were acquiring these capabilities, then those Americans who had become prominent by arguing that we not do the same had served their country badly. By deciding not to build the countermissile and anti-missile forces we could have built, by not making our strategic forces mobile, and by thinking in terms of a technological plateau codified by arms control, they had forced this terrible state upon us.

According to arms controllers, technology itself, if allowed to advance unchecked, would make the problem much worse. The advent of countermissile missiles in both sides' arsenals was only a matter of time—unless either or both decided to forswear them. But this realization had led straight back to the question of Soviet intentions and to the most effective way of safeguarding ourselves if one assumed, as did nearly all Americans, that the Soviets would pursue their interests regardless of what any treaty said. That question, as we have seen, is profoundly subversive of arms control.

If the Soviets really intended to acquire the capability to fight and win a nuclear war, could any treaty really stop them? Could we see everything connected with the qualitative and quantitative improvements in their forces that would indicate such a capability in time to do something about it? And what would we do if we saw danger? Besides, why would we want to get into this deadly game of cops 'n robbers, hide 'n seek, in the inherently disadvantaged role of the hamstrung cop?

No wonder then that arms controllers like Raymond Garthoff, and even chroniclers sympathetic to arms control, like John Newhouse,[7] treated the problem posed by countermissile missiles with such delicacy! The preferred method was simply to exclude these troublesome questions from the arms control process. Some representatives to SALT from the U.S. Department of Defense insisted on asking the Soviets, in effect, to show that they did not intend to use their missiles in a countermissile mode, by agreeing either to low numbers or small sizes of ICBMs, or to limit what they could carry. They asked the Soviets to discuss why they had built the SS-9 in the first place, and to reconcile what their next generation of missiles would appear to be with their intentions.

The Soviets, correctly, deemed that these questions intruded into the very heart of their military plans and policies, and on this ground refused to talk. They were not there, they said, to give away their country's military secrets. If the negotiations were going to continue, they would do so by concentrating on concrete objectives for the future, and with full respect for each side's sources of information. In other words, we could find out what we could and think what we liked, but if we wanted an agreement, we would have to do it in a narrow framework. Incredibly, the Americans in charge of the negotiations agreed with the Soviets that their basic intentions and capabilities were their business. For their own reasons, they wanted the negotiations to proceed and to succeed.[8]

Moreover, arms controllers wanted the talks to proceed without airing the United States' own military strategy before the American people. In 1965, Robert McNamara had publicly stated that, henceforth in case of wars, our targeting policy would aim at the assured destruction of the Soviet Union. In 1967 he had stated publicly that we could not (rather than should not) significantly limit damage from an eventual Soviet strike. Obviously, no American policymaker had dared to make clear to the American people that his policy was to assure that the Soviet Union had the forces necessary for the destruction of the United States! The purpose of arms control was to make sure that this would never change. Indeed, the leading policymakers of the Johnson administration actively and consciously misrepresented to the American people what they were trying to achieve. As they consciously limited the size of American strategic forces and delayed programs for improving accuracy, they bombasted about their commitment to American superiority. As McGeorge Bundy later revealed, "What we did not say so loud was that the principal use of this [American] numerical superiority was as a reassurance to the American public and as a means of warding off demands for still larger forces."[9] But the lowest point this rhetoric ever reached was Richard Nixon's formulation that our forces would be "second to none."

In 1986, Robert McNamara published a little book, *Blundering*

Into Disaster, that makes the same point even more forcefully.[10]
McNamara admits that while he was overseeing the U.S. military's
procurement of strategic weapons, its preparations and operations,
he was convinced that "under no circumstances" could they be used.
Cynically, he gave the American people, and perhaps Presidents
Kennedy and Johnson, the idea that he was making plans that, if
worse came to worst, would avoid the worst. All the while he privately believed that it was basically humbug—he designed weapons that were indeed useless.

How large should U.S. forces be? How accurate? What should
be their purpose if they ever had to be used? How big and sophisticated should be our anti-aircraft and anti-missile defense? Even
if one granted that under prevailing technical conditions we could
do no more than threaten to inflict—and prepare to suffer—irrational
destruction, should we not at least have been trying to alter these
technical conditions as soon as possible? Is Mutual Assured Destruction a condition we suffer only so long as we must, or is it something we want to preserve forever? Obviously the Bundys and
McNamaras of the world think that other Americans can't be trusted
to make judgments on such matters.

During McNamara's years in the Pentagon, especially in 1964–67,
his annual reports discussed these questions with reasonable
clarity—for those who understood the jargon. The same applies to
books like Wayne Smith's *How Much Is Enough?* Nevertheless, the
theologians of Mutual Assured Destruction (MAD) were understandably not eager to put to the public the question: Shall Americans remain undefended forever? Debating such questions in public
rather than among experts, and in jargon, would have subverted
the whole work that Robert McNamara had performed in the 1960s.
Just as importantly, it would have subverted the entire *class* of
officials whom he had made into the leaders of the Pentagon and
the defense industries.

The arms control process, by obscuring these critical questions,
offered the chance to abstract from them. Our arms controllers' only
substantive agenda became the codification of Mutual Assured
Destruction as U.S. policy into the indefinite future. This, of course,
would secure the future of their own class. The most effective way

to further that agenda was to keep it out of the normal channels of public discourse and to transform it into an agenda of abstruse points discussed out of public view in secret with the Soviets. If they and the Soviets talked only about arcane matters, and if the only matters that Congress would debate were the ones framed by U.S.-Soviet agreement, the military policy of the 1960s would sink ever-deeper roots in the U.S. Indeed, there appeared a new language for discussing strategic matters. By its terms and words, alternatives to the military policy of the 1960s could not even be conceived.

Technical Trivializing:
The Artificial World of Verification

Given the intellectual inclinations and political priorities of most of those Americans involved in the arms control process, it was not clear at the outset of SALT what the talks could be about.

Any inquiry into the Soviets' political and military reasons for entering into the arms control process had to be excluded from the negotiations as inherently futile and disruptive. Yet discussion of our own purpose—the maintenance on both sides of relatively small and, above all, militarily irrational nuclear forces—could be (and was) vigorous in private. Were we to try to bring public pressure on the Soviets by "going public" with this line of argument, it would lead to Soviet rejection and would make arms control itself unpopular in the United States. What, then, could the actual talks be about? There was only one subject left: verification.

Information vs. Control

The talks could not avoid one preliminary: the amount of knowledge about each other's activities that both sides would require in order to negotiate an agreement. Since the Eisenhower years, American arms controllers had substituted insistence on our having private *knowledge* about Soviet armaments for the earlier insistence that these armaments be subject to international *control*. Knowledge and control, however, are not one and the same thing. Moreover, U.S. knowledge could not be directly linked to action to enforce agreements because, rhetoric aside, it is impossible to commit a democracy to automatically react to any activity its government considers in violation of a bilateral agreement. Nevertheless, our negotiators chose to consider the amount of *knowledge* available as the practical equivalent of *control*. Any plausibility in this proposition derives from the fact that its converse is obviously true: to the extent that we lack knowledge of a particular Soviet activity, we cannot discuss it—much less hope to affect it.

Thus the negotiators strove to construct some proportionality between the knowledge available and the agreement negotiated—despite the fact that however symmetrical that proportion turned out to be, it would not be terribly relevant. But what could that proportion be?

President Truman had said that there had to be "*immediate* warning of *any* threatened violation. Disarmament must be policed *continuously and thoroughly*. It must be founded upon free and open interchange of information across national borders." (Emphasis added) Clearly, if the U.S. took that seriously, there could be no negotiations. Yet the moment the U.S., resigning itself to reliance upon technical collection, abandoned insistence on cooperative verification to ensure the kind of access to Soviet information that the Soviets had about the U.S., it would always have to worry about the relationship of what it knew to what it did not know. Once having agreed to deal solely on the basis of restricted information, Americans could no longer explain to one another how much access to a particular field would be enough, and how little would be too little. But by then negotiations had become so important to some Americans that they denounced any American insistence that the Soviets "open up." That demand was so unacceptable to the Soviet Union that it was viewed as prima facie evidence of the bad faith of those who insisted upon it. Genuine skepticism about arms control was denounced as warmongering.

At the outset of the negotiations, in response to the most tentative of feelers, the Soviet Union had made crystal clear it would not give the U.S. any information—much less knowledge. It would provide neither "facts" nor the ability to check them out.

In 1951, the Soviets had agreed to a statement of principles on verification of disarmament that Americans took as an agreement that there should be "unrestricted access without veto to all places as necessary for the purpose of verification." The Soviets, however, had reserved the right to decide what would and would not be necessary to verify their compliance. That is why at the time they explicitly rejected the American side's formulation that "verification should ensure that only agreed limits and reductions take place, *but also that retained armed forces and armaments do not exceed agreed levels.*"[11] (Emphasis supplied.) Soviet U.N. representative Valerian Zorin explained the rejection by saying that even though it was eager to enter into arrangements for disarmament, the Soviet Union would never accept control over its armaments. The Soviets would be delighted to show us that they had destroyed the arms they undertook to destroy, the factories where arms production is banned by agreement, and the sites where—by agreement—only a certain number of weapons exist. To do more would be to establish "an international system of espionage."[12] (It is interesting to note that in 1986 at Reykjavik, Mikhail Gorbachev took precisely the same position!)

The Soviet Union has much experience in showing Western observers the face it wishes them to see. For example, according to an article in the February 16, 1925, issue of *The New York American*, the Soviet G.P.U. (forerunner of the KGB) took a group of reporters through Moscow's Lubyanka prison, and left them convinced that the place, "a former first-class hotel," "still bears traces of its ancient comforts." "Sanitary conditions prevail and the food is wholesome." The regime's worst enemy has a comfortable room and spends his time writing fiction. By the same token, *National Geographic* (August 1944) reported from the Kolyma gold fields that the workers were tended to by a dietician! In fact, the fields killed one-third of their inmates every year.

These kinds of restricted "on-site inspections" would leave the U.S. facing even more questions than if we based our approach to arms control purely on our own intelligence sources. At least the

U.S. could expect to control those! Thus, years before it formally did so in July 1968, the U.S. had become reconciled that any and all arms control discussions would have to take place on the basis of the meager knowledge about the Soviet forces gained by U.S. intelligence, and on the basis of bountiful information about American forces published in the American press or supplied by U.S. negotiators.

This asymmetry meant that U.S.-Soviet arms control would become a chess game in which only one participant could see both sides of the board. This means that the shape of both the negotiations and of the agreements would have to be set by the capability of U.S. intelligence.

The negotiations thus provided the American side with virtually no knowledge, no basis upon which to act, which it did not already have. Moreover, the presence or absence of an agreement does not add or subtract from the United States' power to reward or punish in its own interest. But to act in the context of an agreement, a country needs more than a notion of what its interests require. It needs precise proof of specific acts that contravene specific provisions that accurately define its interests.

Any item treated in international law must first be defined. That is, it must be translated into precise legal terms. U.S. officials had to consider how well U.S. intelligence information could permit us to define the parameters of the Soviet weaponry that we wished to limit. Could U.S. intelligence allow us to define all, or even a substantial part, of what was necessary? Even assuming it could, would it provide enough information about relevant Soviet activities so that the U.S. government would know unambiguously that a violation was occurring, and could we know it in time to surmount the difficulty the violation was creating? The answer to these questions was: only a little.

The Americans who first advocated arms control in the early postwar period had wisely warned against agreements based on the U.S. intelligence community's ability to play "cops" to the Soviet Union's "robbers." Those who conceal, they argued, have huge inherent advantages over those who seek to uncover. Even total, direct observation of a country's armaments program, so long as it is superficial, is not enough, because any given activity may occur for any number of purposes. J. Robert Oppenheimer pointed out that it is impossible to tell whether someone is mining uranium for peaceful or for bellicose purposes. Moreover, observation that a country is doing certain things mandated by a treaty is no guarantee that the same country is *not* doing other things forbidden by that treaty. Indeed, occasional corroboration of the occurrence of treaty-compliant behavior may well build false confidence. That is why these early arms controllers had insisted on *controls* rather than on verification, and had argued that to accept less was to practice self-deception.

Magic Assumptions

By the late 1960s, rejecting the earlier wisdom, the new generation of American arms controllers was living by the proposition that knowledge equals control, and that we should have arms control to the limit of our knowledge. With that the U.S. had to ask itself two practical questions: What is that limit? And, what meaning can agreements made within that limit possess? These two questions, especially the second, were uncomfortable. To pursue them honestly would endanger arms control. Shunning such honesty, American arms controllers translated these questions into two assumptions, on which the arms control process since 1967–68 has been built. They are: 1) *For practical purposes, what U.S. intelligence sees of the Soviet Union is all there is to see*; and 2) *For practical purposes, those aspects of Soviet strategic forces encompassed by treaties and thus controlled by them, stand for all the Soviet Union's strategic forces.*

Thus, arms controllers used the U.S. intelligence community's ability to learn about some things that happen in the Soviet Union to perform a kind of magic: intelligence would erase the whole concern about the incompatibility between the Soviets' geopolitical goals and negotiating objectives and our own. It would fill the yawning absence of any U.S. policy for enforcing compliance, and indeed allay concern for the quality of any agreements. If the agreements were *verifiable*, how bad could they be? Verifiability would give us the chance to right any wrongs. Who could doubt we would do so?

This magic, in turn, was achieved by another magic: the U.S. intelligence community let the few things that it knew—or thought it knew—stand for many more things of which it had literally no knowledge. In turn, and by the same token, the arms control process then profoundly affected U.S. intelligence. Let us see how all this occurred.

The advent of the U-2 high-altitude reconnaissance aircraft in 1956 and of the first SAMOS photo-reconnaissance satellite in 1960, along with the expanding American signals intelligence network, proved to be a powerful catalyst in this magic.

The myth of the satellites' near-magical powers became unstoppable when they showed that, contrary to earlier belief, the Soviets had only 14 ICBMs on launch pads in 1962. Banishing the ghost of the missile gap had made possible the resolution of the Cuban missile crisis—which had itself been brought on by a discovery made by high-altitude cameras. Thus intelligence officers started to argue that this kind of knowledge, in the nuclear age, was enough to resolve crises. President Kennedy had brandished the photos and the Soviets had retreated. Both scholarly and popular literature abounded with assurances that the Soviets would never again expose themselves to such humiliations and that the existence of space-based cameras was more than enough to keep them scrupulously faithful to agreements. This obscured the fact that the Soviet Union had backed down not because of exposure or because of an axiomatic nuclear parity, but because of very real U.S. military superiority. Like the cat that, once burned, suffered cold rather than get near the stove, American officials learned the wrong lessons from the Cuban crisis.

In 1962, the Arms Control and Disarmament Agency sponsored a "summer study" on verification that produced an intellectual consensus—that although the Soviets could cheat on arms control agreements, they could not do so significantly before they were discovered. This was not so remarkable given the military and intelligence technology of 1962. The "threat of the day" consisted of primitive, pad-launched missiles. Each took months to deploy. During the time it would take the Soviets to deploy a large force, the satellites of the day—despite the limited amount of film on board—

could be reasonably expected to find most of it in time for the U.S. to react.

Disastrous errors often consist of unwarranted extrapolations of the truth. If one could reasonably have expected missiles and launchers to remain forever frozen in the technology of 1962, if that snapshot were engraved in eternity, then it would have made sense to base national defense policy on U.S.-Soviet agreements to limit the number of launchers/missiles, and to focus U.S. intelligence on observing their construction and operation. But, already in 1962, one could easily foresee that missiles would soon be far more easily handled, that launchers could be reloaded and movable, and that accuracy as well as numbers of warheads would be very important. But the "best and brightest," who became the ruling element in those years, wanted nothing so much as to stop the clock at 1962. Hence the consensus assumed that projected increases in photo resolution, film capacity, rate of recovery, and sensitivity of antennae would translate directly into earlier and even more certain verification of arms control. This consensus helped to make arms control into the very core of U.S. arms policy, which also came to have as its objective freezing the military situation of the mid-1960s; and, when that proved impossible, recreating it.

Technical Keyholes:
What You See and What You Don't

Let us look briefly at the technical means in the hands of U.S. intelligence, at what they can and cannot learn, and at how the inescapable need to use assumptions in order to interpret their "take" leads us to overestimate our knowledge, underestimate our ignorance, indulge our prejudices, and embrace our dreams.

Since SAMOS, the U.S. has orbited three generations of imaging satellites—the latest being the KH-11 series, first launched in late 1976. Their acuity has improved so that they can reportedly discern objects only inches in size. Their orbits have ranged from less than 90 miles to nearly 300 miles high, giving the satellites the theoretical ability to see anything within several hundred miles of their ground track.

These satellites, however, have some limitations that even high officials too often forget. First, not only can a satellite not "cover" or "image" all that it can theoretically see, it cannot even continuously cover the square kilometer directly on its ground track—a line that if drawn to scale on a large globe would be imperceptibly thin. Clearly, thousands of such satellites would be needed to do what former CIA Director Stansfield Turner comically claimed we do routinely: keep track of everything important on the face of the earth! But these satellites are so expensive that the U.S. has always had fewer than a handful in orbit at any one time. They routinely take pictures of sites we know to be interesting, and at most, take one low-quality picture per year of vast countries.

Such snapshots are useful. By looking at tanks, missiles, factories, movements of people, plantings of crops, etc., one might conceivably learn much about what things are available to a government, something about what that government is doing with them, and some hints about what it intends to do. Yet, many of the things that make for military or economic capability normally take place under roof, or are brought outdoors only when imaging satellites are not overhead. Production, even of things as large as ICBMs, takes place where eyes from space cannot see. Development of new weapons and stockpiling of old ones takes place under roof. Even big, outdoor things do not fall easily into the satellites' sights.

The best example of this came along in 1983: the Soviet radar at Krasnoyarsk. This huge installation is unmistakable—once a camera is pointed at it. But the intelligence community did not find it for many months. Yet finding the radar proved to be only the beginning of the controversy about what the Soviets intended by building it. Did they mean to violate the ABM Treaty? More important, do they mean to have an anti-missile defense? While the Soviets and their apologists claim innocence, and while most of the world cries foul, the pictures are silent. Pictures tell but little about intentions, and their tales are inherently ambiguous. Most activities, even if they take place outdoors, also may be observed only partially or with great difficulty. Of course, activities are inherently more ambiguous than things.

To figure out what an object on a picture is, never mind what it means, the analyst needs a key—another picture similar to the one in question, the identity and function of which the analyst already knows. The analyst then assumes that the new object is like the old one. When an object shows up that is unlike anything the analyst has ever seen, he is compelled either to spin airy theories or to ignore it. In other words, photo reconnaissance is so naturally oriented toward the known, that the less the analyst knows about what he is looking at, the more he is likely to fill it with what is already on his mind or to disregard it. When the pictures concern large systems or activities, the results are still more subjective. The analyst may have opinions, but he is certain to have few facts on the Soviet leadership's plans for using the facilities he sees. Almost wholly beyond that analyst's grasp is the question of what facilities have been built under the cover of others, or entirely clandestinely.

What, then, can—and cannot—the satellites see of Soviet strategic forces? They can see research laboratories with known affiliations and measure their size, and, from how busy they are or from new facilities constructed, conclude that they will turn out "a better model" of their standard product. But they cannot tell what is coming, when it is coming, how good it will be, in how many copies it is being produced, or how it will be used. Satellites can see test ranges. If the Soviets allowed them to, they could see missiles being prepared for tests. But, unlike bombers that sooner or later must fly and be seen, the Soviets do not have to show us missiles, and they don't. We do see preparations at test ranges, from which we gather some hints—perhaps useful—about the missiles to be tested.

Satellites see factories where missiles may be produced. But since the Soviets know when the satellites are coming, the satellites never get to count how many missiles come out, or where they go. Satellites see fields where silo launchers are dug, fitted out, and sometimes loaded with missile cannisters in plain view. If the silos are known, in plain view, and in good weather, the satellites can measure them rather accurately, and count them. But they never see all the silos loaded, and have not the foggiest notion whether or not any or all have been loaded or unloaded. Indeed, never seeing the missiles themselves, the analysts *suppose* but do not *know* where they are.

In signals intelligence, antennas serve the function of telescopes. But it is much easier to build, and to place in orbit, very large antennas than it is to build optical telescopes of the same size. Hence, unlike imagery collectors, signal collectors can theoretically work well while far enough away to receive signals from areas comprising thousands of square miles. That is—if the signals are *broadcast*. If, however, the signals are beamed, the antenna, regardless of its size, must be within the beam's footprint. That requires knowing whence the beams originate, their direction, and, at whatever altitude, making sure that the satellites stay in the beams as long as possible. Of course, interesting electronic devices may emit beams from unexpected locations. That is why it makes sense to have many signal collectors orbiting the earth to detect, identify, and report the location of the emitters whose beams they literally run across. This is feasible because, on the whole, signal collectors are cheaper than telescopic cameras.

Signals intelligence, however, suffers from the fact that it can easily intercept huge amounts of uninteresting signals while interesting ones remain hidden or ambiguous. Unlike in World War II, when almost every electronic emission was interesting from the standpoint of intelligence, the electronic environment of the 1980s is tremendously dense, and requires sophisticated judgment to choose which of hundreds of thousands of signals is worth recording, as well as to divide signals into kinds, and to process each kind appropriately. Moreover, modern signals are seldom simple—even if not encoded. Hence, the results of signals intelligence depend much less on the sensitivity of antennas than on the way in which the processing and analysis of signals interact with the signals themselves.

The targets of signals intelligence include not only all kinds of militarily or politically significant communications, but also telemetry. These signals are usually broadcast from airplanes or missiles that are being tested, and relate data on the quality of weapons. Signals intelligence also picks up the actual operating characteristics of electronic equipment, especially radars; and it also identifies and locates, at any given time, the various kinds of equipment that emit significant amounts of electromagnetic energy.

Communications are either broadcast or transmitted along more or less narrow beams. Aircraft in tactical situations have no choice but to broadcast. Long-distance telephone traffic is relayed by wide beams from station to station or through satellites. The intelligence collector must simply contrive to place his antenna within those wide beams, either on the ground or in space. For the collector, the principle is simple: identify the target, figure out what kind of signal it puts out, and place the appropriate antenna there. For the target, the principle is equally simple: check to see if an antenna is positioned to pick up a certain emission, and then either shift that communication to a safe channel, or transmit knowing that someone is listening—which means encryption and/or deception.

Our point here is that *in most cases, the products of technical intelligence do not speak for themselves.* Each picture or intercept becomes meaningful only in the context of a set of assumptions manufactured by the analyst. In practice, a launcher for a particular missile, for example, will be seen as the thing capable of launching that missile, and be regularly associated with that missile. An analyst should judge that something "deployed" if he sees it associated with troops. When working with things the meaning of which is not clear, one naturally tries to draw meaning out of any routine one sees.

In signals intelligence, meaning is more elusive than in imagery. The meaning of most signals is not readily apparent. The telemetry from a weapon being tested may include up to a hundred channels, each reporting the readings of individual gauges throughout the weapon. The matter becomes more interesting when two or more gauges report on each instrument, and the readings differ. Each channel contains a modulated signal that results in a squiggle across a piece of paper. Before the analyst can make use of the information, he has to postulate both the instrument to which each channel refers, and the scale on which each gauge is based. Without these postulates, which contain substantial arbitrariness, the telemetry would be nonsense.

The "vacuum cleaner" approach to communications intelligence involves an analogous problem. Since even modern equipment can record only an infinitesimal percentage of the number of channels that are theoretically available, the analyst and the collector, working together, must first devise priorities in terms of who is using the channels and what subjects are discussed. Second, analysts must postulate the extent to which the intercepted communications represent the much larger mass that is not intercepted.

As they go about their work, analysts—and, even more, collectors of technical intelligence—do not normally contemplate the possibility that the people whose images and signals they are looking at are aware that they are being observed and might act to shape what the intelligence collectors and analysts see. Few U.S. intelligence officials have drawn the right conclusion from the fact that the Soviet Union, soon after the launching of our intelligence satellites, figured out that satellites in sun-synchronous orbits took pictures, and that since the 1960s the Soviets have placed sensitive things under roof when these American satellites were scheduled to pass overhead. The run-of-the-mill explanation is that the Soviets are hiding things—and that is correct. But in fact, by hiding certain things and not others, the Soviets are able to shape our conclusions. By the same token, U.S. analysts were not surprised that after espionage and leaks told the Soviets about U.S. interception of telemetry, the Soviets began to encrypt that telemetry to unprecedented degrees. Nevertheless, U.S. analysts—and, even more, collectors—have been very cool to all suggestions that the Soviets might not just be denying us some information, but biasing that which they choose to let us retrieve.

It just stands to reason that the engineers who had designed "national technical means" have been accustomed to working against nature—picking up ever-weaker signals from ever-farther away, distinguishing signals from noise, and making optical instruments for better resolution, with longer life, and more flexibility—have failed to take deception into account. These achievements are demanding enough by themselves, and the people who do them are seldom concerned with the larger framework in which they work. The analysts, for their part, have the difficult task of making sense out of things the meaning of which is not obvious. They hazard their postulates in order to come up with reasonable explanations. From their position, to consider that the evidence on which they work is not just slim, but may also be bogus, is to condemn themselves to further hedging conclusions that are not firm in the first place. Sisyphus, by comparison, would seem fortunate.

How, then, did the fruits and limitations of our technical intelligence system frame the arms control negotiations that began in the late 1960s? In the mid-1960s, when the missiles disappeared from Soviet launch pads and went into hardened silos and submarine tubes, both military planners and arms controllers went along with the intelligence analysts' convenient—but intellectually sloppy— equation that one site or launch tube equaled one missile. Both groups knew that missiles could be launched from makeshift pads, and that missile tubes, and even primitive silos, could be reloaded. Both knew that the Soviets could do this without the elaborate, "standard" two-way communications links that the U.S. monitors and that the Soviets know are monitored. But military planners shied away from dealing with this fact because it could not be quantified, because it could not be translated into plans to "do something about it," and because it could be as plausibly denied as asserted.

Arms controllers, for their part, realized that focusing intelligence on questions Americans could not resolve would impede the "process" and undermine the intellectual consensus on which it was built, whereas focusing on things we could learn would reinforce both the "process" and the consensus. Hence, as new satellites were planned, intelligence officials had every incentive to concentrate even further on the known at the expense of the unknown: on arms control parameters that we knew well because we had invented them, rather than on a military reality that extended beyond them—but we knew not how far.

So U.S. intelligence fell into the habit of watching and listening to little bits of Soviet reality, came to think it knew it well, and largely forgot about that overwhelming chunk of Soviet reality that they could neither see nor hear. The information U.S. intelligence became habituated to receiving also reinforced the premises upon which it was being sought: missiles could be launched only from silos, there was to be only one missile per silo, and there was one warhead per missile. Bigger missiles (defined as ones that came out of wider silos) were thought to be more dangerous than small ones. The daily business of the talks on offensive arms could only be haggling about the number and size of missile silos and launch tubes on both sides. When anti-missile systems were the topic, the daily business was the even more basic one of defining anti-missile systems out of whole cloth, as it were, in terms of the little bits of Soviet reality evident to U.S. intelligence.

Defining the Terms for the Interim Agreement of 1972

Articles I and II of the Interim Agreement on "strategic offensive arms" were advertised as limiting intercontinental ballistic missiles. Perversely, they dealt only indirectly with missiles by limiting *launchers* for ICBMs. But the agreement did not define an ICBM precisely because, on the basis of what satellites could see about a missile—much less about a launcher—it is impossible to tell unambiguously whether it is meant to launch a warhead to intercontinental range or not. After all, how far a missile travels depends in large part on how much is loaded on it. Hence, the U.S. intelligence community has habituated itself to calling the SS-20 a three-warhead missile with *intermediate* range, that can travel to *intercontinental* range if two warheads are removed. It could just as easily have called it a single warhead missile whose intercontinental range *decreases* to intermediate when two warheads are added. But this is only the most obvious case. The range and carrying capacity of missiles may be increased by changing fuel, adding stages, or setting the engines differently. One can argue that by doing such things the missile ceases to be what it was and becomes "new." But unless international inspectors can view the missiles as they are assembled and fueled, no international agreement could specify the criteria by which any missile, at any given time, should or should not be called an ICBM. Intelligence satellites provide insufficient information for both the formulation of distinctions and the inspection of those distinctions. So these two articles deal with launchers, on the obviously incorrect assumption that a launcher of a given configuration can fire only one kind of missile (and, indeed, that there will be only one missile for it to fire).

But U.S. satellites cannot expect regularly to see any and all means by which any given missile may be launched. If by "launcher" one refers to any means of launching, then any attempt to limit launchers on the basis of intelligence information would have to be judged foredoomed. To be launched, missiles need but to be raised upright, provided with a small amount of electrical power and some data on their position. The equipment for providing these services to a U.S. Minuteman missile has been carried on the back of a jeep, and the Minuteman, fully mobile, has been launched in that configuration.

The equipment for launching a certain Soviet ICBM that the U.S. routinely considered—and still considers—to be exclusively silo-launched, though more extensive, was once in a very small convoy of trucks accompanying the missile (spotted long ago on one of the infrequent occasions when one of our satellites was not where it was supposed to be). Therefore, an honest analyst must admit that so long as the existence and path of our intelligence satellites are known and their coverage does not blanket whole regions, hiding mobile launchers will remain easy, and finding them when they do not wish to be found will remain a rarity. So mobile launchers cannot be defined and monitored.

That is why the articles dealt with "fixed, land-based" launchers. But even that was an exaggeration. After all, land-based launchers may be fixed, but instead of relying for their safety on huge, obvious, concrete-girded holes in the ground, they may rely on the secrecy of horizontal emplacement in warehouses. At the right time, the roofs could be removed and winches could raise the missiles. In sum, then, Articles I and II let the one category of launchers normally visible to satellites stand for all others, which in turn were made to stand for all missiles.

Article II makes only one distinction among launchers: between those for "light" ICBMs and those for "heavy" ICBMs. Of course, it neglects to define "light" and "heavy." How could this have been done, even if the Soviets had agreed? The actual weight of any missile is known only to its owners. Observers can only conjecture. Knowing this, U.S. negotiators substituted the *volume* of the launchers for the volume of the missiles, and the volume of the missiles for their weight, which in turn was a substitution for what they really had to know to be relevant: throw-weight, or how much weight a missile can deliver to what range. This is what they wanted to limit, because they equated a missile's high throw-weight with the capacity to destroy opposing missiles in their silos. Such a missile can be used rationally to wage a nuclear war, not just to cause indiscriminate damage.

Even today, U.S. intelligence can make only an educated guess about the throw-weight of any missile the testing of which is observed under the right conditions. It absolutely cannot prove that its estimates are correct—even to itself. Even if the negotiators had agreed to skip the substitutions and limit missiles to "X" pounds of throw-weight, the Soviet Union could always have told Americans who complained that a Soviet missile exceeded that throw-weight that the Soviet Union knew better than the U.S. what that throw-weight was. So the attempt to limit "heavy" launchers was based on the ability of U.S. satellites to tell the difference between a wider silo and a narrower one, and on the willingness of American negotiators to let that difference stand for the difference they really needed to know but could not define—that between missiles with lots of throw-weight and ones with much less.

However, had the negotiators been able to define throw-weight in a way measurable by intelligence, they would have faced three problems that are even less tractable: defining, in terms of intelligence information, the permissible miniaturization of warheads, the missiles' accuracy, and the numbers in which both missiles and warheads were being produced. Because these problems were not tractable given the information available to the U.S., SALT I was written as if they did not exist.

Let us see what this means. Radars at the end of the Soviet Union's Pacific Ocean test range can measure the ballistic characteristics of reentering Soviet warheads, measuring size and inferring weight. But how much nuclear yield can be packed into each small package? Moreover, warheads tested in one configuration may be used operationally in another—more or fewer warheads on a different missile. But our point is twofold: first, throw-weight is an inadequate measure of a missile's military capacity because of great uncertainty as to how well a nation may utilize it. Second, the radar data about the size of warheads cannot be reduced to formulae that can establish a minimum size or a maximum yield, or a maximum number per missile.

All of this is even more important because a warhead's accuracy is perhaps the most important single determinant of its usefulness. (It is important to remember, however, that greater yield in warheads, especially when combined with greater numbers of warheads can make up for deficiencies in accuracy.) Although analysis of telemetry data from Soviet missile tests—especially when compared with data from our own tests—will yield some reasonable estimates about how precise the missile's accelerometers and post-boost release maneuvers are, still, the results are merely estimates. They cannot be used to confront a Soviet Union that refuses us access to its missile designers' data. So accuracy cannot be controlled.

Even less can the total number of missiles and warheads be controlled because satellites cannot count the numbers produced or stockpiled. Hence cynical negotiators made no attempt to limit production, and were totally silent on stockpiles. Such limits would have been unverifiable, beyond argument. Hence, even if it had been possible, which it was not, to define and therefore to limit the effectiveness of Soviet missiles in terms of intelligence data, the effort would have proved fruitless because of the inability of U.S. intelligence to gather significant information on production and stockpiling. The final evidence that U.S. negotiators did not seriously try is Article IV, which says, "Modernization and replacement of strategic offensive ballistic missiles and launchers covered by this interim agreement may be undertaken." The U.S. would learn later what these words could mean to a Soviet Union intent on having a war-fighting, war-surviving, war-winning missile force.

Defining the Terms for the ABM Treaty

Anti-missile equipment is even harder to define in terms of intelligence data. Quite simply, ABM equipment looks to cameras and sounds to electronic interceptors very much like equipment that can be used for mere warning of ballistic missile attack and for defending against aircraft. Not surprisingly, then, the definitions of ABM systems in the treaty are circular. Article II of the ABM Treaty says that "an ABM system is a system to counter strategic ballistic missiles or their elements in flight trajectory, currently consisting of: . . ." This formula complicates the tautology by making it depend on intentions. Note the use of the word "to" rather than "that can" or "that may be able to." The formula also adds the imponderable of what is and is not a "strategic" ballistic missile. Whereas for the U.S., "strategic" means "intercontinental," for the Soviet Union it means whatever can have a decisive effect on the struggle. Moreover, the formula falsely suggests that the ease or difficulty of intercepting a missile's reentry vehicles is affected chiefly by the missile's range. In fact, ease or difficulty of interception depends on characteristics, the altitude of the trajectory, as well as the size and shape of ballistic reentry vehicles that do not depend on range. Thus, an anti-missile system said to protect against short-range ballistic missiles can also protect against longer-range ones, depending on the size and shape of the RVs. In other words, the ABM Treaty's basic premise, based as it is on a faulty American typology and on the imponderable factor of intentions, is both useless and misleading.

But let us continue with Article II's tautology: "ABM interceptor missiles, which are interceptor missiles constructed and deployed for an ABM role, or of a type tested in an ABM mode." Naturally, the negotiators could not come up with any objective criteria by which to determine the role for which any interceptor missile is "constructed and deployed," nor with any agreed-upon criteria by which to determine what is and what is not "an ABM mode." Indeed, the negotiators tried to deal with the fact that much equipment used to defend against aircraft is inherently useful for defending against ballistic reentry vehicles—with the fact that no firm objective distinction between the two missions is possible—by prohibiting testing of air defense equipment "in an ABM mode." The U.S. delegation thought of some objective criteria: e.g., if a radar is tracking a reentry vehicle, it is "in an ABM mode." But the Soviets refused to agree. Even if the Soviets had agreed, however, the concept of "ABM mode" could not possibly have dealt with equipment that performs both

the anti-air and anti-RV mission without need for special arrangements. This became undeniable when, in 1978, U.S. and Soviet representatives in the Standing Consultative Commission reached a
secret but nonbinding agreement that went some distance in meeting the concerns expressed by U.S. negotiators in 1972. Nevertheless, that agreement has not stopped the calibration of air defense
radars with ABM equipment. Much less has it affected the Soviet
Union's dual purpose surface-to-air missile system, the SA-12.

The Article then goes on to "cover" "ABM launchers" and "ABM
radars" with the same tautological blanket. Such launchers and
radars are defined, respectively, as "constructed and deployed for
an ABM role or of a type tested in an ABM mode." Surely the U.S.
negotiators had seen satellite photographs of Soviet ABM sites and
had been briefed on intercepts of tests of Soviet radars and rocket
guidance systems. These intelligence briefings usually include
reasonable arguments why this or that radar, missile, or launcher
may be intended for ABM work: e.g., the missile is fast enough and
accurate enough; the radar is powerful enough; the tests have
occurred in conjunction with the launching of ballistic warheads,
etc. But none of these arguments should be confused with the pre-
sentation of objective proof. After all, how good and useful does
a missile, radar, etc., have to be for ABM purposes for its owners
to judge it an ABM? This is not an objective technical question, but
a strategic one that the owners alone can decide. At any rate, the
ABM Treaty's negotiators, who "knew an ABM system when they
saw one," did not even try to objectify their understanding of what
distinguishes ABM components from things that may look or sound
like them, but are not. They just couldn't. The job was inherently
impossible, so they just ignored it.

Of course they could not talk about limiting production of ABM
interceptors or guidance radars. Since production of ABM interceptors and guidance radars had to be permitted in order to maintain
limited ABM deployments, any attempt to limit their production
would have had to be based on good knowledge of Soviet production facilities, and that was not to be had via intelligence. They tried
to limit large battle-management radars, but could not overcome
the fact that these are physically indistinguishable from air defense

missile guidance radars, and large early-warning radars. The only obvious characteristic of an early-warning radar is that it be on the periphery of the country and oriented outward. This, satellites can see.

But alas, the ABM battle-management function is also best performed from the periphery, with an outward orientation. In fact, the battle-management network for the U.S. ABM system was on the periphery and oriented outward. Early-warning radars must also detect and track incoming reentry vehicles well enough to predict where they are heading so the people there can be warned. But if they do that job very well, the information they pass can be used directly by other radars that guide interceptor missiles. How well is well enough? It is essential to note that it is impossible to answer this question merely by photographing these large radars and analyzing their intercepted signals. This kind of radar is inherently capable of changing the signals it puts out simply by changing the computer software that runs it. Also, mere changes in software can process what the radar "sees" so as to make the data more fit for early warning or for managing a battle against RVs. Since none of this may be seen or heard by satellites, the ABM Treaty's provisions with regard to large, phased-array radars could constrain only those who wished to be constrained by them.

The scarcity of relevant information about essential matters forced the ABM Treaty's negotiators to focus primarily on deployment. But defining deployment was only slightly easier. In practice, a limit on deployment means no more than that once something is agreed by both sides to be an ABM component limited by the treaty, neither side may set it out for the other side's satellites to see it ready for use, unless specifically permitted. In fact, limits on deployment mean less than meet the eye. Since the treaty does not limit the production of any item whatever, and since intelligence cannot follow an item that is produced, what is limited? Thus, unbeknownst to U.S. intelligence, and totally in accord with the treaty to boot, any and all ABM items may be produced at will and stored near or far from where they may be used. There they may lie in a box, or be kept ready for use. In the latter case, the word "deployment" hides more than it explains. So, in the absence of exact knowledge about production and storage, any discussion of ABM "deployments" has to abstract from much substance.

The negotiators' discussion of ABM components other than those currently in use was even more abstract. Not knowing what laser weapons or optical pointer-trackers might look like or how they might perform, and having no idea whether or how such components might be exposed to intelligence, the negotiators understandably dealt with them simply by agreeing to discuss them if and when they were created.

Defining the Yields of Underground Tests

The negotiations on banning underground tests of nuclear weapons yielding more than 150 kilotons consisted of a drawn-out inquiry into whether the Soviet Union would allow independently manned seismic listening posts at its nuclear test sites. Since the Soviets would not, the real negotiations shifted to within the U.S. intelligence community. U.S. intelligence simply had to decide for itself, by itself, what seismic rumblings from the Eurasian land mass meant. Given the lack of "ground truth" (specific knowledge of how the geology of the Soviet test sites and the earth's crust between those test sites and our own listening posts were affected by the rumblings from explosions of known yield), the rumblings from explosions of unknown yield could not be authoritatively evaluated. Hence, the U.S. had to develop its own (largely abstract) mathematical models for judging our own data. None of the possible models was inherently preferable over any other. But since the Threshold Test Ban Treaty was signed in 1974, the U.S. intelligence community has fought internecine battles over which model to use. It seems that some models find the Soviet Union in violation more often than other models. Since 1974, U.S. intelligence has switched three times to ever less "accusative" models. The problem of Americans negotiating with each other over the standards to be used to decide whether some "thing" or event observed in some way by intelligence fits or does not fit within a provision of an arms control agreement is common to all such agreements. But it is most obvious here.

Defining the Terms for SALT II

Defining the terms of reference for the SALT II agreement was even more complex. American negotiators, seeking to be more specific than they had been in SALT I, devoted more time to the definition of terms than to any other aspect of the negotiations. The treaty itself largely consists of definitions. But once again, the need to frame them in terms of very restricted intelligence information shaped the whole effort. For example, Article II defines ICBM launchers as launchers of missiles with a range in excess of 5,500 km. It is undergirded by the First Agreed Statement and the First Common Understanding, which almost (but not quite) say that if any launcher has ever launched a missile whose range exceeds 5,500 km, all launchers of that type shall be considered as ICBM launchers. Still, the negotiators had to substitute the concept of launchers for that of missiles. Even so, just as in SALT I, SALT II in practice lets only those readily visible launchers stand for all launchers.

The negotiators at SALT II attempted to deal with the fact that missiles can carry multiple warheads. This fact, though well known at the time of SALT I, had not been dealt with then because Americans could not derive any satisfactory way of learning, through intelligence alone, how many and what kinds of warheads the Soviets would place on each missile. At SALT I, the Soviets had refused any sort of regular inspection of missiles, either at the factory or in their launchers, to verify the number and kind of warheads actually in their inventory. So at SALT I, Americans decided officially to ignore this important matter, unwisely assuming that the Soviets would not want multiple independently targeted warheads, or if they did, they would be unable to build them anytime soon. Since by the time SALT II began the Soviets had demolished both assumptions, American negotiators had to choose between scrapping the arms control process or inventing new terminology—"controlling definitions"—that would give the impression that the U.S. could find out much more about Soviet missiles in 1979 than it had been able to seven years earlier.

In fact, however, U.S. intelligence, on balance, had become somewhat less able to perform these tasks than it had been in 1972.

By 1979, the radars at the end of the Pacific test range had been improved, and the number of high-quality reconnaissance photos available to U.S. intelligence had increased. But this merely bolstered performance in areas of secondary importance. The real producer of useful information on multiple warheads is telemetry. By 1979, the Soviet Union was using more encryption, as well as low-power and exotic band telemetry. Moreover, the U.S. had lost some important sources of collection on telemetry. Hence, by 1979 the U.S. could intercept less telemetry than seven years before, and could no longer rely on analysis of the contents of the telemetry stream. Although in 1979 the U.S. was working on new means of collecting telemetry in the future, this did not offset the fact that, given encryption and other Soviet counterintelligence moves, telemetry itself was yielding diminishing returns.

Article II:5 defines *launchers* of MIRVed ICBMs and SLBMs as any launcher of a type "developed and tested for launching" MIRVed missiles. The First Agreed Statement and the First and Second Common Understandings almost—but never quite—say that if any launcher has ever launched a MIRVed missile, it must be counted as a launcher of MIRVed missiles. The truth remains that U.S. intelligence cannot tell unambiguously which launcher launched what in a test. There may be visible preparations around Silo "X," while invisible ones go on for launching out of Silo "Y" nearby. Nor, of course, can U.S. intelligence tell what is in any given launcher. The negotiators handled that neatly in the Fifth Common Understanding, requiring both sides, when they put MIRVed missiles into launchers that had previously not contained them, to modify the launchers so as to signal to the other side's intelligence that the change has been made.

The uninitiated might well wonder why, if the Soviet side is presumed willing to make such notification in good faith, intelligence is needed at all! Conversely, if the Soviet side happens not to be willing to act in good faith, what good can such "intelligence" do? Such "intelligence," it seems, serves primarily as a placebo. This logic reached its *pons asinorum* in SALT II's provision that bombers modified to carry cruise missiles also be fitted with Functionally Related Observable Differences—FRODS, or frauds, for short. No one has yet explained why anyone seriously interested in such weapons' military effectiveness would go out of his way to help his enemy keep track of them.

The Third Common Understanding names the missiles on both sides that are MIRVed. But there remained three problems: associating each missile with one and only one kind of launcher, making sure that the missile carries no more than its allotted number of warheads, and making sure that improvements in accuracy, reliability, etc., do not result in, in effect, filling these launchers with missiles that represent wholly new threats. Beyond these are all the unresolved definitional problems bypassed at SALT I, such as quantity of production. The negotiators dealt with this comically (Article IV.6) by limiting production to "numbers consistent with a normal construction schedule" defined in a Common Understanding as "one consistent with the past or present construction practices of each party." In other words, given the United States' lack of knowledge about "present" or "normal" Soviet missile construction practices, the negotiators simply abstracted from these questions, and established limits for various kinds of launchers on the basis of this abstraction in Article III.

In Article IV.5, they specified what they had supposed in SALT I: one missile per launcher. But, in 1979 as in 1972, U.S. intelligence could have no idea how many Soviet missiles were where, unless the Soviets wished the U.S. to know. Hence, there could be no criteria for judging whether, contrary to Article IV.5, more ICBMs are being supplied to—or stored in—ICBM launcher deployment centers "in excess of a number consistent with normal deployment, maintenance, training and replacement requirements." Moreover, lacking knowledge about what is stored where and agreed-upon criteria for judging such knowledge, who could possibly challenge what is "normal"? By the same token, there can be no criteria for judging whether the Soviets "develop, test, or deploy systems for rapid reload." Since we are not watching constantly, we can have no basis for judging any arbitrarily set rate as "rapid," even if we were otherwise able to set one.

The negotiators dealt with throw-weight by forbidding each side from developing, testing, or deploying any missile with throw-

weight greater than that of the heaviest ICBM that it had at the signing of the treaty. Though Soviet negotiators were willing to acknowledge in private that American estimates of the SS-18's throw-weight
were accurate, they would not officially agree to setting down a
numerical limit. Had they done so, it would not have done the U.S.
much good since they would no doubt disagree about the throw-
weight of any missile the U.S. subsequently found in violation. The
U.S. could have no objective criteria for proving to anyone that its
estimates of the new missile's throw-weight were accurate represen-
tations of reality. Only the Soviets would know that reality.

As regards new missiles, the negotiators agreed that any given
missile would be regarded as "different" from any other if its length,
diameter, launch-weight, and throw-weight differed by more than
5 percent, or if the type of propellant (either liquid or solid) or the
number of stages differed. U.S. intelligence could discern most of
these differences with fair-to-good reliability. But a missile "old"
under these standards could be "new" in every other way—quality
of propellant, materials, reliability, accuracy, penetration aids, etc.
As for the number of warheads per missile, since U.S. intelligence
had noticed how many warheads had been tested with each kind
of missile, it was simple to limit further tests of each kind to the
number of warheads already tested for that kind. But the silent
premise for doing so—that no missile would ever be deployed with
more, or more effective, warheads than it had been tested with—is
wrong. In fact, missiles may be tested below full power many times,
each with different combinations of occupied and unoccupied warhead stations, until all stations and their corresponding release
maneuvers have been tested. The same missile may or may not be
tested a few times at full power with a single heavy payload to simu-
late all warhead stations occupied.

U.S. intelligence had been able to follow release maneuvers
reasonably well through unencrypted telemetry. But it could never
be sure which moves dispensed warheads, penetration aids, or
nothing at all. So, especially after the Soviet Union began to encrypt
the telemetry from its missile tests, U.S. negotiators had either to
give up the pretense of being able to count warheads or recklessly
to *assume* that they could nonetheless distinguish release maneu-

vers, and that there would never be more warheads on any given missile than the maximum number of release maneuvers observed for that kind of missile.

Despite all of this, the negotiators whom President Reagan set to work after the rejection of SALT II (even more than the negotiators at SALT II) had to consider numbers of warheads. The whole objective of missilery is to place warheads on targets and, undeniably, the Soviets had more or less legitimately increased the number and quality of the warheads they could place on American targets. Any arms control agreement that did not deal with warheads would lack all credibility. But since a U.S. presence at the production of warheads (or missiles) continued to be out of the question, the negotiators invented a new political currency: deployed warheads. But as translated into legal currency, this became: "deployed missiles." Further translated into reality, under the constraint that it be arguably verifiable, it was none other than the old SALT I currency of "launchers."

The silent but necessary premises for this translation are: Only the missiles, and therefore the warheads, ready to go on a moment's notice, could ever be useful because war would be a mutually annihilating spasm. Therefore, we may safely treat any other missiles and warheads which may exist as if they did not. Only those missiles, and therefore warheads, in standard, regularly observed modes of deployment will be counted. There may be others, but since we cannot confront the Soviets or the U.S. public with evidence about them, we must treat them as if they did not exist. Only those numbers of warheads that we have "seen" associated with tests of a particular missile, through a combination of telemetry and radar, will be counted as belonging to this missile. Of course, the accuracy and yield of the warheads cannot be taken into account, both because of uncertainties in U.S. intelligence and because counting them would raise uncomfortable questions about why U.S. forces are not comparably equipped. Thus, in the new currency, "deployed warheads" equals precisely the old one of silos plus submarine tubes, multiplied by estimates of the number of warheads. Such estimates are becoming ever less certain as the significance of release maneuvers is obscured by telemetry encryption and by other even more straightforward efforts to deny the U.S. any access to telemetry.

The role of telemetry deserves some attention. No law of God or man compels the Soviets to broadcast telemetry from weapons tests. The data can be beamed, or recorded in a capsule for retrieval. No law ensures that the telemetry that is broadcast is correct. Often, the Soviets broadcast *several* readings for every gauge. This may be so that they can take the average of them, or because they have biased all but one reading and wish to give us a chance to accept the reading most consonant with our own prejudices. In fact, when the Soviets began to encrypt some channels of telemetry but to clear-broadcast others that could just as easily have been encrypted, some intelligence officers asked on what basis the Soviets chose which information to place in which category. In other words, they asked what impressions do the Soviets wish to convey by presenting certain facts to us while hiding others? Although this question is most obvious as regards telemetry, it is equally valid for all information gained by collection capabilities known to the Soviets. But since the question is not answerable because it points to an obvious vulnerability to deception, and is therefore subversive of arms control, it is treated as unimportant.

The penultimate resolution of the negotiators' worries about telemetry was the provision in SALT II prohibiting encrypting telemetry necessary for verification of the treaty's parameters. This formulation, by the way, follows directly from the Soviet doctrine on verification stated by Valerian Zorin in 1951: the Soviet Union would show whatever *it* judged necessary to demonstrate compliance, but no more. U.S. negotiators agreed to this formulation, knowing full well that only the Soviets, not they, would know the parameters to which the encrypted channels referred. Any American claim that encryption of any given channel violated the prohibition would reasonably lack proof.

The ultimate resolution of the telemetry question came after the Soviets encrypted substantially all the telemetry channels from their new missiles. The U.S. declared this a violation, but continued the arms control process nonetheless. The moral of the story is that the U.S. negotiators define the parameters of arms control agreements less for their military significance than to conform them to the ability of U.S. intelligence to gather information. The only certainty, so far as the U.S. government is concerned, is that both military significance and verifiability are less important than the arms control process itself!

Nothing shows this more clearly than the definition of the heavy bombers and cruise missiles to be included in SALT II. Here, the negotiators had even less basis than they had for the case of ballistic missiles to define a given device as useful or not useful in intercontinental war. This is because the range of bombers and cruise missiles depends on such completely nonobservable features as the efficiency of engines and the size of fuel tanks. Gross size can be an indication of range. According to that measure, the Soviet Union's Backfire bomber, and most of its larger cruise missiles, would have to be counted as intercontinental weapons. The Backfire is almost as large as the American B-1, and had been observed, unrefueled, flying about as far as the U.S. B-52, unrefueled. Moreover, intelligence photographs had shown the plane equipped with refueling probes. But the Soviet Union stated that the Backfire's role was regional and naval—not intercontinental, and so, based solely on the word of the Soviets, U.S. negotiators agreed not to count the Backfire. As for cruise missiles, the negotiators agreed on an arbitrary range limit of 600 km, while realizing that any data on the range of any given cruise missile is inherently unreliable, since the flight can be terminated long before the fuel runs out. Moreover, they cordially agreed not to count as having a range over 600 km one Soviet missile, the SS-N-3, which had been observed flying further than that.

The way that U.S. negotiators handled bombers and cruise missiles are the exceptions that prove the rule that they designed the arms control treaties' parameters as at least *tautologically* verifiable. In fact, given the capacities of U.S. intelligence, the provisions regarding bombers and cruise missiles are beyond the possibility of even meaningless verification. The fact that U.S. arms controllers were willing to agree to such provisions shows an unbridled interest in the health of the arms control process, not the safety of a nation. For the sake of that higher purpose, arms controllers were happy to frame the terms of treaties by abstracting not just from what U.S. intelligence does not know, but also by abstracting from what U.S. intelligence *does* know.

*   *   *

The upshot of all this is that American arms control negotiators built an artificial world in which the larger reality of Soviet military power, and the purposes for which it might be used, disappeared as if deliberately pushed out of focus, while the eyes of the American people were directed to tiny tidbits of facts fashioned through the concurrent, mutually reinforcing efforts of the arms controllers, the intelligence community, and the Soviet Union itself. The American people were told that the arms control process controlled Soviet arms. But given criteria according to which new things could be "old" or heavy things "light," and in which key words like "rapid" had precisely no meaning, it was never clear what was to be controlled—other than the thinking of Americans.

Anyone even slightly familiar with the limitations of U.S. intelligence who considers the artificial quantities that the arms control process substituted for Soviet military realities can see in them so many invitations to Soviet deception. As we shall see, the Soviets in fact appear to have taken advantage of at least some of these invitations. But these Soviet deceptions are insignificant in comparison with those that Americans performed on themselves by constructing this artificial world in the first place.

4

What We Expected from the Treaties

How American politicians loaded upon the treaties — which consist of tautologies tied together with allusions — the expectation that our strategic problems would be solved without exertion.

How the treaties were supposed to ratify a convergence of political objectives and be guaranteed by a "network of relationships."

How they were to "guarantee" that American missiles would never be vulnerable to Soviet missiles, that Soviet targets would always be available to American missiles, and that, at least on the highest level of warfare, competition had ended.

The artificial world of verification was built largely by the Verification Panel, a group of high U.S. officials that President Nixon convened in the spring of 1969 under Henry Kissinger. It purported to analyze the weapons systems that would be negotiable, determine the extent to which aspects of those systems were verifiable by U.S. intelligence, and ascertain the effects of alternative treaty language on the character of U.S. weapons programs.

SALT I (the ABM Treaty, the Interim Agreement on offensive weapons, their protocols, and the Agreement on the Prevention of Nuclear War) emerged through the technical elaboration of its terms. And yet, as Kissinger stated in 1972, his panel had the higher function of making sure that the negotiations did not bog down on technical issues. The Verification Panel was pursuing a heavy strategic agenda. SALT I's burden was no less than, in Kissinger's words, to be "a central element" in "a broadly based accommodation of interests with the USSR."[1] It is remarkable that responsible people could believe that the technical tautologies that were their prime product could bear the heavy burden they envisaged for them.

Kissinger explained that the treaty's provisions alone could not restrain a Soviet Union bent on seeking the utmost advantage under them. If both sides strained the agreement's edges, these would not hold. That is why he and other spokesmen for the administration discouraged talk about which side had gained, or would gain, advantage under the agreements as "exceptionally inappropriate." The success of the entire exercise would depend on a rejection, by both sides, of "constant jockeying for marginal advantage." The treaty thus "will either be a serious attempt to turn the world away from time-worn practices of jockeying for power, or there will be end-

less, wasteful, and *purposeless* competition in the acquisition of armaments."[2] (Emphasis added.)

Kissinger, speaking for the President and for the whole executive branch (from which there was no dissent), made clear that for
the U.S., there could be no useful political purpose in increased
military power, and that "there was reason to believe that the Soviet
leadership *might also be* thinking along *similar* lines" because they
had failed to gain military advantage from military competition in
the past. (Emphasis added.) At any rate, the Soviet Union had
proved its intentions by signing the agreements, and by entering
into broad-gauged political and economic relationships that would
serve its interest well "if the entire process unfolded." Said Kissinger,
"We have sought, in short, to create a vested interest in mutual
restraint."[3] (Emphasis added.)

Thus, in Kissinger's words,

> the SALT agreement does not stand alone, isolated and incon-
> gruous in the relationship of hostility, vulnerable at any time
> to the shock of some sudden crisis. It stands, rather, linked
> organically to a chain of agreements and to a broad under-
> standing about international conduct appropriate to the dan-
> gers of the nuclear age. . . . Any country that contemplates
> a rupture of the agreement or a circumvention of its letter and
> spirit must now face the fact that it will be placing in jeop-
> ardy not only a limited arms control agreement, but a broad
> political relationship.[4]

In other words, Kissinger seemed to agree with those critics
of arms control who argue that treaties cannot restrain nations otherwise committed to military superiority—except that he seemed to
argue that the Soviet Union was not so committed. The Bear had
learned the lessons of the nuclear age, and willingly entered into
a mature new relationship with the United States, its propaganda
to the contrary notwithstanding. Neither Kissinger nor anyone else,
however, adduced one scrap of evidence of the Soviet Union's fitness
for partnership in this noble enterprise—other than to point out
circumstances that *should* have been pushing the USSR into a new
relationship, and opportunities that *should* have pulled it there.
Indeed, Kissinger had stated the basis for this enormous, near-

millennialist construct in the subjunctive mood, with a qualifier to boot: "The Soviet Union *might also* be thinking along *similar* lines."[5] (Emphasis added.) Clearly, as in the 1950s, arms controllers were unwilling and unable to argue that the conditions for agreement existed. They stated their proposition as a question. But the wish was the father of the thought—except that in 1972, high U.S. officials acted as if the wish that had become a thought had in turn become reality.

Secretary Kissinger and the Nixon administration expressed a wholly different, even contradictory, set of expectations as well. According to this view, the Soviet Union was well on the way to gaining significant military advantage, and the agreement would stop it cold. The administration used this set of expectations to defend its acceptance of higher ceilings for Soviet missile launchers and submarines, as well as a monopoly of "heavy missiles" for the Soviet Union. Absent the agreement, so goes the argument, the discrepancy between the Soviet and the American numbers would surely have become worse. Kissinger and Nixon recognized the Soviet Union's two-pronged reasoning with regard to numbers. First, to reduce American numbers where superior to Soviet numbers; and second, to maintain those ratios that lay in favor of their own forces.

Nevertheless, Kissinger and Nixon were seduced by the idea that "the spirit" of negotiations would control a totalitarian side in the same manner it would control the democratic side.

The Soviets, the administration noted, had reached parity with the U.S. in numbers of ICBMs in 1970, and were continuing to build ICBM launchers at the rate of 250 per year. The U.S. had stopped building launchers in the mid-1960s. The ratio embodied in the Interim Agreement—of 1,610 Soviet to 1,054 American ICBMs— might look bad, but if compared to the ratio of 2,500 to 1,054 that would exist in 1977, only 1,610 to 1,054 had to look good. The same argument applied to missile-carrying submarines. The U.S. had long since stopped building at 41. The Soviets had in the water, or under construction, some 48, and were building them at the rate of eight per year. This Kissinger characterized as not "the most brilliant bargaining position I would recommend people to find themselves in." By the same token, the Soviets had built 313 launchers for the SS-9 missile, which many feared could successfully attack our missiles on the ground. If they continued to build them, or converted other missile-launchers to the SS-9, we would have "Minuteman vulnerability." If the trend continued and the Soviets could plausibly count on destroying most of our missiles by expending only a relatively small fraction of their own force, they might come to believe that a war could be advantageous. Far better to leave the Soviets with 313 such missiles to none of our own than to let them go on to build the critical 1,000 while we struggled to start up production!

Interestingly, this line of argument paralleled that of the Soviet Union's negotiators: The U.S. should not complain about accepting lower numbers of missile launchers than the numbers permitted to the Soviet Union. International agreements can only reflect the correlation of forces existing at any given time. That correlation had been shifting inexorably in the Soviet Union's favor, and would continue to shift. Thus, although the unequal ceilings might look like a bad deal to Americans in 1972, several years down the road Americans would look back on them and consider them a bargain.

America's negotiators did not probe the Soviet negotiators' interesting attitude by asking why the Soviets thought the *military* component of the correlation of forces would shift in its favor under a treaty whose purpose—on its face—was to keep that correlation constant and equal. Nor did they ask why and how the Soviet Union could restrain itself from promoting or exploiting further shifts in the correlation. Asking questions about the Soviet Union's intentions regarding its future plans for military superiority would have been disruptive of the overriding objective: agreement. Security was defined as sophistry.

Besides, argued America's arms controllers, it would be counterproductive for Americans to project past Soviet behavior into the future. The Soviets should be not blamed, but rather excused, for having sought military superiority. The U.S. had done the same thing in the 1960s, before it had fully realized the "facts of life" of the nuclear age. The earlier American attempt at superiority had inspired Soviet attempts at superiority. America had stopped building missiles for two distinct reasons: First, its leading officials had adopted a strategic outlook that deemed superiority superfluous. Second, the Congress had become less friendly to military expenditures because of the war in Vietnam. So, the argument went, we had no reason to blame the Soviets for having built so many missiles. We and the Soviets had reached the same conclusions on different timetables. We only had reason to be grateful that they had learned their lesson and had now agreed to stop. So what if their numbers at this time were higher than ours?

But American officials who explained what we had gotten out of SALT I, and who claimed that SALT I had kept a "not brilliant" situation from getting worse, never made clear that conscious American strategic choices had created that "not brilliant" situation, and most certainly did not renounce those choices in favor of ones that would reverse the situation. Indeed, they clouded their own direct responsibility for the situation. They said the situation had come to be not because of anything they did, but rather because the American people had lost faith in their government during the Vietnam war. Kissinger argued strenuously that,

> under the impact of the Vietnam turmoil, [our] defense programs were being cut by the Congress every year. Every new weapons program we put forward was systematically attacked or dismantled. As a result, starting in 1970 our defense department was pleading with us to negotiate a freeze on the Soviets lest the disparity in numbers continue to grow. We needed a freeze not only for arms control reasons, but for strategic reasons—we froze a disparity which we inherited in order to gain time to reverse the situation.[6]

So the American people, not the negotiators, are to be blamed for agreements that allow more power to the Soviets than they should have. Admiral Zumwalt, Chief of Naval Operations at the time, quotes Kissinger as saying: "The American people have only themselves to blame."[7] Thus SALT I was presented—and all subsequent U.S. proposals have likewise been presented—as the brilliant handiwork of statesmen who worked from an inferior position that they deeply regret, and purchased time in order to change that position.

How does one reconcile these conflicting explanations of what we were trying to accomplish in SALT I? The authors believe we can discount *both* the political explanation that our dreamy-eyed officials believed the millennium had arrived *and* the military explanation that our valiant officials were just buying time for a reversal of whatever inferiority we suffered. Top U.S. officials did not believe the millennium had arrived because, despite the talk of some on the SALT delegation about how the negotiations had been "incipient collaborative strategic planning,"[8] and about an irreversible turn on the part of the Soviet Union, most believed that détente was only the beginning of a long road that the U.S. and the Soviet Union would travel together. On the other hand, these people were clearly not buying time because they never proposed using that time to build American military superiority. Indeed, they passionately rejected such thoughts.

Some did not want American superiority because they did not believe that the U.S. could, or would, use it for good ends. Victor Utgoff, an official of the National Security Council in the Carter administration, best explained this point of view when he said:

> Even if the United States could attain strategic superiority, it would not be desirable because I suspect we would occasionally use it as a way of throwing our weight around in some very risky ways. . . . It is in the U.S. interest to allow the few remaining areas of strategic advantage to fade away.[9]

Others made the same point, basing it less on political relativism than on pure dogma, straight out of Brodie's *The Absolute Weapon*. Hence, Henry Kissinger:

> What in the name of God is strategic superiority? What is the significance of it politically, militarily, operationally, at these levels of numbers? What do you do with it?[10]

Asking such a question is akin to asking, "What can a man do with a beautiful woman?" Whoever asks it confirms that no answer could possibly mean much. On several occasions since he left office, Henry Kissinger has supplied reasonable answers to his own question: Strategic superiority is the capacity to substantially disarm one's opponent with a first strike, to render retaliation so weak as to be unreasonable, to protect one's own country substantially from such

weakened retaliation should it occur, and, perhaps most significantly, to use this capacity for political coercion. But as Kissinger
himself has admitted in a speech in Brussels in August 1979, his
sobriety came upon him *after* he had left office.

The final proof that U.S. officials were selling rather than buying time lay in their embarrassed reaction to the amendment proposed by Senator Henry Jackson (D-Washington), that any subsequent agreement provide for equal numbers of weapons. Pursuant
to that amendment, the Ford administration negotiated the Vladivostok Accords of December 1974 providing for a maximum of 2,400
strategic nuclear delivery vehicles for each side, and immediately
let it be known it had no intention of acquiring the weapons that
would bring the U.S. up to that number. By the same token, in 1975
the same administration did not object strenuously to the amendment by Senator Edward Kennedy (D-Massachusetts) to close down
the United States' only ABM site at Grand Forks, North Dakota,
even though it was specifically permitted by the ABM Treaty, and
the Soviet Union was modernizing its own ABM site at Moscow.
So, clearly, the administration and its congressional allies were not
interested in American superiority, or even in parity.

In the political realm, the artificers of SALT I stressed present
accords and present ties, and simply projected them into the future.
Because they found the accords useful in their intramural battles
with "hawks," they assumed that their Soviet counterparts found
them similarly useful and would want to continue the process.
Because they so passionately believed in their lectures to the Soviet
delegation that Soviet-American relations should not be a "zero-
sum game" but rather be mutually beneficial, they were willing to
continue to suspend judgment on Soviet military-political intentions and adopt — as a working assumption — that Soviet intentions
were like our own. In other words, that the Soviets, like themselves,
were animated by greater antipathy to their own "hawks" than to
the other side, who were merely competitors who could help to
defeat the real enemy: the "hawks" in both camps. The artificers
of SALT I simply projected onto the Soviets their own international
purposelessness and internal disunity.

In the military sphere, the artificers of SALT I thought they had achieved a blueprint and a warrant for the kind of American forces they wanted. In their reports to the Congress, Henry Kissinger, chief negotiator Gerard Smith, and other spokesmen for the Nixon administration took the existing American forces as "given"—to be changed only at the margin. They assumed that U.S. forces were not to be given capabilities significantly different from the ones they then had, ever. Indeed, this was the overriding virtue of SALT I to its supporters: that while without it, U.S. forces would have had to change in order to survive an enemy attack and to penetrate Soviet defenses, with it, the Soviets would simply *allow* U.S. forces, without radical change, to perform those very functions into the indefinite future. Such a thought would be laughable in a novel, but apparently not in a treaty.

Without a treaty, said Gerard Smith, "U.S. retaliatory strikes might have to penetrate a Soviet defensive screen of some 8,000 ABMs during this decade [the 1970s]."[11] Please note that there was no nonsense here about ABMs being unfeasible. On the contrary, U.S. officials assumed that because of the feasibility of ABMs in the USSR, the U.S. had gone through the expense of placing multiple warheads on its own missiles. Without a treaty limiting ABMs, the U.S. would have to go through great expense to add more warheads and more decoys. This would be a great waste, because the whole process would simply reestablish the destructive capability the U.S. had had. Indeed, Kissinger emphasized, the U.S. Congress must continue to demonstrate its willingness to engage in such waste in order not to have to engage in it—much as we must be willing to devastate Soviet cities in order not to have to devastate them.

But, Kissinger reassured the Congress, the essential step had been taken: ABMs were off the board for both sides, forever. As Smith said, "Neither side is going to try to defend its national territory. This is an admission of tremendous psychological significance, I believe, recognition that the deterrent forces of both sides are not going to be challenged. When you think of the concerns that we have had for the last 25 years about first-strike and counterforce, it seems to me a general recognition by both countries that they are not going to field a nationwide system is of first importance, politically, psychologically, and militarily."[12]

The great cultural struggle that had raged within the U.S. since the dawn of the nuclear age *both* about whether our own nuclear weapons should be targeted against people or weapons *and* about whether we should try to defend against the other side's weapons or learn to live with mutual vulnerability had been settled once and for all. The majority of U.S. officials concerned with national security, whose careers had been made under Robert McNamara, had been vindicated in their life's work. The American ABM system, which the majority of U.S. officials thought to be provocative and ultimately futile, and which they had accepted grudgingly only under political duress, could now be ceremoniously junked.

By precisely the same token, the establishment's decade-long effort against American counterforce weapons had been vindicated. The Interim Agreement, according to Smith, "constrains a number of Soviet programs, and no U.S. programs." Furthermore, "the agreement would be violated if one more ICBM launcher for operational use was started."[13] How prescient, then, had been those American officials who had fought to stop the construction of more American missiles! The agreement proved what they had always said: that the path to security is restraint. Moreover, because the agreement provides a "qualitative constraint" as well, U.S. officials had been proved prescient for having built the *kinds* of missiles they had built. As Smith explained, "It is clear from oral exchanges during the negotiations that both sides understood that Soviet SS-11s and SS-13s are 'light' and that SS-7s, SS-8s, and SS-9s are 'heavy,' and that U.S. Titans are 'heavy' and Minutemen are 'light.' The United States cannot replace Minuteman with missiles of the volume of Titans, and the Soviets cannot replace SS-11s with missiles of the volume of SS-7s or 9s."[14] Since, as we have seen, "heavy" and "light" were synonymous to "counterforce" and "countervalue," respectively, U.S. negotiators believed they had succeeded in persuading the Soviets to drop their preference for winning wars and to take up their own preference for Mutual Assured Destruction. Given this, the fact that the agreement did not constrain the Soviets' programs for accuracy and miniaturization of warheads did not concern the administration.

To have talked of the importance of accuracy and of miniaturization while presenting the argument for SALT I would have been even more subversive of the arms control process than to have done so during the negotiations.

However, in the years *after* the treaty was ratified, such talk became commonplace—in the Congress. U.S. arms controllers opposed proposals for installing the NS-20 guidance system in a portion of the Minuteman force to increase its accuracy. They argued, with some justice, that doing so was against the spirit, if not the letter, of SALT I. Yet the administration pleaded that this increased accuracy was necessary as a minimal response to the Soviet Union's testing of precisely the kinds of replacements for its missiles of 1972 that SALT I's Interim Agreement had ostensibly succeeded in banning. Because of this, the President asked for a limited ability to strike Soviet weapons—in Secretary of Defense Schlesinger's lingo, "limited nuclear options." But the argument against the NS-20 guidance system and all other attempts to give the U.S. some counterforce weapons, made in the face of full-scale Soviet construction of counterforce weapons, shows unmistakably what the purpose of SALT I was: to bind U.S. forces to the ideas of a particular class of Americans. These ideas proclaimed their own validity regardless of what happened in the rest of the world. Thus, while the architects of SALT I were not wholly unconcerned in affecting what was going on in the Soviet Union, their concerns had relatively low "salience" in comparison with their single-minded dedication to keep the U.S. wedded to MAD.

* * *

In all subsequent arms control agreements and negotiations, American officials have sought to redeem pieces of the vision they thought they had realized in SALT I—a vision that the fourfold increase in Soviet strategic missile warheads had shattered once and for all.

SALT II was supposed to correct the chief shortcoming of the SALT I Interim Agreement, namely, that the Soviet Union had produced an offensive threat far greater than the worst scenario that the Americans who negotiated that agreement had imagined.

Instead of building up the number of their SS-9 launchers from 300-odd to 1,000 or so and thus threatening to put one counterforce warhead on every American missile silo, the Soviets were filling those launchers with SS-18s, all of which would be able to deliver 3,000-odd counterforce warheads. Instead of replacing their older missiles with new ones that would carry single, non-silo-killing warheads, they were replacing them with the SS-17, and mostly the SS-19, which carry, respectively, four and six silo-killing warheads. Between 1972 and 1979 the U.S. had gone from the mere possibility that, in the far future, the Soviet Union might try to acquire a war-winning force, to the near certainty that such a force was in the final stages of construction. Thus, SALT II's negotiators and salesmen had their work cut out for them.

In March 1977, President Carter proposed to the Soviet Union that it reduce the number of its silo-killing missiles to a level that, once the U.S. had built 200 MX missiles (10 silo-killing warheads apiece) and had completed fitting 900 Mark-12A warheads atop 300 Minuteman III missiles, would have given the Soviet Union only a moderate edge over the U.S. in the ability to kill "hard" targets. The proposal's key element would have limited both sides to 550 MIRVed ICBMs—the number of ICBMs then in the American Minuteman III force. The Soviets could not have more than a total of 550 SS-17s, -18s, and -19s. But they would be allowed only 150 "heavy missiles," i.e., SS-18s, while the U.S. would be allowed none. That meant that in the short run, the Soviet Union could count on 1,500 counterforce warheads from its SS-18s and 2,300 (6×350 plus 4×50) counterforce warheads from its SS-19s and SS-17s, for a total of 3,800 warheads each with about a 90 percent probability of killing an American silo. In the short term, the U.S. could have its 900 Mark 12As on 300 Minuteman IIIs. In the medium term, the U.S. could convert all 550 Minuteman IIIs to Mark 12As for a total of 1,650 warheads, each with a probability of about one in three of killing a Soviet silo. Only after the MX was to be fully deployed in 1989 could the U.S. trade 600 of these 1,650 for (the then-planned) 2,000 MX warheads with a combination of yield and accuracy comparable to the Soviets' 3,800. The U.S. would then have had 2,000 true counterforce warheads—plus another 1,050 of lesser value—to the

Soviets' 3,800 true counterforce warheads. This is the element the Soviets found ludicrously one-sided, and that the Carter administration later felt it had to apologize for. The Soviet Union contemptuously rejected that proposal.

Hence, once again an American administration faced the fundamental choice about arms control. A few years earlier Paul Nitze, one of the architects of SALT I, had pointed to the incompatibility of American and Soviet intentions as the obstacle to further SALT agreements. It would be technically possible, he wrote, for both sides to agree to scrap all their present ICBMs

> and substitute thousands of new ICBMs, each with a throw-weight . . . of no more than 200 pounds. Within such a throw-weight limitation, an effective combination of yield and accuracy for a single missile to destroy more than one silo becomes inherently infeasible. . . . But such hypothetical solutions have two constraints—verifiability and negotiability. Certain of the more important qualitative characteristics of strategic weapons, such as accuracy, are inherently unverifiable.[15]

Furthermore, he said the Soviets would simply not scrap their SS-17s, -18s, and -19s. In other words, the Soviets want the war-fighting, war-winning capabilities we do not want them to have, and we are in no position either to make them not want them, or to keep them from getting them.

By April Fool's Day 1977, the Carter administration had accepted this fact. But two very different conclusions flowed from it: on the one hand, abandon arms control on the ground that it could not possibly provide the desired military result and hence resolve to achieve our military goals through our own efforts, or, on the other hand, continue with the arms control process, and learn to deem desirable whatever the process might yield—regardless of its effect on the military balance. The administration chose the latter conclusion.

This choice was all the more significant because to make it, the administration had to deny the logic of its own developing understanding of the strategic situation. As early as 1974, in his National Security Decision Memorandum 242, President Ford had begun to follow the logic of the Soviet Union's preparations by focusing a few American ICBMs on Soviet ICBMs. Far from denying this trend, the Carter administration fulfilled it with its own Presidential Decision #59 (July 1980). In fact, it was Carter's Secretary of Defense, Harold Brown, who said in 1979 that the primary requirement of U.S. strategy thenceforth had to be the ability to place on target at least one high-quality U.S. warhead on every Soviet silo. The same Brown had said of the Soviets, "When we build, they build. When we stop, they build." By 1977–80, at least Brown, National Security Adviser Zbigniew Brzezinski, and perhaps Jimmy Carter recognized first, that counterforce was possible—indeed, the order of the day; second, that nothing would keep the Soviet Union from having a full counterforce capability; and third, that they themselves desired it to some extent for the U.S.

Why, then, did they desire SALT II? The fundamental reason was that these officials, and even more the hundreds of subordinates who ran the U.S. government for them, continued to believe in Mutual Assured Destruction. Perhaps the clearest exposition of MAD ever made by a U.S. official came in President Carter's 1980 State of the Union address, in which he said that a single American missile-carrying submarine could devastate the USSR and was, in fact, sufficient for the United States' minimum essential objective: deterrence. According to the MAD dogma, the Soviet Union could do whatever it wanted and not upset this condition—so long as the U.S. took prudent countermeasures.

If the administration had followed Harold Brown's newfound appreciation of counterforce to its logical conclusion, it would have declared arms control a fraud, built several hundred MXs and put them on the United States' railroad network, and built anti-missile devices aplenty. But when it chose to view the United States' strategic predicament through the optic of MAD, the administration did not at the same time explicitly deny the usefulness of counterforce weapons or targeting. It simply put them "in their place" as "hedges" or prudent measures intended to maintain the viability of MAD. Thus the administration made SALT II possible by a kind of schizophrenic choice.

SALT II's American architects then had to construct a set of military objectives that were acceptable to the Soviet Union, arguably beneficial to the U.S., and arguably verifiable. This would involve building an artificial world far more complex than SALT I's. This complexity would obscure to some extent the maximum objective of U.S. negotiators at SALT II: to keep the United States' strategic position from deteriorating much further. After the cow had sauntered out, American negotiators would endeavor to close the strategic barn door a bit. But they were under no illusions about being able to shut it.

The State Department's official explanation of U.S. military objectives in SALT II stressed "strategic forces which are at least equal to those of the Soviet Union," and it also said that "a goal of SALT is to restrain arms improvements" so as to prevent "one side" (i.e., the Soviet Union) from gaining "the illusion of a temporary advantage."[16] The treaty, said the State Department, had achieved these military objectives, because American forces, in being and projected, *were* the equal of Soviet forces. Given the balance that would exist under SALT II, neither side could gain the dread "illusion."

This intellectual tour de force was also performed in the CIA, the Defense Department, and the Arms Control and Disarmament Agency. ACDA's account is the clearest unclassified version of it. On the basis of the "capability index" used in this study, the following observations can be made:

- The U.S. is ahead of the Soviet Union in target destruction capability.

- Both U.S. and Soviet forces will become substantially more capable by the mid-1980s.

- U.S. retaliatory capability after a Soviet strike in the mid-1980s exceeds the current retaliatory capability.

- The capability of U.S. and strategic forces in the mid-1980s is essentially equal.[17]

Let us look closely at how this thaumaturgic index healed the wounds of SALT I:

While there are asymmetries within [sic] the U.S. and Soviet target systems . . . it is not unreasonable to assume an equal number of hard and soft targets for purposes of comparing overall capability.[18]

This, of course, is nonsense.

But the report compounds nonsense by breaking this "equal number" down into 5,000 "soft" and 1,500 "hard" targets. By this token, the roughly 5,000 small, inaccurate warheads aboard U.S. submarine-launched missiles, plus the several thousand gravity bombs aboard U.S. B-52s (all of which the "study" assumes will get through Soviet air defense), can indeed devastate Soviet soft targets, perhaps even more effectively than the Soviet Union could have carried out a disarming strike against American "hard" targets *in 1978*. So, because the study shows that both sides were reasonably equipped to carry out their respective strategies, it concludes that their capacities were equal.

In the mid-1980s, with the conversion of U.S. submarines to Trident missiles, and with the addition of cruise missiles to the B-52 force, the U.S. capacity to strike back—*against soft targets*—after a Soviet attack (that miraculously would strike no submarines in port or bombers on airfields) could indeed have been projected as superior to that of 1978. The "study" does not say so, but assumes that since, in the 1980s, a Soviet first strike would destroy nearly every American ICBM, the U.S. would have nearly zero capability to strike Soviet hard targets; so, in a convoluted way, the "study" boils down to telling the truth!

The truth was that under any circumstances the Soviets could destroy the U.S. military, and under miraculous circumstances the U.S. could devastate Soviet society. So, in the mid-1980s the Soviets would be able to do what they wanted, and the U.S. would be able to do what some of its leaders said it wanted. Since those two things are different (destroying "hard" and "soft" targets, respectively) and since the "index" presumes that these two different purposes were equivalent, *presto*—"the capability of U.S. and Soviet strategic forces in the mid-1980s is essentially equal."

Only somewhat more soberly (but just as surely circularly) the Pentagon, but chiefly the Air Force, saw the limitation of the Soviet threat as essential to the feasibility of the new weapons and systems necessary for the implementation of the new counterforce emphasis, and to the maintenance of vigilance. The MX, for example, was (and in 1987, remains) the United States' first major departure from the strategic forces designed by McNamara in the 1960s. Especially in the late 1970s and early 1980s it was touted as "survivable," because each would have been based in one of many shelters—the others being left empty as decoys. But, advocates of SALT II pointed out, the MX, thus based, could not survive a Soviet attack if that attack hit every one of the places where the missiles might be.

To prevent this saturation, SALT II provided limits in the overall number of launchers (2,250), limits in MIRVed launchers (1,320), and most important, limits in the numbers of MIRVed ICBM launchers (820). As we have seen in practice, this meant limits in the number of silos and submarine launch tubes. To make those limits meaningful, SALT II also limited the number of warheads on individual missiles. This in practice meant the number of "release maneuvers." Also, to provide against surprises like the SS-17s, -18s, and -19s under SALT I, SALT II allowed each side only one new missile. But newness, as we have seen, could not be well-defined. Hence, only if the Soviets were willing to limit the forces by means of which they intended to destroy the forces that we meant to keep from being destroyed, could our new arrangements for making those forces survivable succeed. In other words, our premise was that our purpose could be accomplished only if we succeeded in persuading the Soviets not to seriously pursue their own. So, while no one said—as so many had in 1972—that the Soviets had agreed to solve our strategic problems for us, the spokesmen for SALT II said the same thing with expressions a couple of steps removed from reality: Only if the Soviets acquiesced in our thwarting their will could we successfully thwart their will. In other words, we could thwart their will to prepare to fight and win a war against us only if their will was not serious; i.e., if the Soviets agreed with those Americans who believed in MAD.

According to its architects, SALT II also went beyond SALT I's agreement in principle to respect each other's national technical means of verification by specifically assuring both sides access to each other's telemetry. But as we have seen, there was a catch. The

Soviets could encrypt telemetry and claim that the encrypted channels referred to aspects of the missile's performance not covered by the treaty. No one had the right to be surprised when the Soviets did precisely that.

The U.S. government's official position on these and many other lesser but kindred military provisions was that they left much to be desired. The U.S. government, however, pointedly focused the public's eye as far away as it could from the Soviet Union's concrete military intentions, which were embodied in a Soviet military force reasonably well-fashioned to carry them out. Instead, the U.S. government blamed both countries equally vaguely: "Neither side is ready at this point for far-reaching disarmament schemes."[19] So, the agreement should not be measured "against some ideal agreement that, as a practical matter, given the relationship between the two countries, cannot be concluded at this time." Instead, it should be measured against "no agreement at all."[20] Literally hundreds of spokesmen for the administration in highly classified briefings, as well as on the stump, left no doubt as to what this would mean: some 13,000 to 20,000 Soviet warheads by 1985 without SALT II instead of about 9,000 under SALT II.

But the U.S. government never did explain, either in public or in the most highly classified meetings, how it would cope with the forces the Soviets could legally build under SALT II. Under SALT II, the Soviets would have a minimum of 6,000 counterforce warheads to cover little more than 1,000 "hard" U.S. targets. Altogether, they would have some 7,000 warheads on intercontinental systems over and above what they would need for a disarming first strike against U.S. ICBMs, and twice the number of warheads needed to attack U.S. military targets. Why, then, did American arms controllers believe that the Soviets would go out of their way simply to get more such warheads rather than to concentrate on making the number they already had smaller, more accurate, more reliable, and more survivable? Why did American arms controllers believe the Soviets would pile up useless warheads rather than build their own anti-missile devices? The sad answer is that they themselves thought about strategic forces only as tools for getting arms control agreements. Hence, the U.S. government simply refused to grapple with the internally divisive question: How could the Soviets use the forces allowed under SALT II to their best military advantage? To have done so would have raised the one question our government wanted to avoid most of all—indeed, one might say, the question that the U.S. government entered into the arms control process in order to avoid dealing with directly: How shall the U.S. use strategic forces to its own best advantage?

Clearly, any American could have used the letter of SALT II's definitions and limits to sanction American forces far different from existing ones. The MX, for example, has a throw-weight similar to that of the SS-19, and a volume that allows it to fit into Minuteman silos. It is certainly as "light" a missile as the SS-19. Hence, nothing in the letter of SALT II prevents the U.S. from building 820 MXs— and placing them on the nation's rail network. That alone would give the United States 8,200 survivable counterforce warheads. Doing so would involve no legal or technological issues whatever. But the U.S. government never considered this approach because it would have been a total reversal of U.S. military policy since 1964 and a total negation of the spirit that U.S. arms controllers brought to SALT II. Nothing in SALT II prevents the U.S. from loading swarms of very long-range cruise missiles on hundreds of naval vessels and submarines, as well as on trucks in the northern U.S. But U.S. policy is not to pose to the Soviet Union a threat greater than, or equal to, the one that it poses to us. And so it goes.

In sum, then, the primary military goal of SALT II was to preserve U.S. military policy—in all its ambiguity—from pressures to face the choices before it, and all their demanding consequences. The U.S. got precisely what it bargained for. SALT II allowed U.S. officials to speak of "rough parity," as well as of the irrationality of war, while simultaneously speaking of modernizing to meet the Soviet challenge. SALT II allowed the Army, Navy, Air Force, and Marines to keep their struggles for the military dollar within known limits. Above all, it allowed many American politicians to talk of peace. On the ominous other hand, it allowed the Soviet Union to double its strategic forces between 1979 and 1985.

The political objectives of SALT II, like the military ones, were to make the best of a bad situation for the sake of the arms control process and, not incidentally, to affirm the credentials of those Americans involved in the process. By 1979 the promise of détente — the key component of which had been SALT II — had been shattered. The chief political fruit of détente was supposed to have been a mutually observed code of behavior — solicitude for each other's interests. The Soviet Union's conquests in Asia, Africa, and the Mideast, plus its ostentatious sponsorship of the quintupling of the world's oil prices, showed that "code" to have been an illusion. All but one of the presidential candidates in 1976, Gerald Ford, had denounced détente — and he lost. Proponents of SALT I had promised a bright new world. Proponents of SALT II could not credibly promise any such thing. But they could and did present the treaty as an indispensable attempt to stop a dangerous deterioration of relations. As befits weak cases, the case for SALT II had to be made ferociously.

Common sense demands that agreements on important matters rest on shared objectives. President Carter drew a dreadful picture for the American people: the world was sliding closer to war. He did not mention that the primary reason for this was the relative strengthening of the Soviet Union under the arms control process, or that the Soviet Union might find war attractive. He depicted war as an apolitical catastrophe that threatened both sides equally. The engines of war were weapons rather than the plans of the men who control them. He said that he and Brezhnev had "identical" interests in avoiding war. This identical interest united them in SALT II.

By implication, and spokesmen for the administration drew on it repeatedly, the peace-loving elements in both countries had coalesced against the real enemies of peace in both countries. The Soviet Union was not the threat to peace. Americans who opposed SALT II, who were well known, plus some hazy, unknown "Kremlin hawks," were the threat to peace. In perhaps the most memorable statements of the 1980 presidential campaign, President Carter said that the election would be a referendum on arms control, and that its results would show whether the *American people* were or were not on the side of peace. Shorn of the credibility to promise rewards other than the continuation of the process, advocates of arms control have had no alternative but to threaten Armageddon, and, in effect, to ally with the Soviets against their own countrymen.

*   *   *

The military and political objectives of two arms control agreements outside SALT are also worthy of mention: those of the Biological Warfare Convention of 1972 and of the Threshold Test Ban Treaty of 1974.

The background of the Biological Warfare Convention is one more example of what happens when the U.S. tries to be clever regarding what it believes—always without solid basis—to be Soviet domestic quarrels. In 1971 Victor Lessiovski, a high-ranking Soviet official at the U.N., the man the FBI had code-named Fedora and considered their top penetration of the Soviet hierarchy, told his handlers that a controversy was raging within the Soviet Defense Council over the future of biological warfare. The KGB had supposedly reported that the U.S. was far ahead in the technology of producing, storing, delivering, and countering biological and biotoxin substances. Some elements of the armed forces wanted a big program to overtake the U.S. But the Politburo was hesitating largely because of the cost.

President Nixon and Henry Kissinger saw an opportunity to achieve much at no cost. They quickly proposed to the Soviet Union that both countries do away with their programs in biological and toxin warfare—and destroy all stocks. The Soviets, they reasoned, would be doubly delighted to comply. By so doing they would rid themselves of concern in a field in which they deemed the U.S. superior, and avoid a huge expense. For these reasons the deal would be self-enforcing, as it had to be given the absolute impossibility of positively "verifying" any preparations for bio-toxin warfare by "national technical means."

For the U.S., the military benefits would be obvious: to remove from the world the specter of manmade disease would be no small accomplishment. Also the U.S. would not have to compete to build weapons that it wanted to use even less than nuclear weapons. Moreover, by destroying programs and stocks, the U.S. would retain its presumed edge in technology, further insuring itself against Soviet violations.

The political benefits of signing the convention were even more appealing. What a chance to strike a humanitarian pose before the 1972 elections! What a chance to put the arms control process on smooth tracks! The preamble to the convention called it a step toward "general and complete disarmament, under strict and effective international control," taken by two countries "desiring to contribute to the strengthening of confidence between peoples and the general improvement of the international atmosphere."[21]

All of this, of course, rested on Fedora's tip. But less than two years later, a complex series of events led to the unmasking in the *New York Times* of Fedora's identity and his cooperation with the U.S. government. One might have expected Mr. Lessiovski to seek asylum or to flee for his life. Instead, he happily returned to Moscow, his real job as a Soviet double agent well done. In the Yom Kippur War of 1973, Israel captured—and made available to the United States—Soviet equipment that clearly showed the Soviets were well ahead, not behind, the U.S. in the technology of handling bio-toxin materials.

The Threshold Test Ban Treaty (TTBT), which bans either side from exploding nuclear devices underground with yields above 150 kilotons, never had a military purpose, or even a rationale. After all, nuclear weapons were made big only to compensate for the inaccuracy of delivery systems. As the latter have improved, both sides have decreased the yield of their nuclear weapons. This trend is certain to continue. Insofar as both sides have the need to test devices more powerful than 150 kilotons, they can do it simply by testing the relatively small fission bomb that sets off the fusionable booster material, or by sub-scale testing of the fusion booster. When the Soviets really require a test above 150 kilotons, there are many ways of muffling the seismic "signature" of underground blasts. So, although the TTBT increased the cost of testing nuclear weapons, its military impact on both sides was always acknowledged to be nil.

The purpose of the TTBT was almost exclusively political. The treaty's preamble formally dedicated both parties to "achieve the discontinuance of all test explosions of nuclear weapons for all time" and, of course, the ever-present "general and complete disarmament under strict and effective international control."[22]

One need hardly stress that the U.S. government has not given serious thought to living without nuclear weapons—much less has it considered the implications of "general and complete" disarmament and the power of the international agency that would provide "strict and effective" control. But the words sound noble—if not examined too closely, and so long as the actions taken in pursuance of them are inexpensive. Moreover, such words and deeds may further the arms control process which, unless we think of it too rigorously, may allow us to continue to avert our eyes from a host of unpleasant problems.

5

What We Got

How, by violations, circumventions, but mostly within the letter of the treaties, the Soviet Union built precisely the kinds of forces that we had sought to avoid by entering into arms control in the first place.

How legal terms, even if well drawn, cannot possibly comprehend, encompass, and restrain the uses to which willful men put new inventions.

How American forces did not change despite changing Soviet forces, and how growing Soviet superiority came to be the argument for even more arms control.

How, at the beginning of the 1980s, no one could propose any means of causing the Soviets to adhere more faithfully to future arms control agreements than they had adhered to ones then in force.

How the Strategic Defense Initiative arose as a consequence of the failure of arms control.

By the early 1980s, after twenty years of negotiations and agreements about arms control, the strategic balance was both far less favorable to the U.S. than it had been before, and far different from what American arms controllers had expected it to be. In that sense, arms control had failed. But the arms control process had been so successful *within* the U.S. government that strategic matters came to be discussed exclusively in terms of arms control. The formulation of U.S. negotiating positions and the debates on treaties were the only occasions in which U.S. defense officials peered out from under the budgeteers' green eyeshades, and, if only theoretically, considered the United States' strategic posture.

However, because the intellectual currency of the arms control process could not comprehend strategic matters, neither could U.S. officials fully grasp the changes taking place in Soviet weaponry, or what these changes required of the U.S. The best illustration of this has been the U.S. government's treatment of the Soviet Union's violations of arms control agreements, which has confused legal and military considerations in ways detrimental to the understanding of both. Because most of the Soviet Union's military buildup does not violate any treaties, talk of individual violations abstracts from the dangerous military reality of which they are a part, and has logically led to the conclusion that the violations are militarily insignificant. By the converse of that logic, any consideration of the military significance of treaty-compliant activities has been cut short by noting the fact that they are not violations.

Nevertheless, the existence of violations has engendered both political turmoil and intellectual unease. To resolve these, some arms negotiators, including Paul Nitze, have talked of setting up cooperative events with the Soviets so that the Soviets might turn on radars or fly missiles in ways such that our "intelligence" might pick up data that would lead us to reclassify violations as activities that had been treaty-compliant after all. But many others realized that there is no satisfactory answer to the question: If the Soviets were to violate the *next* treaty, what should we do? Hence, by the early 1980s, even such former stalwarts of the arms control community as Henry Kissinger and Zbigniew Brzezinski had concluded that "arms control is dead"—that is, that we should not look to arms control to diminish the Soviet missile force. The majority of those who, discounting arms control, asked what the American people should look to for their safety, answered: Build devices to shoot down Soviet missiles.

The Nightmare Becomes Real

Arms control, then, has failed as a means of constraining the Soviet Union and succeeded as a means of constraining the U.S. The figures published in the Defense Department's annual report, *Soviet Military Power*, tell much of the tale. As of 1986, the Soviet Union had *at least* 5,720 warheads on its SS-17s, -18s, and -19s, plus some 500 on 420 SS-11s, -13s, and -16s. These, as we have said, possess the combination of power and accuracy required for a high probability of success in attacks against missile silos and other "hard" targets.

That is more than enough to "cover" the 1,000-plus U.S. strategic "hard" targets with two warheads, and still leave the Soviet Union with a huge, land-based reserve force — never mind its sea-based missile force which, as of early 1986, carried some 2,700 warheads. In addition, the Soviet Union's force of 441 SS-20s could not just "cover" every militarily significant target in Western Europe with a fraction of its 1,323 warheads, but also deliver a large number directly to the U.S. How many, we do not know, since each SS-20 launcher has an undetermined number of missiles for refire. To this we must add the Soviet Union's 12 Yankee-class submarines (recently converted to carriers of modern cruise missiles), some 180 Bear and Bison bombers, and over 250 Backfire bombers. All this means, in sum, that a Soviet surprise attack on American forces would leave the United States with considerably fewer than 100 ICBM warheads, with perhaps 25–75 bombers, and with some 2,400 warheads aboard perhaps 15 submarines, while the Soviets would retain nearly all their forces. Given this new military balance, what could the U.S. do?

As Secretary of Defense Weinberger said in December 1984, the U.S. military predicament in the 1980s is precisely the one we had sought to avoid by entering into the arms control process in the first place.[1] Actually, the predicament is much worse than anyone imagined at the outset of the process.

Moreover, the usefulness of American forces remaining after a Soviet first strike would be reduced by Soviet defenses, built largely in accordance with the ABM Treaty. The SA-12 anti-aircraft, anti-warhead system that could be deployed in some 1,000 mobile firing units equipped with perhaps 6,000 missiles could offer solid protection to any Soviet installations that were targeted by fewer than, say, a dozen warheads, and that the Soviet Union chose to defend with SA-12s. This weapon would thus significantly reduce the effect on the Soviet Union of a spread-out American retaliatory strike. Thus, the very existence of the SA-12, plus our ignorance of how many units would be concentrated to protect what targets, compel the U.S. to concentrate its retaliatory strike onto a relatively small number of high-priority targets in order to increase the chances of destroying them. But the effectiveness of such a strike would be reduced by the Soviets' network of nine large anti-missile, battle-management radars on the periphery of their populated zone, tied to the Flat Twin missile engagement radars and their associated SH-4 and SH-8 interceptors. This combination is openly deployed around Moscow, and who knows how many are in warehouses around the rest of the country? Even if this system succeeded in protecting only half these hypothetical targets-of-last-resort, the U.S. would have little to show for the total expenditure of its remaining strategic forces.

Then, of course, since 1980 the U.S. has expected the Soviet Union to test a high-energy laser weapon in space sometime in the late 1980s. No one knows how effective such a weapon will be against American missiles, or how many copies the Soviets would place in orbit during a crisis. But there is no doubt that, when added to the other measures the Soviets are preparing against American missiles, both prior to and after launch, even a small number of first-generation Soviet laser weapons could be effective. Under these conditions, *it was clear by the early 1980s that no American could devise any plan for employing those strategic forces conceivably surviving after a Soviet first strike — no plan that would allow the U.S. to accomplish any reasonable military objective whatever.*

Arms controllers are unwilling to say that, after a Soviet attack, they (or anyone they know) would recommend to the President that he launch the remaining U.S. forces. They are even less willing to specify what targets we should go after; whether, after a Soviet first strike, we should be trying to kill soldiers, sailors, or factory workers — i.e., whom we should be trying to kill, or why we should be killing them. Nevertheless, they profess confidence that because the Soviets could never be sure that a U.S. president would not irrationally launch the crippled remainder of U.S. forces, the Soviets would never seriously contemplate an attack. But since the late 1970s American arms controllers have made this argument with less and less conviction. Sometimes they still claim that thanks to their efforts, the Soviets have removed some 1,000 ICBMs from their silos and have removed 12 ballistic missile submarines from the line. When pressed, however, these advocates uncomfortably acknowledge that they have no idea what happened to these missiles that supposedly no longer threaten us, and are downright sheepish about the submarines' conversion into more formidable weapons — i.e., launchers of very modern cruise missiles. Nor do they mention the fact that the new ICBMs have four, six, or ten times the number of warheads of the ones they replaced.

But many arms controllers remember their promises to the American people about a safer world and a reduction in the tempo of the arms race. Whatever else they may say, when they act as defense attorneys for the Soviet Union, arguing that this or that technicality should absolve the Soviets from charges of having violated this or that treaty provision, they do acknowledge that the world of the 1980s is less safe than that of the 1960s. Their refuge is to blame "both sides," as well as to ask for redoubled American efforts and concessions. Still, they regard the Soviet Union's violations as so many personal affronts. How could the Soviets, they ask, have put *us* in such an embarrassing position? So all told, no major American arms controller has declared himself happy with the arms control process' success in restraining the Soviet Union. At most, they claim that things could be worse.

Conquering the Pentagon

Advocates of arms control have succeeded brilliantly within the U.S. A glance at American strategic forces shows that these forces have stuck close to the logic of Mutual Assured Destruction, despite the consistent flow of American targeting policy away from MAD since 1974. The U.S. has not increased the number of its ICBM warheads since the early 1970s—2,100 in all—or their potency since the Mark 12-A program in the mid-1970s. The number of warheads aboard ballistic missile submarines has remained steady at 5,700 since the late 1970s. Because plans have lagged for substituting some of these warheads with ones carried by MX and Trident II missiles respectively, the U.S. still does not have the ability to threaten large numbers of Soviet "hard" targets on a time-urgent basis. As of 1987, the U.S. had no plans for acquiring a force able to do that.

Hence, although the U.S. has advanced the state of the art of strategic weaponry, and although the technology available to the U.S. would allow us to build weapons fit for whatever rational strategy we were to choose, in the 1980s the U.S. remained equipped with a force that fit no strategy at all—not even Mutual Assured Destruction. Given the Soviet Union's ability to reduce the stock of U.S. strategic weapons even before they are launched, and to defend against the ones that are, the U.S. in the 1980s could not even expect to execute MAD—to count on killing 25 percent, or any set percentage, of the Soviet population. There are no plans in the U.S. for preparing to increase Soviet casualties. Indeed, were the U.S. truly interested in preparing a MAD-consistent defense strategy to maximize Soviet casualties, we would be building enhanced-fallout warheads, and perhaps also warheads to disperse toxins and exotic diseases. That the U.S. is not—as, indeed, it should not be—

building such horrible weapons is indicative of the fact that there is no true interest here in utilizing American weapons against the civilian population of the Soviet Union. The supposed strategy of MAD is mythical as well as immoral.

However, although U.S. strategy does not fit well with any approach to international conflict, the myth of MAD continues to be promulgated as an item of purely domestic political ideology. In short, the United States' strategic agenda in the 1980s, as expressed in its budgets for strategic forces, continued to be that of the late 1960s: to do what is necessary to maintain forces that could sustain a Soviet first strike and still do "unacceptable" damage to the Soviet Union. But more and more, U.S. officials have come to define doing what is necessary less as building weapons that, if used, could accomplish certain things and more as crafting positions for negotiations; and they have come to craft negotiating positions, not with an eye to shaping Soviet forces, but with an eye to domestic political and budgetary battles.

Indeed, Senator Wallop, speaking with Ambassador Kampleman about the U.S. INF proposals of 1987, found that the military equation had been less than a major part of his marching orders. The senator asked why, if the purpose of these proposed agreements was to enhance the military security of Europe, were Europe's military leaders exhibiting so much anxiety about them, and why were NATO's leaders so uncertain of their postagreement courses of action for the defense of NATO and the deterrence of war. Kampleman's honest answer was that he did not entirely know, as this had not been within the negotiator's charge. Here we have an intelligent, able, honorable negotiator who clearly can pursue the goals set out for him. That those goals were unclear or silent about essential matters is not so much the fault of the negotiator as it is proof that for Americans, arms control is a political exercise and not a strategic one.

It is instructive to recall how one part of the U.S. INF position— that there should be 100 intermediate range missiles on either side— came to be. President Ronald Reagan mentioned that number to Mikhail Gorbachev at a summit meeting that he swears was not a summit meeting and feels honor-bound to stick with that number if we cannot get zero. This is neither a military judgment nor one in any way relating to safety. It is the result of a weekend of domestic American politics carried out in Iceland. Since the beginning of SALT I, American policymakers, senior military officers, and the press have tended to look at strategic weapons either as technical-managerial-budgetary phenomena or as things interesting primarily from the standpoint of arms control. Not surprisingly, the arms control perspective has tended to complicate the technical-managerial aspects of weaponry, and has crowded out of the minds of senior officials thoughts about the actual usefulness of weaponry to the nation's safety.

The best example of this is the MX. This missile was first conceived in the late 1960s as a hedge against the possibility that the millennium had not arrived, that the Soviets just might be interested in acquiring large numbers of counterforce missiles, and therefore that we would have to have more than just 1,000 Minutemen. The Soviets' acquisition of counterforce missiles, reasoned U.S. military planners, would imply that our own missiles must somehow be made survivable *and* that they should be given the capacity to "counter" the enemy's hardened missile forces. Thence flowed the indispensable twin requirements for a "follow-on" to Minuteman: survivability and a counterforce punch. To make our missiles survive, we could make them mobile so that the Soviets would not know where they were, or we could prepare to shoot down warheads coming toward them, or, better yet, we could do both. These desiderata were extraneous to missile design. Nevertheless, mobility was not a technical problem, and anti-missile defense was the order of the day in the late 1960s.

Even in the late 1960s the only strictly technical requirement of the MX—achieving a combination of yield and accuracy to destroy a silo—was easy to meet, and all of the several MX designs met it. By 1972 the U.S. could have put in production a three-warhead road-mobile, or a six-warhead rail-mobile, version of the MX. But arms control intervened. We would not need MX because the Soviets would solve for us the problems they had created for us by building SS-9s.

It took until 1974 to figure out that the Soviets would not solve those problems, but complicate them. But by the time that lesson had sunk in, the very arms control process that had delayed the MX had also placed substantive constraints on it: we had already agreed to limit the number of launchers. This meant that we could not fix our problems simply by building as many missiles and launchers as we wanted. So we had to pack as much as we could into as few missiles as we could. This meant that the MX would have to be big—carry 10 warheads, weigh 200,000 pounds, and be difficult to move. Besides, the logic of verification by intelligence satellites—the key to arms control—was against mobile missiles. For the sake of arms control, the Soviet Union had to be able to find out precisely how many MXs we had by using its satellites. To the contrary, however, the key to survivability still had to be denying the other side knowledge of where these huge missiles were at any given time. Thus, between 1976 and 1982, a major industry—and literally billions of tax dollars—went into the impossible task of devising a "survivable" basing mode for MX within these parameters.

None of the seemingly endless variety of "MX basing options" could square the circle: If each missile were shuttled relatively seldom between dozens of widely dispersed, empty, vertical silos, it would be difficult for the Soviets to attack economically. But, the numbers would then be difficult to check. If each missile were shuttled, but more often, within a set of horizontal shelters relatively nearby, the number would be easy to check, but attacking the set would be easier. If the missiles were all in silos very close to one another, they would be very easy to count and would be reasonably survivable, *if* defended. Defense, for that matter, would enhance the missiles' survivability in every basing mode. But the spirit of the ABM Treaty ruled that out as well.

Basing the missiles on the nation's railroads might provide excellent survivability, but many considered it too offensive to the spirit of arms control. U.S. officials have never given this as the reason for opposing railroad basing. Instead, they have spoken of hypothetical public opposition to having missiles rolling through America. At the end of 1986, the Strategic Air Command finally proposed this alternative, but appeared to do so as a "trial balloon."

To be sure, U.S. officials conveyed lack of seriousness about each basing mode by setting forth fantastic requirements for each. For each proposed basing mode, the Pentagon ordered studies of how the Soviets might conceivably attack it with means that existed only in the imagination of the report writers. For each basing mode, the State Department compiled an Arms Control Impact Statement and the Pentagon compiled an Environmental Impact Statement. All possible costs were extrapolated over 30 years using guesses about rates of inflation, civilian and military pay, fuel prices, etc., that attempted to model the future. The results were daunting. General Guy Hecker (USAF), once program manager of the MX, used to regale audiences with the fact that the horizontal shelter basing mode would be mankind's largest construction project – dwarfing the construction of the Pyramids and requiring more concrete than the entire U.S. Interstate Highway System, and with tales of how closely spaced MXs might be protected by piling around them crushed rock approximating the volume of a mountain range. All of this was being said while technology was rendering precise attacks on any and all known sites cheaper and surer. Thus was MX, a project deformed at conception by arms control, born a laughingstock.

Ronald Reagan campaigned for the presidency in 1980 citing, correctly, that the United States had entered a period during which the Soviets could destroy nearly all our strategic forces with only a small fraction of theirs. His term "window of vulnerability" meant nothing more than what Harold Brown, President Carter's Secretary of Defense, had said in his report to Congress for fiscal 1980:

> It is equally important to acknowledge, however, that the coordination of a successful attack is not impossible, and that the 'rubbish heap of history' is filled with authorities who said something reckless could not or would not be done. Accordingly, we must take the prospective vulnerability of our ICBM force with the utmost seriousness for planning purposes.[2]

Candidate Reagan may have understood much less. But the term "window" implied that this dangerous period would come to an end once the U.S. deployed survivable ICBMs, and that he was committed to deploying them. However, as we shall see elsewhere, President Reagan soon became as committed to arms control as his predecessors. Hence, he was no more able to find a survivable basing mode for the MX than they were.

So, like his predecessors, Reagan turned to the disease for the cure. The Carter administration had tied MX to the SALT II Treaty by arguing that its plans for 200 MX missiles gave the Soviets the incentive to agree to the treaty (lest the U.S. build more), and made that number sufficient; for without the treaty, the Soviets' threat to the MX could outgrow the ability of its (arguably) survivable basing mode to cope with such threat.

In 1982 the Reagan administration, embarrassed by its inability to explain how its proposal to build only 100–rather than Carter's 200–MXs would close the "window of vulnerability," and stung by criticism that it was not sincere about arms control, appointed Brent Scowcroft (Henry Kissinger's deputy during the time of SALT I) to explain its own strategic weapons program to the public, and perhaps to itself. The Scowcroft Commission's report rightly pointed out that the MX was needed not just to survive, but also to threaten Soviet reserve missile forces in their silos. Thus, reasoned Scowcroft, our inability to find a survivable basing mode for the MX (within the constraints of arms control, of course) does not mean we should not deploy the MX. Rather, we should deploy it in vulnerable silos in Minuteman fields. Reagan had made the correct decision to deploy 1,000 vulnerable MX warheads rather than 2,000, because the lesser number would not be a serious threat to Soviet reserve forces. Thus, argued the report, Congress' approval of 100 MXs, and their actual construction, would not be enough to present a real threat but would be enough to serve as an incentive for the Soviet Union to enter into a "stabilizing and equitable agreement." Thus again was the angel "bargaining chip" called upon to soothe the political mind by arguing simultaneously both for and against the weapon.

Such an agreement might work out ways in which both sides would be sure of each other's forces, and would be sure that their own could ride out the other's attack. Although this would be in both sides' best interest, said the report, it would be "illusory" to think the Soviets would satisfy this desire, which *we* think mutually beneficial, without the MX. The Scowcroft Commission thus recommended the MX not as hardware that might be useful in military operations to protect the American people, but as a bargaining chip useful in the only meaningful struggle: arms control. In its 26-page report on achieving the strategic purpose of the MX, the Scowcroft Commission used the term "arms control" 62 times.[3]

Lest anyone consider this substitution of arms control for reality to be a delusion peculiar to civilian policymakers, to which the military are immune, consider, among many possible examples, the visits that General Bernard Davis, Commander-in-Chief of the Strategic Air Command, paid to U.S. senators in June 1984, on the eve of one of the Senate's perennial votes on the MX. Vote for the MX, argued the officer who would be in charge of using it, because we are at a crucial stage in our negotiations with the Soviet Union. Without the MX, we will stand no chance of getting the Soviets to agree to limit their threat to all our forces. With the MX there is such a chance. When asked what he could do for the American people with the MX that he could not do without it, the General returned to talk of strengthening the President's negotiating position. The General did not seem to understand repeated requests for his assessment—as the man who would have to use the missile—of what good the missile might do for the American people. Theoretically, 1,000 well-placed MX warheads could prevent several thousand Soviet missile warheads from landing on the U.S. Would that not be valuable? Not really, answered the General. The MX is useful primarily in the arms control process. After all, unless they agree not to do so, the Soviets can prepare forces that would prevent us from ever launching the MX. But once we have deployed some MXs, reasoned the General, we may have persuaded the Soviets to agree not to prepare a force that would render them useless. This line of argument persuaded neither devotees of arms control nor those who prefer to rely on U.S. military power for the country's safety.

The General's point, precisely that of the Scowcroft Commission, resembled less Harold Brown's skepticism circa 1980 than it did the "pure" arms control doctrine enunciated by Gerard Smith in 1972; i.e., that the military policy of the United States shall be predicated on the willingness of the Soviet Union to do us a very big favor. Yet, logically, senators devoted to arms control asked whether by purchasing the MX we might not make the Soviets *less* disposed to do well by us.

Clearly, the Reagan administration's handling of the MX displayed its inability even to think of any weapon that we might build as anything but a means to ask for—but not to compel—favors at the negotiating table. Of course, neither General Davis nor any of his more "responsible" policymaking superiors had addressed the question of how to enforce *compliance* with agreements.

Intellectual Confusion

This rendering of military thought into the make-believe categories of arms control has made it difficult to understand the facts of Soviet noncompliance with agreements, and how this noncompliance fits with Soviet military developments. Although examination of Soviet noncompliance could be enlightening, debating the intellectual categories of arms control has generated confusion.

Here is one example (among many) of this confusion. In 1983, two senators, James McClure (R-Idaho) and Joseph Biden (D-Delaware), drew together, respectively, the case for the proposition that the Soviets were violating SALT agreements, and the case against it.[4] Senator McClure contended that the Soviets were violating the most important provision of the SALT II Treaty—Article IV, Paragraph 9—by flight-testing two new types of ICBMs. Senator Biden argued that Senator McClure was "simply and flatly inaccurate." The SALT II Treaty indeed allows only one new-type ICBM to be developed by either side. The two Soviet missiles that had been tested were sufficiently different from all other missiles to be new types. However, the treaty also stipulates that the differences that determine the newness of a missile—discrepancies of more than 5 percent in length, diameter, launch-weight, and throw-weight between the missile tested and all other missiles—may not be counted as violations until after the twelfth test. Inasmuch as when McClure and Biden spoke the Soviets had conducted only three tests, Biden had a technical point. But McClure had a substantive one. The second new Soviet missile, then known as the PL-5 and now known as the SS-25, differs in throw-weight by more than 200 percent and in length by more than two meters from any other remotely similar Soviet missile. No matter how many times it would be tested, these characteristics would not change.

Neither set of arguments, however, touched the crucial point: while the United States had produced one new missile (the Trident I) and was planning another two (MX and Trident II), the Soviets had produced four fourth-generation missiles and had begun a fifth-generation likely to include six new missiles.[5] Moreover, two of these fifth-generation missiles, the SS-25 and the SS-24, were fully mobile. Neither the liberal Biden nor the conservative McClure addressed the question of what we were going to do about the latest generation of Soviet missiles. Long before the U.S. possessed reliable means of attacking *fixed* Soviet ICBMs, the Soviets had begun producing *mobile* ones.

The Soviets' creation of a new strategic problem long before we had got around to meeting their previous challenge would appear to call for new thinking, not just about building weaponry to intercept in flight the Soviet missiles we cannot prevent from being launched, but also about updating our approach to counterforce targeting. If Soviet missiles are going to be mobile, the combination of accuracy and yield will not be so important in the future as the combination of intelligence and automatic retargeting.

Might this not be the time to reorient American technical intelligence away from monitoring the minutiae of treaties, and toward keeping constant track of mobile Soviet strategic weapons? Might this not be the time to talk about investing in equipment for near-real-time translation of intelligence information to updates of our own missile guidance systems? But, no. Such thinking has been crowded out by the debate on the technical-legal minutiae of violations.

In 1983, Senator McClure also charged that the Soviets exceeded the SALT II ceiling of 1,320 MIRVed missile launchers and bombers equipped with long-range cruise missiles. Senator Biden cited the CIA's count of 788 Soviet MIRVed ICBMs and claimed that the total of MIRVed ICBMs, SLBMs, and bombers capable of carrying cruise missiles did not exceed 1,320. The legal issue hinged on whether one counted the "Fencer"—the Soviet equivalent of the American FB-111 bomber. Once again, however, the legal issue is of little practical relevance. Even if one chose to agree with Senator Biden, one cannot thereby skirt the issue of the threat that the Soviet Union's nearly 6,000 counterforce warheads carried by the Soviet MIRVed systems pose to the U.S., or change the fact that our most potent MIRV—the Mark 12A—is considered to have only about one chance in three against 7,200 PSI Soviet silos. Should the U.S. have a capability similar to that of the Soviet Union? If not, why not? At any rate, how are we going to deal with the Soviet arsenal? Both the liberal and the conservative senators were too closely focused on arms control to deal with such questions of reality.

Senator McClure also contended that the Soviets had violated SALT II by testing the "rapid reload of ICBM launchers" and by stockpiling at least 1,000 to 2,000 missiles that could be refired from standard silos. These missiles could also be fired by "soft" launchers from covert sites. Senator Biden considered this point to be "succinctly rebutted" by the U.S. Defense Department's volume, *Soviet Military Power* (1983), which stated that: "The Soviets probably cannot refurbish and reload silo launchers in a period less than a few days." Biden concluded: "Although the Soviet Union might have a limited capability to reconstitute its strategic forces after an initial firing, there is no real indication of a rapid reload capability." McClure conceded that a legal grey area existed because "the Soviets never agreed upon a definition of 'rapid.'" But both senators were referring to the same data: During the summer of 1980 the United States observed that the Soviet Union routinely practiced reloading its principal missile silos many times during war games. This procedure indeed took a few days.

However, all the parties concentrated on the treaty so fixedly that they missed the point. Whether or not the Soviet practice of reloading offensive or defensive missiles is legally "rapid" is quite irrelevant to American security, as is the difference between a Soviet strategic force actually reconstituted in minutes or days—given the fact that the U.S. force cannot be reconstituted at all! Ever since the beginning of the arms control process in the mid-1960s, the United States has based its entire strategic policy on the notion that each side would have only about as many missiles as it had launchers. The Soviets never formally agreed to this; nevertheless, informally, in a thousand ways, they led us to believe that they did. Now we know that, probably from the beginning, the Soviets had held a wholly different view of the matter.

Thus, not only is it a virtual certainty that the Soviets have available for use many more missiles than overtly deployed launchers, but the implication is much larger and strikes at the heart of the MAD/arms control view of the world: namely, that the Soviets do not share the Western view that nuclear war, if it ever comes, will be a mutually annihilating spasm. While American planning stops in effect at the edge of the contingency of a nuclear exchange, the Soviets are planning and practicing what to do after the first round. If this is not strategically significant, nothing is. Yet, as we can see, the arms control perspective is capable of trivializing even this fundamental factor in the nuclear equation.

Our point already should be clear: by thinking and arguing about Soviet activities in terms of the relationship of these activities to treaties, instead of relating them to security substance, both senators quibbled over trivialities while the strategic position of the United States crumbled apace. Moreover, those who argue in these terms inevitably cast themselves in the role either of the Soviet Union's prosecutors or of its defenders. Senator Biden has strongly expressed the wish, no doubt sincere, that he not be taken as the Soviet Union's defender. But how else can one characterize his invitation not to be alarmed by activities that are clearly threatening to Americans but that might possibly be shielded by some technicality?

In one instance, Senator Biden resorted to redefining the terms of the treaty. He noted that the Soviets had encrypted just about all the telemetry in their tests of the fifth generation of missiles. Article 15 of SALT II prohibits encryption that impedes verification of the treaty. Senator Biden noted that Soviet practices in this respect "raise questions" about whether the Soviets have violated the treaty. Questions? These activities are not questions; they are answers!

Senator Biden said that "Soviet activities in regard to . . . the ban on the [mobile] SS-16 . . . can only make one wonder about

the depth of Soviet interest in maintaining the SALT framework."
In thus "wondering," he was no doubt inspired by the CIA's version of said Soviet activities. According to this version, the Soviets
have some mobile SS-16 missiles (prohibited by the SALT II Treaty)
at Plesetsk. They are ready to be fired. But because they are not being
handled in a way that fits the CIA's definition of deployment, they
are not "deployed." The point, again, is: Why cast about for artificial definitions and technicalities that might becloud the issue of
whether a given Soviet activity is or is not in contravention of SALT?
Why not think—first, last, and foremost—in terms of the strategic
implications of the threatening activity itself?

Finally, Senator Biden, searching for a definition of what a violation of SALT II might be, posited that if the Soviets were to have
more than 820 MIRVed ICBMs, *that* would be a violation. A little
later he noted in passing that by not having dismantled 95 strategic nuclear delivery systems as new ones have joined their forces,
the Soviets then had to have more than the 2,504 permitted by SALT.
Later, when the Soviet Union began to deploy the SS-25 as an explicit
violation of SALT II, Senator Biden, who had earlier taken refuge
in technicalities, took further refuge, this time in silence. Ultimately,
he had no position.

Nevertheless, Senator Biden has conceded that the Soviets have
violated the Biological Warfare Convention of 1972. At the same time,
he described himself as "a strong supporter of the unratified SALT
II Agreement and of worthwhile future arms control agreements."
Clearly, these are contradictions that cannot be bridged with technicalities regarding Soviet compliance.

Senator McClure's position was much more direct, but contains
an anomaly. He so strongly hammered on the fact that the Soviets
are cheating on the treaties that he led his audience to infer that
our strategic difficulties would vanish if only the Soviets could somehow be held to the letter of the treaties. Yet, not even the most
enthusiastic advocates of arms control have argued explicitly—at
least not since the mid-1970s—that the treaties are so well conceived
or drawn up that abiding by them will secure the future of mankind.

In short, even while the strategic position of the United States
continues to erode, men of goodwill find themselves saying things

about arms control that cannot halt that erosion, and that cast them in roles that they sincerely reject for themselves: apologists for the Soviet Union and/or apologists for the arms control process.

Thinking of weaponry in terms of arms control has also made it difficult for U.S. intelligence to understand what Soviet weaponry it sees. We cannot here do justice to this complex subject. Suffice it to say, however, that focusing our intelligence on arms control has enabled the Soviets to hide major military developments behind the screen of minor violations of arms control agreements. The clearest example involves mobile missiles. The Soviet Union, knowing what our intelligence satellites see, has shown us fleeting glimpses that its SS-16 mobile ICBM program, banned by SALT II, continued—though not on a militarily significant scale. Because these discoveries are important for arms control, American intelligence for many years continued to think of the "mobile ICBM problem" as synonymous with the SS-16.

At the same time, however, the Soviet Union was building 441 mobile launchers for the SS-20. Each SS-20 missile could carry a single warhead to intercontinental range, and each SS-20 launcher could launch SS-16s as well as SS-20s. These 441 mobile (SS-20, SS-16) launchers are also able to fire the newest Soviet missile, the SS-25, which also violates SALT II. But, as of 1986, the Soviets have built fewer than 100 launchers that are distinctively for the SS-25. These they show to our well-known satellites. In the past, these glimpses of "forbidden" activities led U.S. intelligence to identify the "mobile missile problem" with the distinctive SS-16 launcher. Today, these "forbidden" glimpses are leading U.S. intelligence to identify the "mobile missile problem" with the SS-25 launchers— whose number is small—rather than with the capacity of the 441 SS-20 launchers to fire a large but unknowable number of SS-25s, -20s, and -16s at the U.S. Intelligence is supposed to warn of danger, and to provide the knowledge needed to do something about it, but talk and resources devoted to this kind of treatment of the "mobile missile problem" do the opposite.

The Soviet Union's activities in the field of anti-missile defense provide perhaps the best illustration of the proposition that the arms control process' terms of reference have proved unable to encompass or to comprehend military reality, and hence have confused American officials who have used them.

Nowhere is this more evident than in the U.S. Arms Control and Disarmament Agency's report *Soviet Noncompliance* of February 1986. The report lists five things that the Soviets have done that are either violations of the ABM Treaty or ambiguous situations of serious concern with regard to that treaty. The large missile detection and tracking radar near Krasnoyarsk is an obvious violation because of its location.[6] The second item is called "Mobility of ABM System Components." The report, noting that the treaty never precisely defines its prohibition of "mobile" ABM systems, goes on to note that the components of the Soviets' dedicated ABM system – obviously referring to the Flat Twin and Pawn Shop radars, as well as the SH-4 and SH-8 interceptors – are "apparently designed so that they could be relocated in months rather than in terms of the years required to deploy fixed land based systems." The report limits itself to charging a "potential violation."

The third item is called "Concurrent Testing of ABM and Air Defense Components." The report notes "the many occasions when Soviet ABM and SAM radars were operating at about the same time." In June 1986, the Soviet Union calibrated the radar associated with the SA-5 interceptor missile with the Pushkino ABM battle-management radar. This makes sense only if the two are to be used together. Nevertheless, ACDA still concludes, as it did in the report, that "the USSR probably has violated the prohibition on testing SAM components in an ABM mode." But since there is no clear definition of "ABM mode," it calls the violation only "probable."

The fourth item deals with the "ABM Capabilities of Modern SAM Systems." The report notes that "virtually any air defense missile system has some level of ABM capability." Hence, it says that "the treaty was not intended to preclude an incidental or insignificant ABM capability, but rather a meaningful or significant capability." Then it goes on to note that the SA-12 is a competent ABM weapon. But since the treaty contains no fixed standards against which to judge at what point an ABM capability becomes meaningful or significant, the report limits itself to saying that this is a serious matter but the evidence concerning it is ambiguous. Legally, this point is unexceptionable. Militarily, it is irresponsible.

The report renders the same judgment regarding the rapid reloading of Soviet ABM launchers, and for the same reason. There is obvious evidence that these are meant for more than one shot. But since there is no information on just how fast the reloading can be done (theoretically, the time is less than one second), and since there are no clear standards, the judgment must be: "Ambiguous/serious concern." Each of these items ends with the words: "This and other ABM-related Soviet actions suggest that the USSR may be preparing an ABM defense of its national territory."

In explanation of this judgment, the report considers the first five items in the context of one another. It notes that the radar near Krasnoyarsk is the *sixth* of its kind, the Pechora class. (Since the report was published, the U.S. has discovered three more Pechora-class radars, bringing the total to nine.) The Soviet Union's possession of all these radars, together with its ability to produce and rapidly transport all the other components of a nationwide coordinated ABM system, plus the ability to back up such a system with the SA-12 and other dual-purpose air defense equipment, leads the U.S. government, alas, not to a conclusion but to a question: "The USSR *may be* preparing an ABM defense of its national territory." (Emphasis added.) It seems to us that only by filtering the above-mentioned items through the distorted medium of the arms control process could one blur their obvious warning into a question. Only by filtering these facts through the optic of a legalism whose motto is to reserve judgment until all "shadow of doubt" has been removed can anyone in a position of responsibility avoid the conclusion that the Soviet Union is making impressive preparations to defend itself against American missiles.

This mind-bending legacy of the arms control process is strongest in the area where legal standards are necessarily weak, not to say nonexistent—that of "futuristic" defensive weapons. As we have seen, the American negotiators of the ABM Treaty sought to ban—or limit to insignificance—all anti-missile weapons then existing or that might ever come into existence. But our arms controllers only hazily defined existing systems, and wholly deferred trying to define future ones. The ABM Treaty does not mention lasers, or particle beams, or optical pointer-trackers at all; indeed, it could hardly have done so in 1972, when such technology was in its infancy. The only possible reference to such technologies is in Agreed Interpretation "D," which states that in the event components based on "other physical principles" and capable of substituting for ABM launchers, missiles, and radars "are created," the two parties would discuss how they might be limited. That is to say, the two parties would try to develop definitions. It must be kept in mind that, in international law even more than in domestic law, the crafting of definitions is no mere technicality. Rather, it is the very essence of deciding what the limitations are and what they are not.

A moment's reflection is enough to realize that in the case of space lasers, to distill reality into legal terms verifiable by national technical means would be much more difficult than it has been in the case of ballistic missiles. Unlike missiles, the characteristics that make lasers fit or unfit for strategic warfare are not discernible through mere observation—even if observation were possible. Observation will yield information on gross size, power plant, and possibly wavelength. But the laser's power, the quality of its beam, its pointing accuracy, its jitter, the time it needs to retarget, and the number of times it can fire can be learned only from direct access to test data.

Hence, suppose for a moment that the Soviet Union placed a number of laser devices in orbit. Discussion of the strategic significance of this event would instantly be distracted by questions of whether a violation of the ABM Treaty had occurred. But on what basis could the Soviet Union be accused of having violated the treaty? There could be little in the way of determining—much less hard proof—that the lasers' mission was ballistic missile defense, or indeed that they were weapons at all. Yet, against this background of legal murkiness and ominous strategic implications, many devotees of arms control, who would not accuse a Soviet laser device in orbit of violating the ABM Treaty, still object to placing American lasers in orbit on the grounds that doing so would violate the ABM Treaty. They do this even though, almost universally, they deprecate the efficacy of American lasers against ballistic missiles.

In short, the difficulty of reducing the reality of modern weapons to legal terms has produced an intellectual tangle of our own making, within which we thrash about even as the Soviets widen their margin of military superiority. It seems to us that since the question of Soviet violations of arms control treaties refers to a framework removed from reality, dwelling on the question only compounds the unreality.

The arms control process also left its legacy on the American political process. Any number of American politicians, since the early 1960s, have chosen to depict themselves to the American people as "standing up for," or being "on the side of," peace in order to inexpensively stigmatize their political opponents as somehow dangerous or on the side of war. As their protestations continued through the 1960s and 1970s, arms control became so much a part of these politicians that to speak of alternatives to arms control is to speak of alternatives to them personally. Whenever anyone discusses the failure of arms control agreements to bring about a safer world, even if one blames the Soviet Union for that failure, one is effectively blaming all those Americans who are responsible for formulating and selling the agreements. That is why so many politicians seem to become more attached to arms control even as that attachment grows ever more patently absurd. They are riding a tiger, and have ample reason to believe that it will devour them if ever they dismount.

This legacy of arms control should be no surprise. Some of the generic difficulties in the path of rational discussion of compliance with arms control agreements were outlined by Fred Iklé in his classic article, "After Detection—What?", in the Fall 1961 issue of *Foreign Affairs*. Iklé's points are well worth reformulating after nearly a generation's experience because they, too, are fruits of the arms control process.

First, unless the violator acknowledges that his activities constitute a violation, politicians in a democracy are likely to feel that the evidence in their possession might be insufficient to convince public opinion that a violation has occurred—at least, that trying to persuade the public would be a thankless task. Moreover, many politicians, having staked their reputations on the agreements, will fear being damaged in the public's esteem if the agreements were perceived as failures.

Second, a political leader who declares that arms control agreements—which are a fundamental part of national policy—have been violated thereby faces the obligation to propose a new, redressive policy, one that will make up for the other side's violations and assure his nation's safety in an environment more perilous than had previously been imagined. Inevitably, such a policy looms as more expensive and frightening than continuing on the arms control track. Few politicians are willing to take this step of personal and political valor, especially if they can rationalize the observed violation as "insignificant." Iklé, in his article, cites Stanley Baldwin's admission that fear of losing an election had prevented him from admitting that Germany was violating the Treaty of Versailles. This remains a rare example of honesty and courage, albeit after the common fact of dishonesty and cowardice.

Third, politicians can always hope—more or less in good conscience—that continuing negotiations will eventually reach the goal of a stable and mutually accepted peace, and that therefore "this is not a good time" to accuse the other side of bad faith and risk driving it from the bargaining table. But when is it a "good time"? Moreover, as time passes and the dictatorship's arsenal rises in relative terms (abetted by the violations), the premium on finding a *modus vivendi* with the dictatorship rises apace. The net result is that the brave declarations that accompany the signing of arms control treaties, according to which this or that action by the dictatorship (usually some form of interference with verification) would cause withdrawal from the treaty, become dead letters.

Finally, these inhibitions are compounded when they are involved in alliance diplomacy among democratic nations. Each alliance partner is likely to find in the other a reason for not pressing the uncomfortable issue of violations.

All of this is to say that in the 1980s, after twenty years of the arms control process, the U.S. is left with a radically worsened strategic situation, with an impaired ability to judge military developments at home and abroad, with a near-total reliance on arms control for our safety and independence, as well as with a growing realization that Americans have precisely zero means for enforcing the terms of any agreement, good or bad.

6

The Reagan Administration, Sincerity, and Arms Control

How President Reagan was convinced to use the arms control process as a cover for his military budget.

How, thereafter, he was pressed to find practical means of demonstrating his "sincerity" toward that process.

How the Reagan administration's arms control proposals mostly replayed old scripts, but also sowed some utopian seeds that the administration would later regret.

How arms control affected the administration's early plans for strategic forces.

How the administration's attention to Soviet violations, and lack of policy for obtaining compliance, mutated into an insistence on "restoring the integrity" of arms control—i.e., on its own strict observance.

How the administration's pursuit of the "integrity" of arms control and of strategic defense has shown once again that no one can advocate two contradictory propositions without discrediting both— there are no parallel convergences.

When, in 1980, candidate Ronald Reagan called the SALT II Treaty "fatally flawed," he may have meant to do no more than use catchy words to demean what his opponent was calling his principal achievement. Nor is it clear what weight (if any) Ronald Reagan placed on the words he spoke charging that SALT I and SALT II had been powerless to stop increases in Soviet missilery, and had legitimized the Soviet Union's acquisition of a first-strike capacity. Reagan did not explicitly say whether he would find a Soviet first-strike capacity acceptable or unacceptable if the absolute number of Soviet missiles were lower.

He did say, even as the Republican platform on which he ran said, that arms control had not and could not ensure the American people's security. That would have to be done by repairing the results of a decade during which, as (former Secretary of Defense) Harold Brown had said, the Soviets had "built," while we had not. If there was a chance for a fruitful agreement on arms with the Soviets, that chance would come only *after* an American buildup. A Reagan administration, he said, would put first things first.

President Carter himself had acknowledged that SALT II was highly imperfect, and Carter would have welcomed a debate on the treaty's minutiae. Such a debate would have forced Reagan to tacitly accept the premises of the arms control process. Having done so, Reagan could have rejected Carter's argument that a bad treaty is better than no treaty only at his peril. But Reagan chose to oppose the treaty on general principles. Still, his political staff kept him from making a big deal of this. A delighted Jimmy Carter, however, forced the issue to the forefront. By Carter's lights, Reagan had made a big mistake. Carter sought to frame the election as a choice between a negotiated solution to America's security problems and a unilateral military one. Having no alternative, Reagan accepted this formulation of the issue, and won the election.

Arms Control As Cover

The Reagan transition teams at both the State and Defense Departments, who had wanted to make Reagan's stated opposition to arms control the centerpiece of his campaign, were unanimous that arms control should be on the new administration's back burner at best. But they immediately confronted a bureaucracy that sought—by any and all means—to keep the new administration from renouncing arms control. The State Department's Bureau of European Affairs and the Joint Chiefs of Staff did not overtly challenge the position on which President Reagan had been elected. Nor, in the last weeks of 1980, did any senior official in these organizations propose, even as a joke, that the administration adhere to the expired part of SALT I and the unratified SALT II treaties. The boldest arms control advocates in the government were only so bold as to say that there was no need to rush to denounce the ABM Treaty because however fast we built anti-missile devices, we could not manage to violate that treaty before it was due for its second review in 1982. Rather, both bureaucracies' objective was to keep arms control alive and as big a factor as possible in the administration's day-to-day life. Hence, both agreed that by all means there should be an American military buildup. However, in order to "cover" this buildup in public opinion at home and abroad, the administration should enter into a new round of arms control negotiations with the Soviet Union.

We "insiders," so argued the bureaucrats, have learned enough from the previous decade not to expect good results. But the American people, and especially "the Europeans," could not stomach the bitter and costly medicine of rearmament unless it was coated with the sweetener of arms control. Thus, we should have a "two-track" policy. In the first instance, this "two-track" policy should be applied to Europe in order to persuade the Europeans in general, and the German Social Democrats in particular, to carry through on their acceptance of the American Pershing II and cruise missiles they had requested. Then the two-track policy should be applied to intercontinental missiles as well. Both transition teams countered that the strength of democracies lies not in dissimulation but rather in unambiguous policies that inspire moral commitment. The previous decades' experiment with arms control had harmed the free world's security. Obscuring that fact in any way could only compound the harm by confusing the choices that free people faced. But Caspar Weinberger and Alexander Haig, Reagan's prospective appointees to head the Defense and State Departments, wholly accepted the bureaucrats' arguments and wholly rejected the transition teams' arguments. When the transition teams were dismissed at the end of December 1980, their arguments left the Reagan administration with them. The "two-track" approach to arms control and strategic policy became a vessel in which the bureaucracy mixed its favorite recipes.

President Reagan appointed no one to any executive office dealing with national security who would raise an objection to the "two-track" approach. Alexander Haig, an aide to Henry Kissinger at the time of the SALT I Treaty, possessed no ideas on this subject that might contradict the ones the State Department would give him. Nor did Caspar Weinberger, who spent his substantive efforts less on strategy and military effectiveness than on a budget policy with Congress that was not about such things. The National Security Adviser, Richard Allen, spent his political capital on quarrels with Alexander Haig that were not over issues; at least if they were, no one could tell. Nevertheless, a major obstacle remained to committing the administration to the arms control process: Ronald Reagan. The proponents of "two track" believed that the President was not really on their side and had to be approached indirectly. Nevertheless, Reagan's own disinclination to detail, his tendency to confuse style and substance, as well as intention and result, made it possible for him to embrace an approach to this subject that he had denounced. But he did not do so easily. How the "turning" of Ronald Reagan was accomplished we may see from a memorandum on this subject from Richard Burt (then Director of the State Department's Bureau of Political Military Affairs) to Secretary of State Haig. This is but one example, but it is typical of the conduct of business in the Reagan White House.

DEPARTMENT OF STATE

ACTION MEMORANDUM

S/S LPB

July 16, 1981

TO: The Secretary

THRU: P -- Ambassador Stossel
FROM: PM -- Richard Burt

SUBJECT: Percy Letter Opposing Withdrawal of SALT II
             from Senate

ISSUE

How to respond to Senator Percy's letter of July 8
(attached).

BACKGROUND

As you told me following the May 21 SALT NSC meeting,
the President stated a preference for withdrawing the Treaty,
and when and how to do so was briefly discussed there and,
subsequently, in the IG. We as yet have no formal read-
out from the White House on this Presidential preference,
so it is unclear to what extent it is a "decision", and I
gathered from your debrief of the meeting to me that there
was no urgency.

Percy's letter urges against a Presidential request
to withdraw the Treaty now because it would elicit efforts
by various Senators to define SALT policy in ways which
would limit the Administration's flexibility and would also
harm relations with our Allies.

DISCUSSION

My own preference would be to avoid withdrawing the
Treaty until we have examined and developed an alternative
proposal. But the interagency reaction could be less
cautious. In the absence of White House confirmation that
the President wants withdrawal soon, I have not pushed for

IG analysis of modalities for doing so. I am concerned, however, that in the necessary clearance of a written response to Percy, the issue would be prematurely raised again.

Accordingly, I suggest you call Percy and tell him:

-- You have his letter of July 8 on withdrawal of the SALT II Treaty from the Senate.

--This issue is now dormant within the Administration.

--You can assure him, however, that there would be consultations with the SFRC if consideration of this issue is revived. And we would in general plan to consult with the Committee on development of SALT policy as key decision points are reached.

--I hope that this phone call will have answered the main concern you expressed in your letter.

Recommendation

That you telephone Percy and make the points above rather than respond in writing to his letter.

Approve _____   Disapprove _____

Attachment:

As stated.

Drafted:PM/SNP:CHenkin:jc
        7/16/81:x21617

Clearances:PM:RWDean
           H:RFairbanks
           EUR:JScanlan
           ACDA/ISP:JTimbie
           C:RCMacFarlane (subs)

Essentially, both Haig and Burt recognized that the President viewed arms control as something that had done harm to the free world and that he wanted nothing more to do with it. But since he had given no direct orders, the two officials felt free to act as if the President had no policy of his own. Hence, they felt free to shape the flow of information to the President and to orchestrate the sequence of decisions coming to him so that, while doing things that would appear to him to be leading away from the policies of the past, he would in fact enmesh himself in those policies perhaps more deeply than any of his predecessors.

The tools that Richard Burt, Alexander Haig, and their allies in the bureaucracy used included the "wise" counsel that only through bows in the direction of arms control could the President quiet the worrisome threats from Europeans that they would destroy the alliance. It is essential to note, however, that these officials themselves were helping to generate and to highlight these threats. Still, nothing was so effective in "turning" Ronald Reagan toward arms control as the promise that arms control talks would be cheap fertilizer for a U.S. military buildup.

Arms Control and Military Planning

Ronald Reagan believed that America had to have a military buildup. But he had no idea what that should mean other than passage of the budget his Department of Defense submitted for his approval. That budget, in turn, did not embody any strategic vision. Rather, it was a compilation of the military services' "wish lists." When, in the spring of 1981, the Pentagon unveiled its Five-Year Defense Program with a price tag of $1.3 trillion, a *New York Times* editorial defied the administration to show precisely how this program would make Americans safer.[1] In the absence of such a demonstration, argued the *Times*, the American people should demand that the administration rein in expenditures that make it harder to tread the only possible path to greater safety: arms control. This challenge was well crafted. The Reagan administration never seriously tried to meet it.

The services' budgets had not been designed, any more than those in the previous three administrations, to fight and win wars while protecting the American people. The services are combinations of "communities" (e.g., Army armor, Navy submarines, Air Force tactical fighters), each contending for a larger share of the budget. A strictly political process, quite unrelated to the nation's safety, parcels out the "defense" dollar among the communities and between the military services. That is why, for good or ill, such vision as U.S. military budgets have embodied in the past generation has been imposed by civilians.

But President Reagan and his Secretary of Defense were committed to nothing so much as to the proposition that the uniformed military knew best. They did not realize that during the 1960s, Secretary of Defense McNamara had wrought a revolution within the officer corps. Rather, Reagan and Weinberger believed that the nation's recent military shortcomings were attributable not to *bad influences* from civilians, but to *civilian influence* simply. They were half right. Hence, they were, *in principle*, closed to advice on military matters that suggested that the $1.3 trillion, five-year defense plan represented the services' mindless self-indulgence. They imagined that they could sell the Congress on the plan simply by arguing that we needed to spend more to catch up to the Soviets.

But then a host of voices following the *Times'* lead asked, "Catch up in what? What for? Precisely what could we do once we had spent this money that we could not do were we not to spend it?" The administration could not and did not try to show that its budget would provide the wherewithal to carry out any plan that, if worse came to worst, would make the American people safer than when Ronald Reagan had taken office.

All doubt about the nonexistence of such a plan vanished on October 1, 1981, when the administration unveiled its project for "strategic forces modernization." The main difference between it and President Carter's was the substitution of 100 B-1 bombers (to Carter's zero) for 100 MX missiles (to Carter's 200). Much of the drive for this shift came from raw, inter-service and intra-Air Force struggles over shares of the budget. Had Reagan given to the Air Force the B-1 bomber (for which the Republican Party had campaigned) while retaining Carter's 200 MXs, he would have given the Air Force a bigger share of the budget than the other services were willing to accept. So if the Air Force was to get both MX and B1, it would have to have smaller numbers of both. This is not a brilliant way to make military policy.

But arms control abetted this mindlessness. If Reagan had bought the 240 B-1s, the number originally planned by the Ford administration—equipping them with cruise missiles and Carter's 200 MXs—he would have had to count these as 440 "MIRVed" delivery vehicles under SALT II's ceiling of 1,320 for such systems. These, together with 550 Minuteman IIIs and 656 SLBMs, would have exceeded the 1,320 ceiling substantially (though not before the late 1980s). Thus, even in 1981 the Reagan administration allowed a combination of inter-service and inter-community rivalry, and respect for an unratified treaty that would not be breached until after it would have expired, to lead it to a strategic modernization plan that made no strategic sense.

Just how little sense the plan made may be gauged by the Reagan administration's rationalization for buying 100 rather than 200 MXs. The Carter figure, said administration officials, would have given the U.S. the capability to threaten so many Soviet military targets that the Soviets might have been tempted to "use or lose" their missiles. That is, 2,000 MX warheads, targeting two-on-one against the 820 Soviet silos that held the SS-17s, -18s, and -19s, could deprive the Soviet Union of the vast bulk of its militarily most useful warheads. One hundred MXs could still threaten Soviet missiles, but could not threaten enough of them to frustrate Soviet strategy. Hence, argued the administration, the Soviets should not be too worried about 100 MXs. This number, they then judged, was a good number because it was most acceptable both to *Moscow* and to the Pentagon's inter-service process!

However, neither proponents nor opponents of counterforce targeting have been able to endorse the commitment embodied in this compromise—a commitment to do counterforce targeting, yes, but to do it ineffectively. Thus we see that arms control induced senselessness into military planning, which, in turn, compromised the intellectual and political bases for the military buildup, for the sake of which Reagan had compromised his hostility to arms control in the first place.

Thus, when in 1981 Ronald Reagan hazarded a few ill-chosen words about how it would be necessary for the U.S. to prevent Soviet victory in the early stages of a nuclear war so as to be able to end it on terms favorable to the U.S., he and his administration lacked the intellectual substance to withstand the charge that he was a warmonger. At that point the White House began to search frantically for something that would deflect that charge, calm European politicians (whose furor the State Department had helped to whip up), and help to sell the Pentagon's budget. A thousand old hands were ready to proffer that something: more arms control.

Arms Control, Budgets, and Bargaining Chips

Like arms control itself, the proposition that the Congress and the public are likelier to vote more money for the Pentagon if the President is engaged in arms control negotiations than if he is not, rests on rejection of both fact and reason. During the late 1970s, the Congress and American public opinion were trying to add money to the military budget *despite* the administration's advocacy of SALT II. The opposition to SALT II, Ronald Reagan among them, was pointing to SALT II as proof of the administration's neglect of a "present danger"–the Soviet counterforce missile force. The opposition to SALT II further argued that there was a way of mitigating that danger: achievement of American superiority in counterforce missiles and in anti-missile defenses.

Note well that both proponents and opponents of SALT II agreed that SALT I had failed. Danger, and the real prospect of dealing with it successfully, logically called forth effort. Contrast this with the situation earlier in the 1970s. When many had believed SALT I was living up to our arms controllers' billing, the Congress – supported by public opinion–had cut one strategic program after another. Congress did this *despite* pleas from Henry Kissinger and Gerard Smith that the terms of SALT I had been negotiated on the assumption that the U.S. would build the very weapons Congress was cutting. In 1972, as he was selling the SALT I Treaty, Kissinger had scorned as illogical the wholly logical expectation that the Congress would take the treaty as a sedative. But, one has to ask, how else is a reasonable person to take assurances that the Soviet leaders' interests and purposes are compatible with our own? If there is agreement on ends (and if there is not, why would anyone in his right mind have signed an arms control treaty), then why spend scarce resources on more violent means? Richard Russell, it seems, knew logic better than either Reagan or Kissinger.

The *practical* linkage between arms control and military budgets, as the Reagan administration was to learn, is as uncomfortable as the theoretical one. While the legislators and journalists who support military projects usually do so because they believe these might do the country some good in a fight, those who most ardently believe in arms control do so either because they believe that weapons and fights are futile, or because they would rather not think of such things. When the Reagan administration began to pursue arms control alongside its military buildup as a means of asking people to vote for a buildup whose purpose, it loudly claimed, was to eliminate the need for that very buildup, it had to pay the price of confusion. The first installment of the price—discrediting the idea that weapons are to be bought because they might have to be used— the administration paid willingly.

In return, liberal congressmen and senators gave the administration a wider margin of victory for its military proposals in 1981 and early 1982 than they otherwise would have. But by mid-1982, the very people whose support the administration had bought, e.g., Senator Mathias, were complaining that the administration was not trying hard enough for an arms control agreement. After all, their aim was arms *control*, not arms. Their votes had pushed forward certain military programs. But they had not brought control. They felt betrayed.

Interestingly enough, no MXs were rolling off production lines, either. The procurement cycle does not deliver weapons for many years. Arms controllers can sell their votes many times before they see the dreaded weapons come off the lines, but arms control proposals and commitments to delay weapons can happen quickly. If such commitments do not come, arms controllers can and do charge insufficient zeal. This is exactly what happened to the Reagan administration in 1982. Having succeeded once, American arms controllers stepped up their pressures. The administration then had to prove its "sincerity" by formulating proposals that the arms control constituency judged acceptable to the Soviet Union. But from the moment in May 1982 when the administration formulated its Strategic Arms Reduction proposals, its own strategic programs began to suffer the fate of "bargaining chips."

This fate has two aspects. First, the bureaucracy and the Congress become reluctant to put scarce resources into things that are being bargained about, and will possibly be bargained away. Therefore, they settle on stretching out the research and development process and, at most, agree to token deployments. After all, if the weapon is really meant primarily to be used as a "chip," it may be able to fulfill that role without the Congress' having to incur the expenditures and inconveniences of building it. The United States, in fact, has never fully deployed any weapon ever described or treated as a bargaining chip. The nature of such chips is that they don't get used. Why should they? Once a weapons system is fully built and deployed, "the threat" it represents at the negotiating table has been carried out. It ceases to be a threat. Second, the bureaucracy and the Congress tend not just to delay, but also to modify, programs that are being negotiated in order not to forestall progress in the negotiation. Why should they do otherwise, given that the programs' principal purpose is to advance the negotiations?

Thus in 1985, only two years after the "bipartisan Scowcroft Commission" had supposedly achieved consensus on the indispensability of 100 MXs for arms control, congressional arms controllers successfully argued to their colleagues – and to the Reagan administration, who agreed with them – that only 40, and surely no more than 50, should be built. The previous year, once again with the administration's agreement (and even praise), they had conditioned permission to begin production of the first 21 MX missiles on the administration's engaging in negotiations with the Soviet Union. Had the Soviet Union refused negotiations, the burden would have been on the administration to prove not just that it was not at fault, but that the MX had any usefulness at all. After all, without negotiations, who needs a chip? By 1985, however, the Soviets were eager to come to the table to fry fish far larger than the MX; that is, to make sure that the administration's only potential answer to its buildup, the Strategic Defense Initiative, would become a "chip."

The practice of making each step of a U.S. weapons program dependent on the arms control process took its most extreme form in 1985, when the House of Representatives stipulated that the administration could not test an anti-satellite device if negotiations about barring that device were under way, while at the same time the Senate stipulated that the administration could not test an anti-satellite device *unless* it was engaged in negotiations to ban it. Thus, one house would have allowed the Soviets to veto our ASAT program by negotiating, while the other would have allowed them to veto it by *not* negotiating. Clearly, the Reagan administration's first ostensible reason for rehabilitating arms control—the proposition that genuflections in its direction are necessary to secure congressional support for military budgets—proved to be the reverse of the truth. Having revived the myth of arms control, the administration felt obliged to feed it the bone and sinew of American military preparedness.

New Proposals, Same Effect

President Reagan's proposals of May 1982, announced in a speech at Eureka College (his old alma mater), broke decisively with previous American efforts, which had only legitimized an increase in armaments on both sides. Heretofore, Americans had used the wrong currency in arms control, and had accepted inequality. This time, said Reagan, the U.S. would insist on deep reductions, by almost half, and on absolute equality in the things that actually kill: warheads. Both sides could have only 5,000 warheads on a maximum of 850 deployed missiles for each side. Reagan's proposal made sense on the surface, but only on the surface.

That is because in reality, all warheads are not created equal. The most common warhead in the U.S. arsenal, the 40-KT Poseidon warhead, yields only about one-twentieth the explosive power of the most typical warhead in the Soviet arsenal, that atop the SS-18, mod 4. Missiles, for their part, are almost as unequal as warheads. The Soviet SS-18 carries *seven times* the payload of the Minuteman III. As we have seen, that means that as the Soviets' performance in guidance and miniaturization approaches ours, the military potential of each SS-18 approaches seven times that of each Minuteman III, and perhaps twice that of each MX. We have already mentioned how inadequately the term "deployed missiles" allows us to comprehend the number of missiles or warheads that the Soviets might be preparing to launch against us. For these reasons, as well as because the START proposal would have included SALT I's prohibition against building any new fixed launchers (which locks in the Soviet monopoly in big missiles), Reagan's START would have frozen the U.S. in precisely the same inferior position that SALT I and SALT II had done.

In fact, START would have been considerably worse. Suppose for a moment that the Soviets had accepted, and adhered to, START's limit of 5,000 warheads. All warheads on the Soviet side, of course, would be on ICBMs and fit for counterforce. We, for our part, would have perhaps 20 ballistic missile submarines with 320 missiles, Reagan's 100 (rather than Carter's 200) MXs, and 430 Minuteman IIIs. That would make a total of 550 things which, if destroyed, would leave America disarmed. Under START, the Soviets would have nine warheads to devote to each of these 550 things. Today, they have about five for each of our 1,200 or so strategic aim points. Even the Carter administration's Director of Political-Military Affairs, Leslie Gelb, using this kind of analysis, denounced START as imprudent, as did Herbert Scoville, president of the leftist Arms Control Association.

The Reagan START proposal was also imprudent because it did not proceed from any sense of what we might want to *do* with the warheads that the agreement would have wanted us to have. If Reagan had made his START proposal with the intention of building 500 MXs—which the proposal would have permitted us to have—the balance under START would have looked different. But given that U.S. forces under START would have been, *at the very best*, the ones announced in the Strategic Modernization Plan of October 1981, the U.S. would not even have the capacity to carry out an attempt at Assured Destruction, much less any rational military strategy. The START proposal by itself—assuming the Soviets accepted and adhered to it, and that the administration had been determined to do everything possibly allowed under it to maximize American power—would have remedied SALT II. But START is a catchy title, with catchy headlines that hide the Reagan administration's refusal (or inability) to think in terms of maximizing American power.

The administration's proposal for Europe, the "zero option," was even catchier, but just as mindless. In 1977, President Carter had agreed to European governments' requests to offset the Soviet Union's growing superiority in conventional armament, as well as its deployment of a growing number of new, accurate, three-warhead SS-20 missiles, with 108 single-warhead, Pershing II ballistic missiles and 464 single-warhead cruise missiles. Since the SS-20 force was expected to top 400 launchers, each with more than one missile (and therefore with well over 2,000 warheads) it was clear to friend and foe alike that the United States' 572 warheads were pure tokenism. The U.S. purpose was political solidarity in NATO.

Nevertheless, the Reagan administration's first key decision on arms control in 1981 was to explain to our European allies that we were interested in placing intermediate-range missiles in Europe only to make the point in the negotiations that the Soviets should get rid of their SS-20s. It was never clear why anyone thought that such a point would be driven home by an exercise that we knew would end in military inferiority worse than that which had existed when we began it. At any rate, President Reagan declared that while we would be happy with a deal that left either side with precisely the same number of intermediate-range missiles in Europe, we would be happier if the number agreed upon was low, and happiest of all if the Soviets would agree that both sides would have zero such missiles. His purpose, declared Reagan, was to rid the earth of such senseless weapons.

The Soviets' violent rejection of the "zero option" was predictable. Why should they agree to negotiated parity in a field in which the U.S. had already foreclosed the option of challenging their superiority? The Soviets accused the U.S. of using the proposal as a screen behind which to place missiles in Europe—which was correct. These attacks gave American arms controllers, eager to preserve the "process," incentive to shape U.S. policy so as to prove U.S. "sincerity" toward arms control both to the Soviets and to the Europeans. Thus did the Soviets exact a high price for the deployment of 572 American warheads in Europe. In addition, the Soviets could not help but note that the Reagan administration proposed both START and the "zero option" in Europe with utopian rhetoric about the uselessness of military force and the need to eliminate nuclear weapons from the face of the earth. As we will see, they learned how to use the Reagan administration's own words to help move it in the direction they want it to go.

Thus the Reagan administration's arms control proposals, superficially different from those of previous administrations, had the same effect—to confirm the U.S. government's acceptance of military inferiority and to demonstrate the U.S. government's poverty of political-military thinking.

The Reagan Administration's Intentions and Its Evaluation of the Soviets' Intentions

The total sacrifice of substance for the sake of rhetoric embodied in the Reagan administration's arms control proposals could be partially justified if their purpose were totally cynical. But no one could apply such a label to Ronald Reagan. Nevertheless, an administration's words and proposals, regardless of the purposes for which they are spoken, provide warrants for various groups within the U.S. government to push for policies they want, and think they can justify in terms of the President's words. Most important, the words of public figures are the currencies by which democracies transact daily business. Let us then look more closely at the rhetoric with which the Reagan administration accompanied its proposals.

In his talk at Eureka College, President Reagan set the goal of reaching "a new understanding" with the Soviet leaders, who, he said, have "an overriding interest in preventing the use of nuclear weapons." That literally means that the Soviet leaders' interest in preventing the use of nuclear weapons *overrides* all of their other interests. Yet, common sense counsels that their interest in preventing *our* use of such weapons is clearly greater than their interest in preventing their own use of them. Despite common sense, the notion that the Soviet Union shares the views of American arms controllers is so attractive that the President's offering it made it into instant conventional wisdom. As an editorial in the *New York Times* (May 16, 1982) observed, such statements signify "recognition that nuclear weapons uniquely cannot be instruments of policy." Secretary of State Haig made the same point in an official release. In the nuclear era, said Haig, "total victory by military means has become a formula for mutual catastrophe."[2] Did the President and his Secretary of State really think they were speaking for the Soviet leadership, as well as for themselves? They surely gave that impression.

While both Reagan and Haig were publicly touting the Soviet leaders' good sense, they were arguing, both loudly and tacitly, that nothing we can ever do on our behalf will ever assure our safety. This staple, embodied in Ronald Reagan's formula "A nuclear war can never be won and must never be fought," has enervated U.S. defense policy. So, while proudly asserting that under Reagan "America has rebuilt her strength," the administration let it be known that under the Reagan administration the American people would have to seek their safety in negotiations, just as before. Indeed, according to the Reagan administration's public line, America's renewed strength was sufficient to bring on negotiations, nothing more.

Hence, Haig summed up the administration position when he said, "We cannot claim that we are too weak to negotiate and at the same time insist that we are strong enough for a policy of all-out confrontation."[3] Nor did the administration argue that this condition was bad and that we would endure it only so long as it would take us to rid ourselves of it. Hubert Humphrey, twenty years before Ronald Reagan, had made a similar argument, drawing from it the conclusion that this imperative to negotiate arms control was good, rather than tragic, because the Soviets were under the very same imperative. Note that to hold this position in the face of the historic and technological facts of 1982 required acts of faith more heroic—

and a utopian streak more pronounced—than was necessary for Hubert Humphrey to hold that position in 1961.

But no one in American public life has argued the opposite case more forcefully than Ronald Reagan, even as President. In his first press conference as President, Reagan indicated the impossibility of cooperation with the Soviet leaders, who "reserve unto themselves the right to commit any crime, to lie, to cheat." In 1981, not even the State Department, speaking through Alexander Haig, could deny that the Soviet Union's violation of arms control agreements was logically an impassable barrier to making new ones.[4]

President Reagan (in the very speech in which he announced his arms control proposals, based on his presumption that the Soviets have an "overriding interest" in it) mentioned the unfortunate fact that "the Soviet Union has not been living up to its obligation under existing arms control treaties." He mentioned the use of yellow rain against Laotian villagers by Soviet proxies, as well as the Soviets' use of chemical and toxic weapons in Afghanistan in violation of the Geneva Convention of 1925 and the Biological Warfare Treaty of 1972.

What did Reagan conclude from this? His speech to the United Nations on June 17, 1982, is as close to an explanation as he has ever given: "Evidence of noncompliance with existing arms control agreements underscores the need to approach negotiation of any new agreement with care." Or as Lawrence Eagleburger (formerly Henry Kissinger's aide, then Undersecretary of State for Political Affairs under Reagan) put it: "We have to do a better job" of arms control.

Soviet Violations and Reagan's Interim Compliance

Given that the United States has precisely zero means of forcing the Soviet Union to comply with old agreements, much less new ones, and that the Reagan administration realizes, at least to some extent, that Soviet political intentions and military programs aim at supremacy, one may ask what the Reagan administration—or anyone—could mean by doing a "better job" of arms control. Presumably, the first element of a "better job" would be to enforce compliance. To the authors' knowledge, the administration from the

President on down has consistently refused to confront the fact that we have zero means of enforcing compliance. The administration has escaped this confrontation by translating questions about *compliance* into ones about *verification*.

Two events are sadly illustrative of this self-confusing tendency. In the spring of 1985 there was a grand arms control euphoria spread by the White House. President Reagan hosted a large congressional leadership breakfast to send Ambassador Max Kampleman, Maynard Glitman, and John Tower off to Geneva. In an atmosphere of mutual praise and self-congratulation, Senator Wallop asked of the President:

> "Mr. President, why on the heels of your recent report about Soviet treaty violations are we asserting confidence in their willingness to abide by any new agreement? Is it too much to ask them to come into compliance, and if so, why then would we be confident they will comply with the terms of the new treaties?"

The President responded, "Well, you can be certain I won't submit a treaty to the Senate which is not completely verifiable!"

In the spring of 1986, as if to reassert this principle as his executive mandate, Ambassador Paul Nitze embraced it not only for the U.S., but for the Europeans as well. The Ambassador and General Rowny had been traveling to allied capitals explaining the newest U.S. proposals. Senator Wallop met Ambassador Nitze in Geneva and inquired if he had been speaking of compliance in conjunction with verification. His response was, "In our opinion, the allies get very nervous about compliance. We don't bring it up, and they don't ask. Its importance must be assumed by future leaders."

The authors must assume that the President and his highest appointees know the distinction between verification and compliance. Yet they refuse to acknowledge it because if they did, they would also have to acknowledge that they have no more means and no more will to enforce a new arms control agreement than they have to enforce old ones. Hence they, like their predecessors, are merely creating problems for their successors.

What the Reagan administration has meant by "a better job"

in arms control may be seen in its reaction to the undeniable facts of Soviet violations. President Reagan and his chief appointees did not go looking for such facts. Since the SALT debate of 1979–80, members of Congress (primarily senators), as well as a few members of the NSC staff, had been pressing the intelligence community for details on Soviet activities that they claim violate arms control agreements. Despite the wealth of details, those in the executive branch responsible for declaring that violations had occurred were very reluctant to do so. Between 1981 and 1984, Senator James McClure, usually joined by various numbers of senatorial colleagues, wrote twenty-three letters to President Reagan, as well as to the two directors of the Arms Control and Disarmament Agency—Eugene Rostow and Kenneth Adelman—asking the administration to acknowledge various Soviet violations. Many were never answered, while the others received responses that were contemptuously *pro forma*. The Arms Control and Disarmament Agency, whose verification bureau Kissinger had neutralized and Carter had dismantled, touched the subject only indirectly. Its General Advisory Committee (GAC), a body of presidentially appointed outsiders, conducted a study of Soviet violations quite outside of bureaucratic structures.

The only case that by 1982 was an exception to this rule, yellow rain, is actually a good illustration of it. Since 1976 the U.S. State Department and the CIA had received a flood of reports from Laotians and Cambodians about Vietnamese aircraft spraying a yellow powder that caused certain violent symptoms, usually leading to death. The official U.S. reaction until 1981 was that these reports were not credible because the witnesses had an axe to grind against communist forces, and because no *known* chemical warfare agent caused the symptoms that were being reported. Only when U.S. intelligence dispensed with its political prejudice and asked whether *any known substance, if used in chemical warfare*, might cause the reported symptoms did it come up with a candidate substance— mycotoxins—that it later identified in blood samples of victims and in samples of terrain that had been attacked.

In other words, the Reagan administration, like its predecessors, possessed more evidence that the Soviets had been violating other arms control agreements than it possessed desire to publicize those violations. Moreover, they had far more desire to publicize them than any sense of what to do about the situation that would result from such publicity.

Not until the Congress, as part of the Armed Services Authorization Act for fiscal 1983, passed a legal requirement that the President report on Soviet violations of arms control agreements, did the executive bureaucracy begin to grapple with the questions, "Shall we or shall we not actually declare *this* or *that* Soviet activity a violation? And if not, what label do we put on what the Soviets have been doing?" Is it or is it not threatening?

So, in January 1984 the administration submitted to the Congress a list of seven violations that ranged from the trivial (e.g., failure to declare military maneuvers in Europe) to the vital (e.g., the radar at Krasnoyarsk). It did so apologetically, saying publicly and privately that it was doing no more than was required by act of Congress. Indeed, the administration was doing less than required, since the Congress had asked for a full accounting, and the administration was delivering up only violations that were absolutely undeniable. The list had been made up by a very, very reluctant inter-agency team. Both the classified and unclassified versions of the report were written as a collection of seven legal briefs, in which the case for the Soviet Union was clearly made. Nowhere in the report was there any indication that each of these violations (as well as others) fit with other Soviet activities not cited as violations in a way that would enhance Soviet military capabilities.

This reticence had deep roots. When the administration first presented its classified case to the Senate Intelligence Committee, Senator Daniel P. Moynihan (D-New York) repeatedly asked what could possibly have led the Soviets to undertake so obvious a violation as the Krasnoyarsk radar, given the marginal military value of that radar all by itself. He kept stressing that, by itself, the radar could not be worth endangering the U.S.-Soviet relationship. But the administration team's responses never mentioned the simple fact that the Krasnoyarsk radar was the sixth of its kind, and that together with many other activities, that radar was radically changing the military balance in the Soviets' favor.

But why this reticence? In the very same congressional session, Senator Patrick Leahy (D-Vermont) spoke for many others when he said that the administration had made a sound case that the Soviet activities mentioned were indeed violations. Breaches of important treaties are serious events, said Senator Leahy, and he asked what the administration was planning to do. The administration's answer shocked everyone in the room: "We are here to ask you and your colleagues about that, Senator." This answer shows beyond doubt that the administration itself was treating the violations as political hot potatoes rather than as serious threats to national security. And thereafter few of the politicians in the room ever considered trying to do otherwise. Those who did quickly realized that the administration would fight with all its strength any attempt to consider the military consequences to the U.S. of the failure of arms control.

No sooner had the Reagan administration delivered its half-hearted report on violations than the White House's and the Pentagon's spokesmen on Capitol Hill enthusiastically conveyed one message loud and clear: The violations issue is totally extraneous to that of the administration's defense budget. No one should use the fact of Soviet violations to ask what new or different military measures the U.S. should take. To do so would be to call into question the adequacy of the administration's proposed budget for the country's military needs, and therefore to question the adequacy of the people at the top of the administration. Any opening of that question would be an unacceptable infringement on the responsibility of the nation's military leaders to make military plans.

In fact, of course, the administration in general, and the Pentagon in particular, were worried lest Soviet violations—an unpleasant fact from the outside world—intrude upon the cozy compromises by which they were living. That is because, though citing the legal fact of violations might strengthen the administration's hand a bit when asking for defense budgets, to discuss their military significance is necessarily to discuss the weaknesses of the administration's military planners. Whereas in early 1981 the Reagan administration would have been able to carry on such a discussion without impeaching itself, casting all blame on its predecessors, once Ronald Reagan had staffed the administration with men tied to the past, that course was no longer open to it.

Throughout 1984, congressmen, senators, and the press continued to find the administration reluctant to pronounce itself on violations. The administration, for example, refused for a year to release to the Congress, even in its classified form, the GAC's comprehensive report on violations. This refusal had nothing to do with the protection of intelligence sources and methods, and everything to do with the fact that the report not only listed some 30 violations or serious compliance problems, but noted that they fit a pattern: the Soviet Union has been and is pursuing certain military goals, and simply does not let treaty commitments stand in the way of achieving them. This was a fact that the administration could not (and did not wish to try to) refute, but which it heartily wished it did not have to confront, because doing so would have obliged it to question the adequacy of its own plans and personnel in the field of national security affairs. Hence, when in 1984 the White House finally gave in to pressure to release the GAC report, it sought to diminish the report's significance not by quarreling with it, but by giving the impression that somehow it did not fully represent the administration's position.

The Reagan administration's position on violations, at least in 1984 and 1985, came to be that it "would not stand for them," and that it demanded they be "resolved"—whatever that might mean. Of course, the very fact that the administration had declared certain Soviet activities to be violations was a break with the pattern by which previous ones had been "resolved." That pattern had involved the "discovery" that the real problem with the treaties was that their requirements were imprecise, and therefore subject to interpretation under which Soviet activities might not be illegal. "Resolution" of "compliance issues" had also traditionally involved the discovery that intelligence information did not allow the issue, as newly framed, to be resolved beyond the shadow of doubt, and the acceptance of token Soviet activities in the field as having "gone some distance in the direction of allaying concerns."

By the mid-1980s, however, there were simply too many people who knew the process well enough not to be mystified by it.

That is why Paul Nitze (quickly and with some embarrassment) disowned his own suggestion, reported by the *Washington Post* in 1985, that the U.S. resolve the issue of the Krasnoyarsk radar by intercepting a signal from it at a time agreed upon with the Soviet Union, and then declare that the signal was unfit for anti-missile work.[5] So the Reagan administration struggled aimlessly with the issue of violations, half-comfortable because it fit the President's political identity, and fully frightened because it logically demanded a style of governing that its principal members did not possess.

In 1984 and 1985 the Department of State, with no dissent at all from the military, and in the face of objections from Reagan's civilian appointees in the Department of Defense, convinced the President that the only possible path to "resolution" of Soviet violations, which the Department of State defined as "restoring the integrity" of the treaties and of the arms control process, lay in the United States' exemplary compliance with those treaties. This counsel was appealing because it could be sold to different domestic constituencies on grounds pleasing to each. The verbal commitment to "restoring the integrity" of the treaties played reasonably well to those conservatives who had harped on Soviet violations. Also, the fact of exemplary American compliance gratified and strengthened immeasurably the position of liberals within the administration who, since 1982, had led President Reagan to agree that to keep alive our negotiations, we had to abide by SALT I, even though it had expired; by SALT II, even though it had not been ratified on Reagan's own advice; and by the ABM Treaty, even though the Soviets were violating it.

The reader will recall that the purpose for which President Reagan had agreed to this "interim restraint"—to the uncertain extent that he did so deliberately—was to cover his military buildup politically. But if his original agreement to "interim restraint" did not raise in his mind the question of how such restraint would affect that buildup, the State Department's proposal of a policy of strict, exemplary, *unilateral* compliance certainly would have raised that question in any open-minded individual. Yet it seems that the President was convinced not to open his mind to this question. Surely the Reagan administration has not added up the political and mili-

tary costs of this restraint, much less released to the public an esti-
mate of those costs. In its defense, we must note that the
administration's leading personages do not consider themselves
competent to judge military questions, make no attempt to do so,
and therefore cannot calculate the military costs of restraint.

Nevertheless, the policy of "interim restraint" has been a total
fraud—literally, the doing of things under pretenses both wholly
false and intended to obfuscate the truth. First, those who have
urged it have done so claiming that it is for an "interim" period.
However, they do not have in mind a particular length of time or
a set of events that would end the interim. Instead, they want the
notion that what they do is only for a short time to shield their decision to abide by certain rules from substantive questions about the
worth of those rules. After all, so goes the argument, although we
may or may not (but please don't ask which) believe that the rules
are harmful in themselves, we abide by them not for their sake and
not so long as to make them part of the scenery, but only until we
can clarify whether fruitful negotiations are possible. Neither in public, in private, nor, one suspects, in their heart of hearts, do officials
like George Shultz envisage concrete circumstances that would end
that "interim" period and call forth a definitive judgment on the
worth of the arms control process.

Second, those who have urged interim restraint have done so
claiming that we would maintain it only so long as the Soviet Union
did the same—this while the U.S. government is awash with facts
about Soviet violations of agreements, and about Soviet military
capability beyond the very *imagination* of current U.S. military leaders
to counter. Lastly, though some Republicans do not think much of
this, the authors believe that no democrat should take lightly any
administration making the law of the land out of agreements with
a foreign power that the U.S. Senate has rejected, just by adding
the word "interim" to them.

Before it had a name, the policy of interim restraint had already
affected the formulation of the President's Strategic Forces Modernization Plan of October 1981. That plan's total failure to convince
the Congress and the public that it would achieve worthwhile results
gave President Reagan the incentive to overcome nearly unanimous

opposition from his top appointees, and shift the ground of discussion on strategic matters by announcing the Strategic Defense Initiative. But even as the President was putting the finishing touches on his speech of March 23, 1983, the administration's advocates of interim restraint convinced him, fraudulently, that America's first moves toward strategic defense had to be shaped by adherence to a treaty the purpose of which was to make sure that the U.S. would never have such defenses. They were able to do this in part because President Reagan and his Secretary of Defense, Caspar Weinberger, have never acquainted themselves with the major details of defensive weaponry—American or Soviet. Thus the President's science adviser, George A. Keyworth, the Defense Department's Robert Cooper, and National Security Adviser Robert MacFarlane convinced Reagan that given the state of technology, anti-missile defenses could at best be researched in the 1980s, developed in the 1990s, and deployed in the next millennium.[6]

Thus President Reagan found it possible to accept a definition of his Strategic Defense Initiative as a research program. His advisers told him, and he accepted, that because technology would not allow the U.S. to build or develop anti-missile defenses in the 1980s, the U.S. could, fortuitously, have its arms control cake while eating, or at least chewing over, SDI. Whereas the building of American strategic defenses would have been (and could only have flowed from the recognition of) the death of arms control, an American SDI program *defined as research* could be a great incentive for the Soviets to talk about arms control. Thus through SDI, the U.S. would spend relatively little and build no weapons, and exercise leverage in arms control. By any other name, SDI would become the ultimate bargaining chip of the 1980s.

At this point we must make a substantive digression. The notion that the United States needs, and could have, a space-based anti-missile defense was not born on March 23, 1983, in the Oval Office. It matured in the late 1970s in the minds of several technologists and students of strategic weaponry, including these authors. We realized that the strategic vision that had brought the United States the SALT agreements, as well as the force structure that made sense only in terms of these agreements, was deeply flawed, and that at any rate, it had failed even to bring about the situation at which it had aimed. We asked how we Americans might get out of the predicament in which the Soviet Union's 6,000 counterforce warheads, mobile missilery, and growing anti-missile defenses had placed us.

We calculated that politically or industrially it would be futile for us simply to try to match the Soviets in offensive forces. Even if we succeeded, we would remain perilously inferior because of the unalterable fact that we would not strike first. Given this paramount fact, we went to industry to see whether *current* technology could provide us a means of defending against this *current* problem. We found, in short, that as early as 1980 the American aerospace industry possessed the technical wherewithal to manufacture space-based laser weapons, each of which would be able to destroy any missile ever built or designed in a second or less at distances of up to 3,000 kilometers. In addition, current technology would allow the U.S. to immediately build a ground-based, anti-missile system and mobile ABM units better than those now in production in the USSR. Alas, we also found that the Pentagon had grown into a way of conceiving and doing its business that multiplies the years and dollars required to translate ideas into systems. In 1980, Senator Malcolm Wallop introduced the first of several amendments that in the following two years led to a provision of law directing the Secretary of Defense to build—not research, but build—space laser weapons as quickly as possible, and to the establishment of a space laser weapon program office. By 1983, space-based laser defense had become a household term, referring not to a far-off prospect to meet hypothetical needs but rather to the sole practical alternative available to meet a pressing need.

The President's mention of strategic defense in March 1983, however, and his establishment of panels to define what he had meant by his words, shifted the right to speak authoritatively on the subject of defenses to people who, for whatever reasons, do not take our strategic predicament seriously. They obscured the connection between anti-missile defense and current needs, and redirected the programs that had grown under the guidance of the Wallop amendments ever farther away from practical weaponry. They did so by arbitrarily inflating the definition of the Soviet threat that American defenses would have to face, as well as by complicating the performance requirements. Foremost among the inflated requirements is the stipulation that to be worth building, any directed-energy weapon must be able to deposit 100,000 Joules cm² of radiant energy at 3,000 kilometers. The actual resistance of real missiles is considerably less than one hundredth of that amount. The foremost complication has been the stipulation that instead of building individual weapons and sensors as soon as they can meet the requirements (even inflated ones), we must wait to build anything until we can build a totally integrated system that can attack missiles and warheads in all phases of flight. All of this, of course, put off protection into the next millennium.

Another complication stemmed from imposing the requirements of arms control upon the long-standing programs that, after 1983, came under the authority of the new Strategic Defense Initiative Organization (SDIO). But what could these requirements be? As we have seen in Chapter 3, the ABM Treaty's negotiators were unable to specify what an ABM interceptor or radar was. Much less could they define which directed-energy weapons and optical sensors could "substitute" for ABM components then known. Clearly the arms controllers within the Reagan administration who sought standards by which to restrict work on SDI could find none in the letter of the treaty. They therefore wrote complex ones of their own, inspired by the spirit of the treaty (or at least by what they thought that spirit should be) to bind American, but not Soviet, programs. They had neither the information, the will, nor the power to apply those standards to Soviet programs. Moreover, they appointed bureaucrats to sit in judgment over any activities that the Strategic Defense Initiative Organization might think up in the future — activities unforeseen in 1984, much less in 1972 — to make sure that they were shaped according to "the treaty." By this mechanism, the SDIO ordered (among many other silly things) that the electro-optical detector for the Army's flying optical radar be delayed and split into two separate development programs, that the SDIO drop plans to test a ground-based laser against a U.S. missile just lifting off its pad, and that a space-based laser pointing and tracking device be deprived of its infrared seeker.

We must emphasize that the administration's arms controllers could not have done any of these things with so little opposition had not their sympathetic colleagues already redefined SDI's protective fruits into the next millennium. A largely uninformed Congress, fearful of challenge, became the administration's uninformed ally in delaying defense achievements.

The relationship between arms control and the practice of gold-plating requirements for strategic weapons is complex. Each fosters the other, and both push strategic weaponry into a future far enough removed so that actions that in the present would be called irresponsible seem permissible with regard to that future. To equivocate about whether the country shall have weapons that will protect American lives next year, or whether a given military command will have the weapons it was promised for next year, is a serious matter. To play politics with nonserious programs is all in good fun.

A Tale of Two Treaties

By 1984, the fact that arms controllers within the Reagan administration were compiling reams of regulations restricting SDI in the name of the ABM Treaty came together in the minds of many with the fact that the Soviet Union was openly violating that treaty and with the fact that many other violations amounting to preparations for the defense of Soviet territory could not be called violations because American arms controllers were making good cases that the treaty permitted these Soviet activities. This logically led to the question: Just what *does* the actual text of the ABM Treaty allow and prohibit? And, by the way, would the treaty allow the U.S. to do the things that the Soviet Union is doing, which we have not called violations, but which our arms controllers say we must not do lest *we* violate the treaty?

Several civilian officials in the Pentagon raised these questions officially, and an inter-agency group was set up to answer them. Arms controllers in the administration were caught in something of a bind. If they pushed for a strict interpretation of the treaty— not just of the "agreed interpretation D" but of the whole treaty— they would in effect be pushing for calling the Soviet Union in violation of just about every section of the treaty, including everything having to do with air defense missiles. They would also be preparing for calling the forthcoming Soviet high-energy laser a violation. How, then, could they maintain that a treaty so totally violated by the Soviet Union should be honored by the U.S.? On the other hand, if arms controllers pushed for a permissive interpretation of the "agreed interpretation D" and its requirements, that permissive spirit might spread to other areas, and they thus would be helping to grant license for Americans interested in protecting their country to do just about whatever they wanted. This would be just as big a defeat. Under the circumstances, and given the presumptive requirements that what is sauce for the goose is sauce for the gander, arms controllers seemed to be in a no-win situation. They ended up arguing for the restrictive interpretation, citing—correctly—their own intentions in framing the treaty. They lost.

Judge Abraham Sofaer, the State Department's legal adviser, was called upon to review the arguments. He ruled that despite our negotiators' intentions, "agreed interpretation D" (and, by reasonable implication, the rest of the treaty) allowed both sides to do nearly everything that the Soviet Union was doing, and everything in the field of directed-energy weapons and optical sensors that our arms controllers had prohibited the SDI organization from doing. In other words, while American arms controllers had succeeded in enforcing one particular ABM Treaty upon the U.S. government, one in which they believed deeply, there was another ABM Treaty, the one whose words had actually been negotiated, signed, and ratified. This other ABM Treaty has more than provisions that differ radically from those of the first. *Above all, it has a wholly different spirit and effect on the defenses of whoever lives by it* — as can be seen by the obvious differences between what the Soviet Union is doing to protect itself against missiles and by what the U.S. is not doing. Thus, Judge Sofaer's opinion made it crystal clear that as far as international law is concerned, the U.S. would be on sounder ground adhering to the permissive, or Soviet, interpretation than to that of the American arms controllers. In other words, international law would apply minimal restrictions, if any, to a U.S. Star Wars defense.

Then came something even more demystifying. Unfortunately,

most of it happened behind closed doors. American arms controllers dropped their double pretense of trying to constrain Soviet weaponry and of concern with international law. They called upon their raw bureaucratic power, and upon the identification they had built over the past generation with the U.S. government's establishment, and challenged President Reagan to choose between them and the deep blue sea. George Shultz presented to the President threats eagerly gathered up from like-minded people in Europe that if President Reagan were to accept the "permissive interpretation," he would soil his hands with the corpse of the Alliance. They argued to the President that to abandon the *intentions* of the American architects of the ABM Treaty would be to abandon the policies and, above all, the people, who had made the postwar order function — the very people whose company and approval Ronald Reagan preferred! In effect, Ronald Reagan was presented with the choice of following Judge Sofaer's factually correct interpretation, but of doing so in the company of people with whom he does not feel comfortable, or of staying with people he admires — on a comfortable path — though at the cost of twisting words a bit. Reagan chose comfort. Others would explain his contradictions.

The public announcement of this decision came from Secretary of State Shultz on October 8, 1985. It tersely declared, in President Reagan's name, that although the "permissive interpretation is legally correct," the U.S. would follow the "restrictive interpretation." This surely raised more questions than it answered — questions that the administration earnestly wished not to confront in public — e.g., why should the U.S., though literally nothing constrains it, and though the Soviet Union is doing quite something else, shape its military programs in the image that American arms controllers sought but failed to embody in the ABM Treaty? For reasons best known to themselves, however, the winners of this battle for Ronald Reagan set down the answers to these questions in a lengthy, closely held National Security Council document that the President signed. It is written in the first person, and is worth examining in detail.

The document says:

> Recently, we reexamined the ABM Treaty and the associated negotiating record in great detail. In the process, we have

gained new insights into how this treaty can objectively be interpreted. This, however, does not signal any lessening in resolve that this nation will remain in full conformity with its treaty obligations.

This paragraph says that we now know what the treaty really means and that this country is as committed as always to fulfilling its obligation to it. But, it lays the groundwork for disregarding the fact that the treaty's real meaning does not commit us to follow the path that the President, in this document, has decided to follow. The document then continues:

What our recent analyses have led me to believe is that while the ambiguities involved could permit the technical, legal debate to continue, our initial and unilateral assertions about what the ABM Treaty did restrict concerning advanced defensive technologies is not clearly demonstrable in the terms of the treaty as written, nor in the associated negotiating record. Our assertions about this portion of the treaty were not, at the time, shared by our negotiating partner. Rather, the record indicates that they were resisted by the Soviet Union. These assertions reflected more our hopes for what could result from the treaty, made in the context of our assumptions about the future at that time, than an objective assessment of what was achieved and mutually agreed by the signed treaty document.

The document tries to add as much sugar-coating as possible. There are "ambiguities." The "technical, legal debate [could] continue." The fact that the Soviets' different interpretation was true "at the time" of the ABM Treaty leaves room for hope against hope that today it might no longer be quite so true. To assert such a hope explicitly would invite laughter. But the weasel-wording guards against that. Still, the bitter pill for arms controllers is that the ABM Treaty is not what "we" (i.e., American arms controllers) had hoped, assumed, and indeed lived by. Well, then, the reader naturally asks, now what? Here is the answer:

All this being said, over the last two years and working under the constraints as we interpreted them at the inception of the program, our technical community met my guidance and has designed our SDI research program to conform to a more restrictive view of our ABM Treaty obligations. This has entailed some price with respect to the speed of our progress, the overall cost of the program, and the level of technical uncertainty we face at each step in our research. But, nonetheless, they have crafted a program which, if consistently supported with the appropriate funding as requested, will permit us to achieve the goals set for it.

Plainly, and quite contrary to what the administration had led the American people to believe, this closely held document says that the United States shaped the SDI program—from its inception—not to achieve the protection of the American people, but to conform to a treaty the purpose of which is to keep the American people undefended in perpetuity. This, translated from the bureaucratese, means that we have been spending more of the taxpayers' hard-earned dollars than we would have had the administration's purpose been the protection of American lives. In other words, the administration has consciously wasted money. It also means that the administration has consciously put off the time when Americans would have protective weapons, and that it has increased the chances of those weapons not working right.

The sugar-coating here is thin and transparent. The program nevertheless is supposed to "achieve the goals set for it." What, the reasonable citizen eagerly asks, *are* those goals so wonderful as to overcome the fact that the program's results are to be technically uncertain, more expensive than need be, and above all, pushed ever farther back, like Tantalus' apples? Alas, the bureaucrats are not about to answer:

> I have carefully evaluated the price that the U.S. must pay for keeping our SDI program within the bounds of our current plans. I have weighed these costs against our overall national security requirements.

If this document had been written for publication, or even for distribution to Congress, its authors might have imagined their readers—the citizen, or his elected representative—saying, as they read the above passage: Tell me, Mr. President, what *are* these cal-

culations that the advisers to whom you have handed these responsibilities have made about *our* safety? We want to follow you, but
we are neither stupid nor mere subjects, and we are younger than
you. Our lives are at stake if yours is not. We want to know why
you think it is wise to take this direction. We are glad to hear that
there *are* careful evaluations behind this decision of yours. *What are
they?*

Alas, the words that follow are not those of a democratic leader
who rules by convincing people to do the right thing, but those of
a bureaucrat who either does not know, does not care, or is ashamed
of the reason why he is doing things, but who nevertheless wants
the people to give him authority and money, and really resents being
asked about specifics:

> Based upon this I have decided that, as long as the program
> receives the support needed to implement its carefully crafted
> plan, it is not necessary to authorize the restructuring of the
> U.S. SDI program towards the boundaries of treaty interpre-
> tation which the U.S. could observe.

Once again, there is a reference to a "carefully crafted plan" that
the document would have us believe makes unnecessary the things
we could do under the real ABM Treaty, and by implication (but
only by implication) allows us to achieve the same results as if we
did them. But the reader will remember that on the very same page
the document had spoken of a "price" to be paid in speed, cost,
and technical uncertainty, and that the document had refused to
say what that price might be. The reader has learned in daily life
to beware of hidden "prices," and would naturally want to *compare*
what we are doing under this "carefully crafted plan" with what
we could do under the real ABM Treaty, and quite possibly with
what we could do if we decided, as is our right, to do away with
that treaty altogether. But alas the document's author wants to foreclose the reader even asking such questions:

> This being the case, the issue of where exactly these bound-
> aries should lie is moot, even though in my judgment a
> broader interpretation of our authority is fully justified.

There could be no better example of how arms control has crippled our government's ability to think. This document literally tells the federal bureaucracy to not even *think* about what we would be fully justified in doing in the field of ballistic missile defense. This Presidential Order not to think marks as insubordinate, and "not a team player," any employee of the U.S. government who, in exchange for his salary, thinks about how to protect the American people who pay him. But why? What good do we gain by giving up the option even to think about what we might do on our own behalf? What higher agenda has our bureaucracy that might justify this intellectual obscurantism? Right below we read the answer:

> Under this course, there can be absolutely no doubt of the U.S. intention to fully meet its treaty commitments.

But what sort of justification is this? If the document has made anything clear, it is that the "restrictive interpretation" is *not* our treaty commitment, and that the course we are following is the *personal policy commitment* of the class of people who had tried to write that commitment into the ABM Treaty, but failed. It is false to pretend that this personal policy preference became a national obligation simply because American arms controllers, having failed to convince the Soviets, succeeded in convincing Ronald Reagan. At best it is a policy that the President has chosen for its own sake. As the document continues, it makes this case:

> As we do so, we will continue to demand that the Soviet Union correct its behavior and come into full compliance with its obligations, especially in those cases like the construction of the Krasnoyarsk radar and their telemetry encryption, among others, in which there are no grounds for doubt about their non-compliance.

To that, one is inclined to say "good luck," and to remark at the intellectual dishonesty of the author who wrote this document in Ronald Reagan's name, and at Ronald Reagan's absence of mind in signing it. Does anybody believe these things are going to happen? Besides, of what does this "demand" that the Soviets desist consist? How long does the author of the document propose that we wait to decide that the Soviets are not complying with it? If and when that time comes, what would the author propose we do to fulfill the objectives of the policy? Alas, the pretense here that this is a policy is not even halfhearted. The document's substantive part concludes with a perverse reference to the power of example:

> In sharp contrast to Soviet behavior, our clear and principled restraint with respect to our own SDI program, and the price we are prepared to pay in exercising that restraint, demonstrates, by our deed, our sincerity towards negotiated commitments.

In fact, however, the document has shown that it is U.S. policy *not* to be sincere, not to be respectful of the truly undertaken international commitments of the U.S. Instead, the document proves that it is U.S. policy to respect a wholly different set of *domestic*, personal commitments, and to hide the fact that these are domestic rather than international commitments, with a "sincerity" that is downright Orwellian. Or, perhaps, the document shows there is no policy at all.

The document ends with a promise for the future about strategic defense that is all arms control and no protection. On the basis of what follows, only a heroic act of faith could lead anyone to believe that so long as President Reagan's thinking is done by the same people, the President will disentangle America's defenses from an arms control net labeled "Made in the USA." Note how many hurdles are in one small paragraph.

> I can envision that in the future the day will come when our research will have answered the questions necessary to permit us to *consider* going beyond the restrictions that we have and will continue to observe under the current research program. At that time . . . the United States will have the *opportunity* to *reassess* the guidance that I have set forth in this document. At that time, *in accordance with long-standing U.S. policy and after consultation with our allies,* we will *discuss and, as appropriate, negotiate with the Soviet Union in accordance with the terms of the ABM Treaty.* (Emphasis added.)

Extra Miles

The SDI program proved its worth as a bargaining chip in late 1984 when the Soviet Union agreed to enter arms control negotiations with the sole avowed objective of stopping America's moves toward anti-missile defenses. Note we do not say "stopping SDI." That is because the Soviet Union knows better than the American public that the SDI, as defined by the Fletcher Panel[7] and as understood by the Reagan administration, is not a program to build anti-missile defenses, but rather a research program that puts off the choice of whether to build such defenses. The Soviet Union knows as well as does the Reagan administration that perhaps the principal reason why the administration formulated SDI as a nondeployment program was its wish to satisfy constituencies both in the U.S. government and in the country that yearn for arms control. Hence, the Soviet Union's objective in the negotiations has been to keep SDI from *becoming* what most Americans think it already *is*.

Since the opening of the latest round of negotiations in January 1985, the Soviet Union has huffed and puffed about how SDI is the obstacle to all good things. The Reagan administration, for its part, has made brave noises about never, never abandoning SDI. But the Soviet Union knows that the Reagan administration has already shaped SDI to further the arms control process, and that it is willing to go further to delay the day when SDI becomes a program for building American anti-missile weapons. The only question is, "How far?" Certainly the State Department is willing to go very far, while no one prominent in the Reagan administration is particularly interested in making SDI into a program to build anti-missile weapons immediately. Hence, the operative question for the Reagan administration is: To what extent can we satisfy the Soviet Union's demand for assurances that the U.S. is not preparing any anti-missile defense, and indeed that it continues to adhere to the spirit of the ABM Treaty, while at the same time keeping the domestic political rewards associated with the President's noble promise to defend the American people?

President Reagan wants to appear simultaneously as the man who rebuilt America's military power and the man who furthered the arms control process. He evidently believes that these two contrasting images actually enhance one another. Ronald Reagan knows that if he were to formally "bargain away" SDI, he would lose both his only major incentive to the Soviet Union in arms control and his only claim to doing something about the terrible strategic predicament he inherited. So, there is no prospect that he will agree to an explicit treaty to reduce SDI beyond the very limited terms in which it was conceived. Yet, Reagan is under much pressure from American arms controllers to give the Soviet Union some assurance that SDI will not move out of its ruts. This he is quite willing to do—quietly. But the Soviet Union demands that his capitulation be public, and thus that it destroy the powerful political image of SDI. The President is unwilling to grant this, but he is willing to negotiate. That is quite all right with the Soviet Union, so long as Ronald Reagan effectively agrees to keep SDI in its neutered state of endless "interim." This the President has been willing to do.

Meanwhile, President Reagan's continuing legitimization of the arms control process gives both to the Soviet Union and to American advocates of arms control the leverage they need to force the Reagan administration toward "interim" compliance with the spirit of arms control.

Reagan's first formal response to these pressures, in June 1985, was to declare that for the sake of negotiations, he would go the "extra mile" with the Soviet Union and continue to observe all arms control agreements, even though he had once denounced these agreements and the Soviets for violating them. As we have seen, he had already more than paid America's dues to the ABM Treaty. In June 1985 he paid his dues to the unratified, violated, "fatally-flawed" SALT II Treaty by ordering the cutting up of Poseidon submarines in order to keep the total number of U.S. strategic nuclear delivery vehicles below a SALT II ceiling that the Soviets had exceeded! Obviously, he would have to remake this decision every time new weapons covered by SALT II came off American production lines.

It was inevitable, then, that after December 30, 1985, when the SALT II Treaty would have expired had it been ratified, President Reagan would have had an increasingly difficult time justifying the dismantling of American weapons to stay within a treaty that had expired, that had never been ratified, that was being violated, and that he had described as "fatally flawed." His own rhetoric was so flagrantly at odds with his policy of "interim restraint" with regard to SALT II that it became a major burden to him to reply to continual congressional demands that he explain the contradiction between his words and his deeds. In addition, as the end of his term came into view, he felt increasingly uneasy about passing on to his successors the unconstitutional practice of adhering to unratified treaties. So on May 27, 1986, he announced that although at that time he would order the cutting up of two more Poseidon submarines, in November 1986 the "extra miles" would come to an end with regard to SALT II. However, there was far less to this decision than met the eye. While renouncing the letter of SALT II, Reagan did not renounce its spirit. Having renounced the treaty, he made it clear that he and the establishment for which he spoke had no answer to the question: What worthwhile things would you do without the treaty that you are refraining from doing because of it? The final proof, if any were needed, came in a Presidential Report to the Congress dated August 5, 1986. In that report, President Reagan explains that despite his decision of May 27 not to abide by the terms of SALT II,

> we will exercise utmost restraint as we modernize. . . . We do not anticipate any appreciable growth in the size of U.S. strategic forces. . . . We will not deploy more strategic nuclear delivery vehicles or more strategic ballistic missile warheads than does the Soviet Union.[8]

He did not point out that in order for the U.S. to even approach Soviet numbers, growth in U.S. forces would have to be not just appreciable, but downright dramatic. Instead, Reagan emphasized that he has no military vision that would require even "appreciable growth," and indeed, that his vision requires "interim restraint" for the sake of his "highest priority": an arms control agreement that would bring about "equitable reductions. This," says Ronald Reagan, "is the most direct path to achieving greater stability and a safer world."

President Reagan thus announced that he was ready for a variety of formal and *informal* agreements with the Soviet Union to limit arms. This indicated his willingness to negotiate on the basis of the agenda that the Soviet Union had submitted on January 15, 1986, and explained beyond the possibility of misunderstanding on June 4, 1986. As we shall shortly see, this well-crafted plan made use of much of Reagan's rhetoric to involve the U.S. in negotiations to achieve Reagan's "highest priority" at a simple price: an American commitment to continue to adhere to the policy of American arms controllers toward the ABM Treaty while the Soviet Union continued its peculiar "observance" of that treaty.

With his credentials for "toughness" bolstered by his *pro forma* decision on SALT II, President Reagan came under constant temptation to satisfy the many constituencies in the executive branch who do not want American strategic defenses by continuing his "interim" compliance with an ABM Treaty that exists only in the minds of American arms controllers.

Why Ronald Reagan approaches arms control—and, indeed, apparently all other hard choices—by simultaneously embracing contradictory propositions is beyond our scope. We can only note that as regards arms control, he has not just spoken loudly on one side of the question while quietly acting to the contrary; rather, he has spoken loudly on *both* sides of the question. His actions on behalf of arms control, however, coupled with his words, have revived the prestige of arms control in America. Yet the extravagance of his claims about arms control may have done more to undermine that revived prestige than even the contradictions between his words, and between his words and deeds.

7

Reykjavik and Beyond

How the Soviet Union's arms control proposal of January 1986 asked the U.S. to do disastrous things, but followed the Reagan administration's line so closely that the administration could not reject it without at the same time impeaching its own record.

How the administration was reduced to quibbling with the proposal, thus guaranteeing both that U.S. strategic programs would continue to be ratcheted down, and that pressure to show sincerity toward arms control—by not telling the truth about it— would continue.

How the Soviet Union trapped the administration at Reykjavik, and forced it to commit publicly to living for at least ten years by an interpretation of the ABM Treaty that the two sides' "experts" would come to an understanding about.

Finally, how, after Reykjavik, the Reagan administration found itself pressed to either accept the full logic of the Soviet position or commit to building anti-missile devices.

On January 15, 1986, the Soviet Union began a diplomatic offensive that reached its climax in the events surrounding the Reagan-Gorbachev meetings in Reykjavik, Iceland, between October 8 and 10, 1986. In January it presented a comprehensive set of proposals, ostensibly to accomplish the very goals of deep reductions in strategic nuclear forces that the Reagan administration had advocated. Its price: the U.S. must make a formal commitment to curtail SDI. In June 1986 the Soviet Union made clear what had been implicit in its January proposal: it would not require the U.S. to scrap all research into anti-missile defenses — only that the U.S. commit itself formally not to build and deploy any.

The American media, mirroring the Reagan administration, judged this to be a significant Soviet concession. After all, the Soviets were asking the U.S. merely to continue its current *actual* policy with regard to SDI. This, argued the Soviets, echoed by the Western press as well as by parts of the Reagan administration, was a good and magnanimous offer. Throughout the spring and summer of 1986 the Soviet Union kept up diplomatic pressure for "progress on arms control," said that improvements in U.S.-Soviet relations were contingent on such progress, and hinted broadly that something was deeply wrong with Ronald Reagan for standing in the way of a summit meeting that would produce both progress on arms control and improvement in U.S.-Soviet relations. Then, in August, the Soviet Union seized an innocent American journalist in Moscow and held him to ransom. The price of his release was a Soviet spy in the U.S., and, as it turned out, Ronald Reagan's agreement to meet with Soviet dictator Mikhail Gorbachev in Iceland in October. At that meeting, Gorbachev presented essentially his January proposals in the form of a draft agreement, and forced Ronald Reagan to choose between furthering the image of "arms reducer" that he had carefully built up since 1982 – but at the cost of publicly forswearing SDI – or of upholding the image of SDI at the cost of shattering his image as an arms reducer.

The Soviet Union's proposal to gradually eliminate nuclear weapons by the year 2000 neatly sawed off the rhetorical limb on which the Reagan administration had been climbing since 1982. Because the administration had already gone so far out on the limb of arms control, the Soviet proposals were able to follow the administration's rhetoric closely. Hence, by January 1986 had President Reagan already been inclined to try to discredit the Soviet proposals, he would also have had to impeach much of his own record regarding arms control. Yet to the extent the administration quibbled with parts of the proposals, or dragged its feet, it could plausibly be accused of passing up opportunities for agreement on bases not so different from its own, out of excessive attachment to weaponry, and out of plain insincerity.

The Soviet Proposal

Gorbachev's general proposal was

> a step-by-step and consistent process of ridding the earth of nuclear weapons to be implemented and completed within the next 15 years, before the end of this century.[1]

Ronald Reagan had begun his presidency by identifying the Soviet Union as evil, and the Soviet Union's first-strike weapons as the principal threats to free people. He had prescribed a remedy: an American "margin of safety," i.e., American military superiority. Since 1982, however, President Reagan has talked as if the threat to mankind comes from an impersonal, apolitical source: nuclear weapons themselves – regardless of who possesses them. In 1983 he went so far as to reformulate the United States' programs for ground- and space-based anti-missile defenses – which had begun in 1979 as a means of extricating the U.S. from an unfavorable strategic situation, and which the Congress had pushed vigorously in 1981 and 1982 – as a generalized effort to rid the Soviet Union as well as the U.S. of the threat of nuclear weapons.

The administration's official policy, however, reiterated by Secretary of State Shultz on national television on January 16, 1986, was that the United States would not "unilaterally" defend itself against ballistic missiles, but would do so only as part of an agreement with the Soviet Union to phase in defenses for both sides. Should the Soviet Union lack sufficiently sophisticated means for defending itself against ballistic missiles, President Reagan has repeatedly indicated that he would favor providing it with those means.

The Reagan administration's arms control policies therefore placed Gorbachev in a good position to argue in favor of his own proposal somewhat along the following lines (not a quotation):

> We agree with you that nuclear weapons themselves are the danger in the world. But while you propose to remove the threat from one source, ballistic missiles, by a negotiated introduction of yet other kinds of weapons, we Soviets propose to get rid of the threat of nuclear weapons from all sources. We also plan to do it by negotiations. But we propose to do it without the additional expense and destabilization inherent in building yet another class of weaponry. You have stated that you are serious about negotiations, and have acknowledged that we are serious. But we suspect you may be using negotiations as a screen behind which to build awesome new weapons. If you are sincere, prove it by using negotiations to cut weapons rather than as a vehicle for justifying yet another class of weaponry.

Specifically, Gorbachev proposed a 50 percent cut in nuclear weapons during the first five years.

Up to 1982, President Reagan had ably argued that the arms control process had endangered the U.S. because it provided political cover for the Soviets to acquire missile warheads peculiarly able to disarm the U.S. He also had argued that the SALT agreements were fraudulent because they purported to limit military capabilities by limiting the number of launchers. This has not worked and can never work because there can be many more launchable missiles than standard launchers, and these can be loaded with warheads the number, yield, and accuracy of which make all the difference in the world.

Since his START proposal of 1982, however, President Reagan has come to argue that the primary fault of previous arms control agreements was that they did not mandate "deep cuts" in warheads. The proposal, at least as understood by the public and by the State Department (though not by the Defense Department), treated all warheads as if they were alike. Moreover, like previous U.S. negotiating positions, it took into account the fact that we have had no idea how many missiles or warheads the Soviets have had, and hence sought to count only the warheads atop the missiles we saw in those launchers the Soviets chose to reveal to our satellites. Thus, in practice, the START proposal's currency, "deployed missiles," was identical with "overtly deployed launchers."

The Reagan administration's arms control policies placed Gorbachev in a good position to argue in favor of his own proposal somewhat along the following lines (not a quotation):

> Let us cut nuclear weapons deeply, and, finally, be rid of them altogether. We agree that warheads are the thing to cut, that they are all equally nasty, and that deployed missiles and bombers are the correct measures for counting. Our very first move, the one by which all of us will show our sincerity, will be to eliminate U.S. and Soviet missiles in Europe. In 1981, President Reagan proposed a "zero" option. We Soviets now accept. We will remove all our missiles from the European continent, if you remove yours. Do not try to wiggle out of your own proposal by saying that since the missiles we take from Europe would be just a short rail trip out of range of Europe, hence we must destroy them all. We all know—and you have agreed—that a nuclear war, as you have said, "cannot be won and must never be fought." It would be a mutually annihilating spasm, allowing no time for movement. If you insist on arrangements that make sense only in terms of a prolonged nuclear war, it will be only because you have an obsession with nuclear war-fighting. At the same time we eliminate missiles in Europe, let us cut in half our warheads aimed at each other. You choose the ones you will cut, we choose the ones we will cut. If you insist on dictating our cuts,

rather than on going ahead with the business of reduction, it could be only because you prefer seeking a unilateral advantage to actually cutting nuclear weapons. Remember: you have said that nuclear war cannot possibly be won, that these weapons are not usable. If you really mean that, and are not playing games, you will not insist on equal levels of armament, but will agree to equal cuts in armaments; you will agree that one warhead is as bad as another and will be delighted to be rid of half the ones aimed against you.

Gorbachev has proposed that this first stage, as well as the second—which would eliminate all nuclear weapons aboard deployed means of delivery with ranges over 1,000 km—and the third, at the end of which "there would be no nuclear weapons on earth," would be subject to "appropriate verification," including "on-site inspections whenever necessary."

This would undoubtedly mean that the Soviets would announce destruction of missile silos, or even, possibly, the dismantling of missiles, for our satellites to observe. Occasionally, international teams would be invited to see that something the Soviet authorities claim they are doing is, in fact, being done. Conceivably, on-site inspection might mean that international inspectors would be allowed to invite themselves for a low number of visits to one or more out of a list of installations previously agreed upon, just as Valerian Zorin had promised in 1951. It is inconceivable, however, that the Soviet Union might grant international teams free access to places that were *not* on the agreed-upon list, without notice, at times of these teams' own choosing.

Prior to 1982, President Reagan had denounced an analogous arrangement: SALT II's prohibition against encoding missile test data—not any and all such data, but only that which is necessary for verifying compliance with the agreement. As Reagan had foreseen, the Soviets decided that in the case of some missile tests, almost *none* of the data was necessary for verification, whereupon they encoded virtually *all* of it, thereby denying us access to it.

But since 1982, and especially since June 1985, President Reagan has accepted everything connected with arms control as, on balance, adequate *despite* the Soviet Union's violations.

Thus the Reagan administration's policy toward verification made it difficult to denounce Gorbachev's plan as unverifiable, and the Soviet Union as inherently untrustworthy. This has enabled Gorbachev, and anyone who stood with him, to argue that his plan was verifiable, along the lines of past verification arrangements, somewhat along the following lines (not a quotation):

> Let us extend past and current verification arrangements into the future. You say they have served the cause of peace in the past, and serve it in the present by laying the bases for further cooperation. We agree, though we suspect you may be saying this only to gain time to build more weapons. We are even willing to agree in principle to on-site verification, and to discuss the details. Now *prove* whether you are sincere by adhering to something even more revealing than this long-standing satisfactory arrangement for verification *while actually reducing weapons*! If you balk, you prove yourself a fraud.

Gorbachev did not have to argue that by accepting his plan Reagan would ensure that both of them would win the Nobel Peace Prize!

Gorbachev's price for instantly making President Reagan the man who ended the Soviet Union's nuclear threat to Europe, who cut in half the nuclear threat to the U.S., and who began to stuff the nuclear genie back into its evil bottle, was a renunciation by the United States and the Soviet Union of "the development, testing, and deployment of space strike arms."

The U.S. intelligence community is unanimous in pointing out that the Soviet Union has built an easily observable infrastructure for the ground-based defense of its territory against ballistic missiles. The well-known battle-management radar at Krasnoyarsk is but one of nine of its kind—a set of devices much bigger and more advanced than the radars that used to serve our old ABM system. The Soviets have placed in mass production all the other components of the system, as well as a surface-to-high-altitude missile system for protecting that vast majority of targets that would be lightly attacked. The intelligence community also expects a Soviet space-based laser weapon of unknown capacity in 1988 (announced as a Mars probe!).

The intelligence community worries that all this would much reduce the number of U.S. warheads arriving on Soviet targets from a U.S. arsenal already crippled by a Soviet counterforce strike. American advocates of strategic defense have long stated that the U.S. cannot endure the Soviet Union's possession of a much superior counterforce sword and of a monopoly in anti-missile shields. They have argued that only by building strategic defenses can the U.S. escape this predicament. Hence, Secretary Weinberger has repeatedly declared that anti-missile defense is now "the very core" of U.S. strategic policy, and Ronald Reagan has made innumerable vague statements that the U.S. would have ballistic missile defense just as soon as the research, development, and testing are complete.

Nevertheless, the administration's position—both officially and actually—is *not* to build anti-missile defenses. On the contrary, it is to *defer* deciding *whether* to build anti-missile defenses until the 1990s. In the meanwhile, the President and the Secretary of Defense have authorized the Department of Defense to go "extra miles" to make sure our current research does not have current or practical application. Under this policy, long-standing programs have been stripped of any features that might produce any weapon, or any component of any weapon, useful for defense against ballistic missiles. Other programs that had been ready to produce weapons or sensors have been recycled into long-term research efforts. The administration is at pains to draw the distinction—as sharply as possible—between "pure" research, which it is doing, and development, which it sincerely eschews as strategically, technically, and politically premature.

Hence by virtue of the administration's position, Gorbachev was well placed to argue his own, somewhat along the following lines (not a quotation):

> You win. Go ahead, waste your money if you must, researching anti-missile weapons, so long as you promise that you will do no "development testing and deployment." We— and, we suspect, your public opinion—ask why you want to spend all that money for protecting against nuclear weapons once you have embarked on a process that has a strict timeta-

ble for eliminating all nuclear weapons. Perhaps it is because you are not sincere, or because you want to enrich your friends in the aerospace business. But, at any rate, *you must continually prove that your research shall have no practical application, and that you shall make no specific preparations for deployment.*

The Case for the Proposal

It is easy enough to imagine the arguments of those in the White House who advised the President to describe Gorbachev's proposal as "positive," and as the basis for further negotiations. By so describing the proposal, President Reagan was able to claim to have turned around the Soviet buildup that had increasingly endangered the American people for a generation. By his personal combination of toughness, conciliation, and bold innovation, he showed the Soviet leaders there is no use competing with Ronald Reagan's America. This personal "Reagan" factor, the administration argues, has done more to bring the Soviet leadership around than mere American weapons could have done. Merely talking about SDI has proved more than sufficient to compensate for his reduction of President Carter's proposed 200 MX missiles to 50!

How can we fault the Soviet proposal, White House aides might ask. As regards strategic defense, it allows us to do everything we wanted to do anyway for at least seven, maybe ten, years—longer than any of us plan on being in our jobs. As regards offensive weapons, accepting the Soviet proposal will let us claim that we have closed the "window of vulnerability" that we were elected to close. "Minuteman vulnerability" and the aging of the B-52 force have been constant reminders that we have not yet done what we were elected to do. Now, under the Soviet proposal we could scrap these vulnerable things and prepare to replace them with mobile, survivable, single-warhead Midgetmen in the 1990s. Meanwhile we would get a 50 percent reduction in the Soviet threat! Sure, we would like to be able to get rid of the Soviet counterforce warheads. But look at the problem another way—if we dismantle a large proportion of our Minutemen and B-52s, those Soviet SS-18s will have much less to shoot at. In the meanwhile, we can research Stealth bombers and Midgetmen missiles as a hedge against the process turning sour five years down the road. But that will be somebody else's watch.

As for Europe, of course our 572 Pershing and Cruise warheads don't begin to counterbalance the Soviet intermediate forces in Europe. We put them there primarily to reassure Europe of our continuing commitment. How much more would our political objectives be fulfilled if we could show that as a result of withdrawing these 572 warheads, we had caused the Soviet Union's 441 SS-20's 2,646 warheads, plus refires, to be pulled out of range! The nuclear threat to Europe would still exist, but part of it would be days instead of minutes away, and the political climate would have improved. Ronald Reagan would surely win the Nobel Peace Prize, and his judgment on talking about SDI would be vindicated.

Some might have objected that the United States would suffer even if the Soviet proposal were honestly implemented. How would we defend ourselves and our allies against Soviet conventional forces much bigger and much more willing to take casualties than our own? How many millions of young men would we have to draft? How many hundreds of billions would we have to spend on tanks and planes? Others might have pointed out that in the more likely event the Soviet Union cheated, acceptance of the proposal would be a deadly trap. As Secretary Weinberger has noted, in the past and present the Soviets have built precisely the kinds of forces that we had sought to prevent by entering into the arms control process in the first place. What would happen if the Soviets were to treat agreements arising out of their new proposal as they have treated the agreements now supposedly in force? What would we do? What could we do? Whatever we do five years hence would be under the shadow of the forces the Soviets had built while the U.S. was marking time. Given how far behind we now are in counterforce offensive weapons, in air defense, and in ballistic missile defense *systems* (as opposed to BMD technology), if we gave the Soviets another five years' free ride, their lead would be literally insurmountable.

The Case Against Rejecting It

White House aides might then have to remind everyone around the table that, to reject the Soviet proposal, the Reagan administration would not only have to pass up concrete political advantages, but also would have to impeach its own policies on arms control, and force the military to do things it does not want to do.

First, President Reagan, having publicly forsworn referring to the Soviet Union as the "focus of evil" in the world, having said that Gorbachev shares the objective of a peaceful world, and having said nuclear weapons are bad things, could not now plausibly take up Andrei Sakharov's thesis that *totalitarian regimes*, not weapons, threaten the peace of the world. The President reaffirmed the inevitability of arms control negotiations with the Soviet Union after the Soviet Union shot down a civilian 747 airliner. He reaffirmed it after each of his own reports charging the Soviets with violating arms control agreements. On what pretext could he now justify saying that the Soviet leaders are not primarily interested in peace through arms control? How could he explain reversing himself? Besides, the primary reason we embraced arms control in 1981–82 was still applicable—we believe that, in order to win support for our military programs from European domestic public opinion, we cannot afford to sound any less committed to arms control than the Soviet Union. To reject the entire Soviet proposal would be to reject the very possibility of arms control. We just can't afford that. As for a world wholly without nuclear weapons, we all know that will never happen. We will never have to face the insoluble conventional problems that would ensue. But it's best not to say so up front. Let us give this problem to panels of experts who, in due time, are sure to report that the problems with verification are insurmountable. But the dream of a world without nukes is too nice for us to shatter.

Second, in order to quarrel effectively with the Soviet proposal's specific provision on offensive arms, we would have to undo everything we have done to protect ourselves against the charge of being war-fighters. Yes, it's true that the Soviet proposal would increase the Soviets' already enormous advantage in *usable* nuclear weapons. But to say so publicly would be to admit we believe that nuclear weapons are rationally usable, and nuclear wars reasonably winnable. We are not willing to advance that argument. If we *did* advance it, we would be asked why we have not proposed providing the U.S. with as high a percentage of such usable weapons as the Soviets have. We don't want to have to answer that question. People just would not understand the complex interplay of our military's budgets and equities that have made for so much continuity with the McNamara era. So, either way we quarrel with this part of the Soviet position, we lose.

Third, the problems with verification are indeed obvious, and we can surely bring them up as needed to keep from being stampeded into something we really can't live with. But we just can't afford a thoroughgoing critique of the Soviet proposal on the basis of verification and compliance. If we say that, not knowing how many Soviet weapons of any given kind are *produced*, it is inappropriate to deal on the basis of the quantities of the kind we see "deployed," people will ask why we are bringing this up now. We've negotiated for years as if the problem of clandestinely stored weapons did not exist. How could we bring it up now? If we were to argue that the most modern and militarily significant developments—accuracy of offensive missiles and the precision mechanisms of defensive weapons—can be tested and built without tipping off traditional technical intelligence methods, we would cut the ground out from under *all* future arms control. Precisely the same would happen if we even raised the question of what we might do were we to find the Soviets cheating. No one has any answers to that question, no one. This administration will not, for any reason, let itself be accused of undermining the arms control process.

Fourth, as regards defensive weapons, the White House aides might continue: If the Soviet offer is bad for us, so is our SDI program. When we chose members for the Fletcher Panel, we decided that we would oppose proposals like those of Senator Wallop or Zbigniew Brzezinski to actually build the anti-missile defenses we can build now. We knew that the Soviet Union was producing a variety of anti-missile devices, and that there was danger that in the near and medium term the Soviets would have defenses while we would not. But we decided that we would give technology and arms control a chance to bring us a system of mutually agreed-upon total protection rather than scrambling unilaterally for whatever protection we might manage. Moreover, from the very first, we decided that SDI would not be allowed to upset our current military programs for at least the remainder of this decade. If now we were to

attack the Soviet proposal, and demand the right to start developing anti-missile weapons in the next five years, we would have to
reverse all that. Which military account would we raid to get the
money? Are we willing to stop setting an example for the Soviets,
to give up the hope that this new class of weaponry will develop
in a mutually stabilizing manner—and are we willing to say so publicly? Are we willing to admit that the Wallops and Brzezinskis of
this world had the right approach—and we the wrong one—all
along? Why should we be willing to do that?

The Road to Reykjavik

Having publicly associated itself with the "positive elements" of the
January 1986 Soviet arms control proposal, the administration
acknowledged that Gorbachev had "put the ball in our court." Conscious of the high domestic political price attached both to accepting it or to rejecting it, the administration settled on quibbling with
it. The President would agree that all nuclear weapons would be
eliminated some day, but added that this would depend on an
"improved balance in conventional forces"—presumably on the Soviets' willingness to reduce their 180 ground-force divisions to something closer to the United States' 20! The Soviet proposal for
eliminating all medium-range missiles from Europe would be made
contingent on a unilateral cut in Soviet medium-range missiles in
Asia. The Soviet proposal of a 50 percent cut in both sides' deployed
long-range warheads would be left to simmer while the U.S. pushed
a ban on multiple-warhead mobile missiles—which the Soviet Union
has (the SS-24) and which the U.S. does not. The Soviets could be
expected to reject all of this as unilateralism, and to demand concession on SDI. The U.S. would counter by proposing an agreement to abide by the ABM Treaty for at least seven and a half more
years. But the arguments on the meaning of the ABM Treaty could
be expected to drag on.

　　In short, the administration would have been happy to mark
time with the Soviet Union at the Geneva talks. Time would be a
respite from its own internal contradictions, and would carry the
Republican administration's arms control image safely through the

Democrats' attempt to recapture a majority in the U.S. Senate in November 1986. Precisely for those reasons, the Soviet Union pressed continuously for a forum in which the Reagan administration would have to resolve those contradictions, or show its disarray, before November. To President Reagan's desire for a summit that would demonstrate his achievement of good U.S.-Soviet relations, the Soviets opposed Gorbachev's challenge: "But we did this in Geneva [in November 1985], . . . why meet again in order just to talk?" Gorbachev wanted a showdown on arms control. Finally, as part of the agreement to release the captured American newsman Nicholas Daniloff, the President agreed to a summit meeting (though it was not to be called a summit) that would be a compromise between what he and Gorbachev wanted. The meeting would be a pre-summit summit—at most a mini-summit. Of course, when he met Gorbachev at Reykjavik, Reagan found the Soviet leader with a familiar agenda: the Soviet proposal of January 15; and a familiar demand: Let us discuss it. At this point, Reagan could have taken the proposal and said that he would consider it as an agenda item at the full summit later, but that now other items should be discussed. Instead, Ronald Reagan, Donald Regan, and George Shultz judged that it would be more difficult to explain to the public why they refused to discuss a concrete Soviet proposal than to discuss it. Gorbachev got Reagan precisely where he wanted him.

The Trap

It has become commonplace that by handing Reagan his detailed proposals, Gorbachev sprang a trap. But given that the Soviet proposal had been made public over nine months before, and that the Soviet Union's obvious agenda was to press it on the U.S., the "trap's" only camouflage was that the Soviet Foreign Ministry had allowed the U.S. State Department to convince itself—and Ronald Reagan—that this would not happen.

At any rate, Gorbachev began the meeting by proposing the total abolition of intermediate-range nuclear forces in Europe (Reagan's "zero option"), plus a cut of 5,000 in warheads as deployed ICBMs and SLBMs (largely Reagan's START proposal) to begin immediately and to be completed in five years, in exchange for the United States' reaffirmation of the strict interpretation of the ABM Treaty for a period of fifteen years. Reagan countered by proposing that Gorbachev's proposed cut of offensive missiles be followed by the total abolition of long-range missiles in another five years, while the reaffirmation of the ABM Treaty would be for only ten years, would prohibit only deployment, and would allow everything except that. Gorbachev countered by agreeing to the total abolition of long-range missiles, and by proposing the total abolition of all nuclear weapons by the year 2000. Reagan agreed in principle, and both Reagan and Gorbachev agreed to ban all nuclear tests. But Gorbachev wanted to specify that the price for all this, the extension of the ABM Treaty, would specifically restrict anti-missile work to laboratory research and testing. Here Reagan disagreed, and the talks broke down. Meanwhile, small groups of Soviet and American experts had actually been working through the night to draft the details of a treaty embodying these principles that the two chiefs might have *signed* (!) had they come to the agreement they were precipitously approaching.

It is doubtful that Gorbachev expected Reagan to agree on the spot to embody the subject of the talks into a treaty, sign it, and push it through the U.S. Senate. Indeed, the language he used on Moscow television to describe the meeting shows genuine surprise that Reagan came as close as he did to agreement. Had Reagan "gone all the way," and had the U.S. Senate followed him, Gorbachev would have achieved a set of advantages perhaps amounting to a decisive victory over the U.S.

1. First, all those political elements in the West that work to reduce the size and effectiveness of Western military forces would have been strengthened.

2. Without testing, the development of new U.S. nuclear weapons for counterforce purposes would have been stopped, and the reliability of the U.S. nuclear stockpile would have commenced to decline. The Soviet Union would have suffered none of these effects because, given the United States' inability to understand seismic rumblings from the Soviet Union, the

U.S. could not possibly make credible charges of Soviet violations, much less do anything to keep the Soviet Union from testing at will.

3. U.S. intermediate-range forces would have left Europe, further skewing the military balance in that region to the Soviet Union's favor. But that balance is already so far in the Soviet Union's favor that the military effects of the pullout would not have been great. The political effect, by contrast, would have been catastrophic. Much of the European establishment literally put its political life on the line in the early 1980s to obtain the right to deploy these American weapons on European soil. By withdrawing them, the U.S. would have shown that these weapons were not important to Europe's security after all, that the European conservatives who had championed their deployment were fools, and that the European far left that had opposed deployment had been correct all along. By doing so without consultation, the U.S. would have shown itself dangerous to Europe. The pro-U.S. position within European politics would have been totally discredited.

4. The U.S. would have begun a drastic reduction in its already outclassed offensive missile forces. Although the treaty would have allowed the U.S. to substitute, on a 1 for 2 basis, new and better systems for the ones taken out of service, experience indicates that this would not have happened, and that the Congress, believing peace had arrived, would find more convenient uses for the money. The Soviet Union, of course, could have continued to produce offensive missiles at will. Who would know? Who could stop it? Who would dare point it out?

5. The U.S. defense establishment would have realized that defending against Soviet ballistic missiles was now off the nation's agenda and would have acted accordingly, killing any prospect of anti-missile defense in the forseeable future. The American public, which by all accounts is strongly convinced of the need for such defense, would have been told unmistakably that its conviction had been mistaken, and that Ronald

Reagan had raised false hopes on March 23, 1983. Of course Soviet anti-missile defenses would have continued to grow, but given the very limited amount of information about them that U.S. intelligence can gather and ABM treaty vagaries, the U.S. would not have been able to prove violations in this field. Moreover, experience shows that even if abundant information were available, most American politicians could not bring themselves even to try to bring violations before the American public until many years had passed since they themselves had expressed great confidence in the treaty.

But Gorbachev had not come to Reykjavik prepared to reap such a huge harvest. Instead, he had come prepared to ripen the crop. In this he succeeded. The meeting, and Ronald Reagan's eagerness to characterize it as a success, committed the Reagan administration even more deeply to the Soviet proposal and put it in the position it dreaded most—that of having to reject arms control altogether, or of agreeing to implement the Soviet purpose bit by bit.

On the first point, Ronald Reagan and his entire administration, spurred by Gorbachev's charge that the meeting had failed because of Reagan's pathological attachment to SDI, went out of their way to characterize the meeting as a great achievement. "We are," said Reagan to the American people, "closer than ever before to agreements that could lead to a safer world without nuclear weapons."[2] Even as Gorbachev's messages, conveyed to the American people through innumerable channels, were trying to undermine Reagan's standing as a man of good faith, the President felt compelled to strengthen Gorbachev's credentials with the American people by giving the impression that two men of goodwill had done their best in good faith to stuff the nuclear genie back into the bottle, and had almost pulled off the miracle. Thus the President, under pressure from the growing utopian sentiments that he himself had nurtured in the land since 1982, fed those sentiments once more. Surely this feeding would strengthen them yet further, and make the Soviets able to demand more next time.

As regards nuclear testing, the "near-agreement" to abolish it completely would just as surely make it harder for Ronald Reagan to insist on adequate verification provisions as conditions for ratifying a treaty to limit both countries to tests under 150 kilotons. Once the precedent of nuclear test bans with sham verification was established, the maximum yield permitted could be reduced, and the path to renewing and maintaining the United States' nuclear stockpile could be progressively squeezed.

To seriously harm the United States' relationship with Europe, it was not absolutely necessary to actually remove U.S. intermediate-range nuclear forces from Europe. It was enough for President Reagan publicly to declare such forces dispensable – suddenly and without consultation – for Europeans to conclude that their efforts on behalf of deploying those forces in the first place were misplaced and that the U.S. could not be trusted. Of course, many Europeans had urged Ronald Reagan again and again to propose the "zero option" in the first place, and had long urged him to be more receptive to Soviet arms control proposals. It was anything but proper for these people to be outraged when President Reagan took their words seriously. Many Europeans had enjoyed talking anti-nuclear talk, confident that President Reagan would not allow the logical consequences of their words to materialize. To them, what the President almost did at Reykjavik was brusque reality-therapy. Nevertheless, the mere talk of removing U.S. intermediate-range nuclear forces from Europe, and of abolishing nuclear weapons, raised for Europeans the prospect of having to face overwhelming Soviet conventional forces, and of having to choose between militarizing their societies to meet the challenge, or accommodating the Soviet Union. Gorbachev could be confident that having gone so far, Reagan could not easily turn around and once again rally energies for cooperation to right the military balance – whether conventional or nuclear. Given this, Europe could be counted on to see more clearly than ever that it will have to make its plans for the future without counting on support from U.S. nuclear forces. Not bad for a weekend's work in Iceland!

Given that U.S. strategic offensive forces had already been crippled by arms control thinking and that the U.S. showed no sign of breaking out of the *intellectual* constraints of SALT, Gorbachev did not need a signed agreement to keep those forces stagnant.

Reagan's words before, during, and after Reykjavik were eminently usable by any American who wished to fight against any plan to increase U.S. strategic forces.

On the critical subject of SDI, Gorbachev positioned himself to achieve his goals via an "understanding" with the Reagan administration rather than through a treaty that would have to be submitted to the Senate. Gorbachev believed that "SDI was held up to shame in Reykjavik"[3]—that is, that the President had conceded that anti-missile defenses cannot give the U.S. "secure protection against a nuclear strike" except, of course, if offensive forces were reduced by arms control. But Gorbachev made it clear that there would be no reduction of nuclear forces without some curb on SDI, and Reagan accepted in principle the notion of a curb on SDI. The only remaining question was, how much of a curb? Reagan offered "that we [the U.S.] continue our present research, and if and when we reached the stage of testing we would sign a treaty that would permit Soviet observation of such tests."[4] The next question was: How would "research" be defined? But Reagan had already agreed that there would be a U.S.-Soviet agreement, the avowed purpose of which would be that for at least the next ten years, the U.S. would have no defenses. The only question on the table dealt with how Americans should think about the period after 1997! Gorbachev realized that the U.S. political and bureaucratic process would multiply the effect of any detailed arrangements whatever on this matter that reflected a fundamental agreement that the U.S. would not deploy strategic defenses. Of course, he also realized that the U.S. political system can produce sharp changes, and thus sought to arm the anti-strategic defense forces in the U.S. with the most powerful tools he could give them.

Gorbachev demanded some assurances that the U.S. would make no preparations for the years after 1997. That turned out to be too specific for Reagan. The President preferred a mere reaffirmation of the ABM Treaty, with its ambiguities. The President explained this as follows:

> What Mr. Gorbachev was demanding at Reykjavik was that the United States agree to a new version of a 14-year-old ABM

Treaty that the Soviet Union had already violated. I told him
that we don't make those deals in the United States.[5]

But Ronald Reagan was protesting too much. Despite early reports
that, subsequent to the summit, the U.S. proposal to extend the
ABM Treaty had been "de-emphasized,"[6] the U.S. State Department and the White House never stopped informally negotiating
terms. On February 1, 1987, "administration officials" announced
that Paul Nitze had met with Y. P. Velikhov, the Soviet Union's chief
anti-SDI campaigner, to work out an "agreement on what kinds of
space weapons and tests are banned by the ABM Treaty," and that
"American and Soviet negotiators have agreed in Geneva to set up
a special working group to discuss what research, development,
and testing are allowed for defensive systems by the 1972 Anti-
ballistic Missile Treaty."[7] In other words, whatever public agreement Ronald Reagan reaches with Mikhail Gorbachev on how to
interpret the ABM Treaty of 1972, these U.S.-Soviet working groups
will already have worked out the effective details that will actually
bind us. This will be precisely the "new version of a 14-year-old
treaty" that Reagan promised not to negotiate. Thus the Reagan
administration once again did precisely the opposite of what the
President declared to the American people. Let us be clear about
what it did.

The Reagan administration negotiated precisely "a new version"
of the ABM Treaty. But, contrary to the plain requirement of the
Constitution and of the Arms Control and Disarmament Act of 1961,
the administration did not plan to submit the products of the U.S.-
Soviet working groups to the public for discussion, or to the Senate for ratification. It pretends that the working groups are only
clarifying each side's understanding of a principle already ratified
by the Senate in 1972—that there shall be no anti-missile defense.
It pretends that it—alone and without Soviet concurrence—is making decisions on how to restrict U.S. anti-missile work, and that it
is legitimate to enforce new details in new circumstances because
any "restraint" is only for the indeterminate "interim" period during which a comprehensive agreement is presumably to be worked
out. Yet, as we have seen, the ABM Treaty of 1972 has embodied

that principle of "no defense" only for those who believe in it. Now we see that the Reagan administration's discussions, about what the treaty really means are carried on by believers, who use the discussions as an aid in their domestic struggle to impose their vision on U.S. policy.

Of course the Soviet Union is there to help in this enterprise. Making "a new version" of the treaty by retrospective definition and without ratification is also easier because the policymakers do not have to worry about arguing that the restrictions they accept for the U.S. are such that U.S. intelligence can have a reasonable chance of monitoring whether the Soviet Union is observing them. They do not even have to present their decisions to Ronald Reagan except as the already-formed consensus of his bureaucracy. Thus, reality is not as Ronald Reagan describes it: "We don't make those deals in the United States." Rather, after Reykjavik, the deal Ronald Reagan protested we would not make *is* the deal we are making. Indeed, during the Reagan administration, arms control has come to consist exclusively of "those deals."

Ronald Reagan, in a letter dated May 26, 1987, argued to Senator Wallop that the Geneva meetings on the meaning of the ABM Treaty are innocuous because their results are not legally binding. But either Ronald Reagan was being consciously deceptive or he does not know how arms control works inside his own administration. In the Reagan administration, arms control does not consist of treaties, but of policy elaborated with reference to the principles of arms control and in "independent," "informal" consultation with the Soviet Union.

The Asses' Bridge

Those who simultaneously advocate mutually contradictory positions cannot help but discredit all those propositions—as well as themselves. If it did nothing else, Reykjavik made unmistakable the contradictions between the Reagan administration's various words and deeds on arms control. As Gorbachev himself pointed out on Moscow television, if Reagan is really sincere about the likelihood of eliminating ballistic missiles and nuclear weapons, why is he so keen on having SDI? If, as Reagan explained on U.S. television, he wants SDI just for insurance against Soviet cheating, and really means it when he asks, "Why are the Soviets so adamant that America remain forever vulnerable to Soviet rocket attack? . . . Why does the Soviet Union insist that we remain so—forever?"— then, why does Ronald Reagan say he believes that an agreement to eliminate nuclear weapons is just around the corner?

Given that Reagan seems to think that we will still have to defend against the Soviet Union despite its willingness to perform the greatest act of disarmament in history, what conventional military measures would Reagan recommend for a nonnuclear world? What "insurance" might he recommend against the Soviet Union's possible cheating with regard to battlefield nuclear weapons? If Reagan does not plan to push to deploy anti-missile defenses before ten years—certainly he has not pressed his bureaucracy to do the utmost with the materials at hand—why would he think twelve or fifteen or eighteen or more years inappropriate?

As a *New York Times'* editorialist asked: "What does he plan for Star Wars that could not be pursued in 10 years of research limited to the laboratory?"[8] The *Times'* editorial then drove home its challenge: Ronald Reagan, by his own account, "had the chance to eliminate Soviet and U.S. medium-range nuclear weapons in Europe, to work toward a test ban on his terms, to halve nuclear arsenals in five years, and to agree on huge reductions later. He said no." He did so for the sake of a program the feasibility of which he himself describes as an open question, and which he has repeatedly refused to make into something other than a "bird in the bush." The *Times* then noted: "Perhaps an argument can be made that this visionary bird in the bush is worth the sacrifice of the Soviet bird in the hand. But so far the President has not made the case, only asserted it."

But how could one rationally choose between the delusion of arms control, and a strategic defense program that this delusion has turned into a sterile caricature? Neither is real. The public debate that would follow a presidential decision to do everything necessary to actually build and deploy anti-missile defenses would inform the American people about what they could and could not do for themselves, and would force politicians to approve what defenses we could build or to propose concrete alternatives. By the same token, the new debate that would have followed either acceptance or rejection of the proposal the Soviet Union pressed on Ronald Reagan at Reykjavik would have been as good for our democracy as the SALT II debate was, because this new debate would have forced politicians to place their bets on concrete arrangements either for arms control or for anti-missile defense. A direct political choice between building anti-missile weapons and agreeing to the Soviet proposal would have been most healthy for our democracy. Instead, the administration, unsure of what it thinks, and afraid of the American people's reaction to the unpleasant truth that we cannot "jawbone" the Soviets into not wanting military superiority, again opted for the arms control process. But by cleverly trying to avoid choice, the administration committed itself to continually trying to prove its "sincerity" toward the arms control process by not telling the truth about it. Fortunately, the logic of the choice between arms control and strategic defense now is so powerful that it shines through the Reagan administration's maladroit obfuscation.

8

The Necessity for Choice

How the Reagan administration is attempting to evade the fundamental choices before it, and why, in the interest of the United States, it—or its successor—should face these choices.

Obfuscation has always been indispensable to creating the delusion of arms control. As we have seen, American arms controllers framed detailed agreements in terms of the relatively insignificant things that U.S. intelligence could see rather than in terms of the much more significant things that U.S. intelligence could not see. On the level of national policy, they succeeded in shaping U.S. forces according to their own view of the world on the basis of an indefinite suspension of questions such as: Of what use is an agreement that we enter into in order to bring about one kind of military balance if the Soviets enter into the same agreement in order to establish another kind of military balance? What is the Soviet Union planning to do in case of war? Will the forces that the agreements specifically allow the Soviets to have, plus the forces the Soviets can have because of obvious limitations of U.S. intelligence, and of obvious limitations in the United States' ability to enforce agreements, be sufficient to allow the Soviets to successfully execute their strategy according to their lights? What should we do when we notice that the Soviet Union is in the process of acquiring what it needs to make its strategy work? What should the U.S. be preparing to do in case of war? What forces must we have to do that? We can make any kind of deal—but how can we make any kind of deal stick? How can we cause the Soviet Union to abide by future agreements when we cannot make it abide by current ones? In short, American arms controllers have abstracted from reality by obfuscating it.

Nevertheless, the debate that accompanied the ratification of both parts of SALT I shed some light on arms control. Ratification forced American arms controllers—Kissinger, Nitze, and Smith—to face reality in public if only for a little while, and to make firm pledges about what the treaties would accomplish. They told the American people that if the Soviets did certain things and failed to do others, we would withdraw from both parts of SALT I. Of course when the Soviets acted precisely as they should not have, the arms controllers' solution was to negotiate SALT II. But SALT II's exposure to public scrutiny was downright enlightening! President Carter uttered brave words about how the Soviets' building of a single strategic nuclear delivery vehicle, a single new missile beyond those permitted by the treaty, their encrypting a single telemetry transmission, would cause the U.S. to consider the treaty null and void, and to look to its own capacity to defend itself. But, given the record of SALT I, few believed the arms controllers' protestations about SALT II. The SALT II debate effectively discredited arms control. In the Senate, supporters of arms control dreaded the prospect of having to vote on SALT II, and were delighted when President Carter withdrew it from consideration. When President Carter ran his campaign as a referendum on arms control and lost decisively, the aura surrounding arms control seemed to have been dispelled.

That fog returned thicker than ever, though, when President Reagan, acting on what historians will record as a textbook example of suicidal political advice, decided to remove arms control entirely from the Constitutional and legal framework that had placed limits on obfuscation. Since 1981, arms control has consisted not of agreements with the Soviet Union, but of American military policies derived from American bureaucratic preferences and domestic politics and shaped to a great but undefinable extent in the name of possible future agreements with the Soviet Union. It has consisted not so much of sham deals with the Soviet Union as of arrangements within the U.S. government and among American politicians, in the name of sham deals with the Soviets – in other words, of a double sham!

The Founding Fathers wrote into the Constitution that treaties would become effective only after the Senate had agreed to them by a two-thirds margin. They did this because they wanted to foreclose the possibility that Presidents would try to do things within the United States for which they did not have sufficient domestic support, by making treaties with foreign countries. The Constitution's provision for ratification of treaties makes sure that this way of making one's policies the "law of the land" will require as much deliberation and consent as other ways of law making. The Congress that enacted the Arms Control and Disarmament Act of 1961 was acutely conscious that strategic weapons was one field in which the U.S. government would be tempted to use an international agreement—or the prospect of one—to shortcut the arduous process of domestic policymaking. Everyone knew that a great domestic struggle was under way to determine what our strategic forces should be equipped to do, and what our strategy for employing them should be.

Everyone knew that the advocates of arms control generally tended to espouse what Herman Kahn in those days called "Minimum Deterrence," or other variants of what later came to be known as MAD. The Congress therefore carefully wrote into law that only arms control treaties, duly ratified, would be allowed to affect U.S. military forces and policy. Private agreements between U.S. and Soviet negotiators would not do. Neither would "restraint" in anticipation of an agreement or of ratification. Certainly modifying a ratified agreement so as to include or "specify" restrictions that had not explicitly existed before would not do—that would be "bait-and-switch." Of course, "understandings" would do least of all. To do any of these things would amount to using the foreign policy process as a means of shortcutting the domestic political process—as a way of depriving the American people of their sovereign right to know and to choose the path that they would follow in strategic affairs.

Yet, since 1981 President Reagan has allowed his administration to do precisely what the Constitution and the law forbid. As a result, the American people do not know—even as Ronald Reagan probably does not know—how or to what extent the arms control process has affected what weapons we do or do not have, and our plans for the future.

Since arms control always involved the suspension of judgment, the substitution of known for unknown quantities, and the abstraction from the most essential elements of the strategic equation, it always fostered political irresponsibility. But the practice of two Presidents—since the withdrawal of SALT II from consideration by the Senate—of arms control without treaties, of shaping U.S. forces and above all U.S. politics, in the name of mirages and afterglows of treaties, is the very definition of political irresponsibility.

A fine example of how presidential irresponsibility fosters congressional irresponsibility is the letter that 57 senators sent to President Reagan in January 1987 urging him to adhere to the terms of the unratified, expired, violated SALT II Treaty. Nearly all the senators who signed the letter would fear for their political lives were the SALT II Treaty itself to come before the Senate for ratification. None would relish defending the treaty as a good thing in and of itself. Far fewer than 57 would actually take Jimmy Carter's political bet and vote for it. Yet all urged the President, on his own hook, to "find" what they themselves would not dare affirm by vote: that the Soviet Union's behavior has been sufficiently "restrained" as to warrant living by the American arms controllers' spirit of that treaty.

In January 1987 a group of four senators, led by Dale Bumpers (D-Arkansas) and John Chaffee (R-Rhode Island), introduced a bill to prevent the U.S. from purchasing weapons in excess of the ceilings of SALT II. If the bill ever comes to a vote, this may prove to be a somewhat more responsible exercise. How responsible depends on whether the bill's opponents make the debate over the bill into what it should be—a debate on whether SALT II and arms control are appropriate instruments by which to seek peace and security, or whether they are hallucinogens that can only render us impotent before Soviet reality, but cannot change that reality.

Of course the exercise would become truly responsible if the administration were to offer a military alternative to SALT II. Note that Ronald Reagan, in formally declaring the end of his formal adherence to his informal policy of "interim compliance" with SALT II, indicated that he would, only somewhat less formally, continue to restrain U.S. offensive forces for the sake of arms control, and that these forces would not "grow significantly." Why then, a senator might ask, if we are de facto not going to have forces significantly different from those that we were going to have under SALT

II, should I not grab for myself the political credit for "standing up" for arms control and for getting along with the Soviets? This question will continue to be politically potent so long as no one offers a plan for building U.S. offensive strategic forces that are significantly different from those that were conceived and built according to the intellectual constraints of SALT.

A more important example concerns the ABM Treaty, and its possible abrogation, or extension in duration, or extension in scope through "redefinition." It would be impossible to convince the American people that decisions of such national importance should be made by a few American arms control enthusiasts meeting with Soviets in the manufactured fog of the arms control process, and ratified by a presidential image. Such decisions in fact properly belong to the American people's elected representatives – preferably in the context of a national electoral campaign.

Indeed, the administration's enforcement as the law of the land of any version of the ABM Treaty embodied not in the words of the treaty but in the private hopes and dreams of American arms controllers is legally and constitutionally improper. Adherence to one version of a treaty while the Soviet Union builds its defenses under another version is no kind of international law, but rather the use of international law as an excuse. Since definitions are the operative heart of treaties, to apply an old treaty to things that were not defined at the time of its ratification by agreeing, albeit tacitly, to new definitions is to make a new treaty. To try to pass off a new treaty as an old one is democratically unforgivable and constitutionally invalid.

Doubly invalid and contemptible would be a policy toward defensive weapons and the ABM Treaty such as Ronald Reagan is following towards offensive weapons and SALT II. To wit: the Reagan administration might well loudly declare that it will adhere to the "legally correct interpretation" of the ABM Treaty, that is, the "permissive" interpretation. But, as in the case of SALT II, this declaration is likely to be coupled with a quiet statement that the Reagan administration will continue to exercise "restraint" with regard to defensive weapons, and in fact will not be acting much differently under the legally correct interpretation than it had acted for years under the strict interpretation, because the administration would continue its quiet efforts to reach a long-term arms deal with the Soviet Union. In other words, the administration would thus try to cover the policy of arms control without agreements (or "interim restraint") with one more layer of fog. Of course, the policy of "arms control without agreements" is itself a layer of fog generated to hide inability to formulate real policy in the field of defensive weapons.

Just as in the case with offensive forces, choices regarding anti-missile defenses can be truly responsible only if they are concrete. So long as political leaders do not place before the American people the possibility of actually building and deploying anti-missile defenses, discussions of possible restrictions for such defenses will remain abstract, and politicians will lack the incentive to seriousness that can come only from popular interest in what protection they will actually get or not get.

Alas, the partisans of arms control know this, and can be expected to try to avoid specificity. In a February 3 article in the *New York Times*, two consultants to the Arms Control and Disarmament Agency sounded the old siren song: arms control and ballistic missile defense are compatible after all! If only those who want anti-missile defense will agree to be bound by the strict, American arms controllers' view of the ABM Treaty for the next ten years, those arms controllers might agree to support funding in Congress for the 100 ABM launchers and missiles at a single fixed site as allowed by the ABM Treaty.[1] This offer is clearly calibrated to the Reagan administration's penchant for trying to have its cake while eating it too. By accepting such an approach, the administration could claim at the same time that it is deploying the first stage of SDI while, out of the other corner of its megaphone, pointing out that it has broadened and deepened its commitment to the ABM Treaty. Having allowed the U.S. to slide into a deepening strategic predicament, and itself to slide into a deepening political predicament for the sake of posturing about arms control, the administration now is advised—as drunks are sometimes advised—to cure its hangover with a "hair of the dog that bit you."

Alas, if arms control has a future, it lies precisely in proffering such temptations to weak officeholders who are eager to avoid choice. Such "decision makers" do not have it in them to sign a treaty and defend it before public opinion. How, in the late 1980s, could even great communicators persuade the public that it should agree to a treaty because they would steadfastly guard its integrity and make sure that it delivered the fruits for the sake of which it was signed? They themselves have long since made it impossible for such appeals to be credible, by continuing military policies that make sense only in the context of treaties, even after the Soviet Union had violated them, even after an unratified treaty expired, far more strictly than the terms of the treaties themselves require! Indeed, it has now become apparent that the penchant of both Presidents and Congress is to react to Soviet treaty violations not by seeking to restrain the Soviet violators, but by placing further constraints on American behavior. If ever anyone who supported the United States' arms control policies from 1981 to this writing assures the American people that he knows how to enforce the next arms control agreement, he will first have to explain why he did not even try to enforce the agreements that were theoretically already in force during his time in office. Such an attempt would be both instructive and amusing. But it is unlikely to be made.

The appeal of arms control comes from its lack of concreteness, from its invitation to build an imaginary world in one's own mind. The more concrete the terms of a treaty, the more experience with the arms control process, the more one looks at the alternatives to arms control, the more the delusion vanishes. As the delusion vanishes, our task becomes clear: to defend ourselves as best we can.

The authors cannot here set forth in due detail the kinds of strategic offensive and defensive forces on which the United States should rely for its security, rather than relying on arms control. Each of the authors has done so separately;[2] here we can only present an outline.

As regards offensive forces, the American people must begin by realizing that the Soviet Union has fielded new systems more rapidly than we, and thus, as it were, has skipped a generation on us. Americans have been *arguing* (some twenty years, now) about whether or not to purchase forces to try to strike Soviet silos in order to deter war by threatening Soviet reserve forces, and to limit damage to the U.S. In the meantime, while we have argued, the Soviets have *developed* a new generation of mobile missiles. Soviet silo-based missiles—if indeed there are any—would be fired in a first strike, and reserve forces would be mobile. Therefore, in order to perform their missions of deterring war and limiting damage to the U.S., our offensive forces must have not so much the combination of yield and accuracy needed to break silos, as they must have intelligence information comprehensive enough and timely enough to constantly keep track of Soviet mobile missiles. Along with this, they must have rapid automatic retargeting systems to keep our missiles constantly pointed at their ever-moving targets. The automatic, constant retargeting systems are not so difficult to build, but supplying them with the intelligence information is a real problem. Nothing in our hands today allows us to perform such a mission, and nothing is under development. There is no shortage of promising technical approaches to doing the job. But senior U.S. intelligence managers have committed the U.S. intelligence budget to continuing indefinitely with systems originally conceived to monitor a world characterized by arms control. We may expect to have the intelligence systems we need for the counterforce needs of the late 1980s and 1990s some five years after a radical shift in the intelligence budget. We believe that such a shift is long overdue.

Reliance on counterforce alone, however, is insufficient both militarily and morally. Because the U.S. will not and should not consider making maximum use of counterforce missiles through a first strike of its own, a U.S. that relied on counterforce would always be at a disadvantage vis à vis a Soviet Union for which "seizing the initiative" in warfare is virtually a religion. Given this, the U.S. has no alternative but to add a substantial anti-missile shield to its counterforce sword.

Such a shield need not be perfect to be perfectly effective. To begin with, it must provide doubt in the minds of Soviet military planners that a first strike on their part would prejudice the United States' ability to fight, survive, and win. Although no defense measure is likely to insure us against irrational, militarily meaningless attacks on populations, even a rudimentary anti-missile defense would begin to protect the American people against the collateral damage from Soviet missile strikes against U.S. military forces.

If a democratic government does not make an earnest attempt to shield the population against the terrible collateral effects of war, it cannot reasonably expect that population to support any military effort whatever or, for that matter, any serious foreign policy. The chief obstacle to building an anti-missile defense for the U.S. has not been a technical one. Rather, it has been the delusion that safety may be had through arms control.

The authors, however, recommend to the American people that it is past time to be sincere about arms control, i.e., to tell one another the truth that it has been a delusion, and to be serious about strategic defense—that is, to build a strategic defense now. Truth, however painful or awkward, must be our first line of defense.

Notes

Chapter 1

1. Comments of Henry Rowen at the conference "Explaining Soviet Compliance Behavior," Conference Digest, Center for International Security and Arms Control, Stanford University, February 14, 1986.
2. See the seminal article of that title by Fred Iklé in *Foreign Affairs* (Fall 1961).

Chapter 2

1. John W. Wheeler-Bennet, *Nemesis of Power* (London: MacMillan and Co., 1961), pt. II, ch. 2, passim; J. H. Morgan, *Assize of Arms* (New York: Oxford University Press, 1946), ch. XI, passim. For a contrasting point of view, see R. Staar, ed., *Arms Control: Myth Versus Reality* (Stanford, Calif.: Hoover Institution Press, 1985).
2. It is impossible to miss the parallel between these developments and those that occurred under the SALT I Interim Agreement of 1972. That agreement forbade the replacement of "light" missile launchers with "heavy" ones. The Soviets promptly began replacing launchers for the SS-11 missile with ones for the SS-17a and SS-19, whose capacity was, by various measures, four

to six times that of the SS-11. The Soviets called these new missiles "light."

3. Bernard Brodie, et al., *The Absolute Weapon* (New York: Harcourt Brace & Co., 1946).

4. U.S. Department of State, *Bulletin*, November 19, 1951, pp. 799–803.

5. Walter MacDougall, *The Heavens and the Earth: A Political History of the Space Age* (New York: Basic Books, 1985).

6. Jerome Wiesner, "Setting the Moratorium Record Straight," *New York Times*, January 3, 1986. This line of argument by Wiesner is typical of arms controllers who encourage public officials to enter into agreements regardless of how vague as "a first step," and then excuse the Soviet Union's breach of the agreement on the ground that it was indeed vague.

7. U.S. Senate, *Congressional Record*, September 8, 1961, p. 17531.

8. Ibid., pg. 17552.

9. Ibid., pg. 17524.

10. U.S. House of Representatives, *Congressional Record*, September 19, 1961, p. 19053.

11. U.S. Senate, *Congressional Record*, September 8, 1961, p. 17524.

12. Ibid., p. 17643.

13. Ibid.

14. Ibid., p. 17552.

15. Ibid., p. 17524.

16. Ibid.

17. U.S. House of Representatives, *Congressional Record*, September 19, 1961, p. 19059.

18. Ibid., p. 19061.

19. Ibid., p. 19063.

20. U.S. Senate, *Congressional Record*, September 8, 1961, p. 17610.

21. Ibid., p. 17527.

22. U.S. House of Representatives, *Congressional Record*, September 19, 1961, p. 19054.

23. U.S. Senate, *Congressional Record*, September 8, 1961, p. 17520.

24. Ibid., p. 17526.

25. Ibid.

26. U.S. House of Representatives, *Congressional Record*, September 19, 1961, p. 19058.

27. Ibid., p. 19102.

28. U.S. Senate, Hearing before the Committee on Armed Services, 92nd Congress, 2nd Session, June 28, 1972. Military Implications of the Treaty on the Limitations of Anti-Ballistic Missile System, p. 287.

Chapter 3

1. Alexander Dallin, et al., *The Soviet Union and Disarmament* (New York: Frederick A. Praeger, 1964), p. 22. For example, Alexander Dallin, arms controller and respected expert on the Soviet Union, contends the Soviets believe that "the risks of a 'forward' policy, combined with an arms race, are greater than the price of postponement of such communist victories as would require Soviet involvement abroad or could precipitate such involvement." His statement was made after Soviet military actions in Berlin and Hungary, after the Soviets placed missiles in Cuba while they were effectively nursing a war against the U.S. in Southeast Asia, and prior to actions in Angola, Afghanistan, and Nicaragua.

   Thomas Schelling, *Arms and Influence* (New Haven: Yale University Press: 1966), pp. 224–25. Schelling, another noted proponent of arms control, described the position in which leaders of adversarial nuclear weapon states find themselves in an "awful position." He says that the leader is "a victim of a special technology." Schelling's assumption is that both sets of leaders share the same motivations and moral propensities.

2. Schelling, ibid.

3. *New York Times*, November 14, 1969.

4. Raymond Garthoff, "SALT I: An Evaluation," *World Politics*, 1978, pp. 1–25.

5. Ibid.

6. V. D. Sokolovskii, *Soviet Military Strategy*, Third Edition, ed., Harriet Saft Scott (Stanford Research Institute, 1975).

7. John Newhouse, *Cold Dawn: The Story of SALT* (New York: Holt Rhinehart Winston, 1973).

8. But to succeed in what? We will consider that at greater length in ch. 4. Note also that one part of the U.S. military, the Air Force, at this time was pressing the U.S. government to be allowed to build heavy ICBMs. Thus it did not wish to de-legitimize heavy ICBMs in the course of the negotiations, but to use the Soviet SS-9s as a lever for obtaining similar missiles on the U.S. side.

9. McGeorge Bundy, *Papers to the Annual Meeting of the International Institute of Strategic Studies*, September 6, 1979.

10. Robert McNamara, *Blundering Into Disaster* (New York: Pantheon, 1986), p. 35.

11. Quoted by De Sutter, "Arms Control Verification" (Ph.D. diss., University of Southern California, 1983), pp. 173–80.

12. Ibid.

Chapter 4

1. Henry Kissinger to U.S. Congress, June 15, 1972.
2. Ibid.
3. Ibid.
4. Ibid.
5. Ibid.
6. Henry Kissinger, *The Economist*, February 3, 1979, pp. 17–18.
7. *On Watch* (New York: The New York Times Book Co., 1976), p. 319.
8. Raymond Garthoff, "SALT I: An Evaluation," *World Politics*, October 1978, pp. 1–25.
9. Quotation in George Will, *The Washington Post*, February 22, 1979, p. A-17.
10. U.S. Department of State, *Bulletin*, October 2, 1972, p. 37d.
11. *Documents on Disarmament*, May 26, 1972, U.S. Arms Control and Disarmament Agency (Washington: GPO, 1973), p. 211.
12. Testimony before the Senate Armed Services Committee, June 28, 1972; *Military Implications of the Treaty on Limitations of Anti-Ballistic Missile Systems and the Interim Agreement on Limitations of Strategic Offensive Arms Hearing*, 92nd Congress, 2nd Session (Washington: GPO, 1972).
13. U.S. Senate, June 28, 1972.
14. U.S. Department of State, *Special Report No. 46*, May 1972.
15. Paul Nitze, *Foreign Policy* (Winter 1974–75) p. 140.
16. U.S. Department of State, *Special Report No. 46*, May 1972.
17. "Arms Control and Disarmament Agency Study on U.S. and Soviet Strategic Capabilities through the Mid 1980s," August 17, 1978, as in *Documents on Disarmament 1978*, (Washington: GPO, 1980), pp. 512–520.
18. Ibid.
19. U.S. Department of State, *Special Report No. 46*, May 1979, p. 1.
20. Ibid.
21. *Arms Control and Disarmament Agreement*, 1982 Edition, U.S. Arms Control and Disarmament Agency (Washington: GPO, 1982).
22. Ibid.

Chapter 5

1. Caspar Weinberger, speech, Department of Defense, December 1984.
2. U.S. Department of Defense, *Annual Report, Fiscal 1980*, p. 81.

3. The White House, *Report of the President's Commission on Strategic Forces*, March 1983.
4. Senators James McClure and Joseph Biden, 1983. Senator Malcolm Wallop, "Soviet Arms Control Violations—So What?," *Strategic Review* (Fall 1983).
5. The "first generation" of Soviet ICBMs, consisting of the SS-6, was deployed beginning in 1960. The second generation, the SS-7 and -8, began in 1963. The third, the SS-9 and -11, began circa 1967. The fourth, consisting of the SS-17, -18, and -19, began in 1975. The fifth, including the SS-24, -25, and -26, began in 1984.
6. This radar is located some 2,000 miles from the Soviet border in the direction of which it faces. Hence it is an uncontestable violation of Article VI(b), which forbids new, large radars except on the "periphery" of national territory. However, as we have pointed out, location on the periphery does not hinder performance of an ABM battle-management function.

Chapter 6

1. Editorial, *New York Times*, June 16, 1981.
2. Department of State, Bureau of Public Affairs, *American Power and Purpose*, no. 388, April 17, 1982, p. 3.
3. Ibid.
4. U.S. Department of State, *Arms Control for the 1980s*, July 14, 1981. Clearly, in Ronald Reagan's words regarding the Soviet Union's motivations on arms control, political expediency and utopianism coexist with passionate anti-communism. But, for whatever reason, Reagan has chosen not to impose discipline on his own contradictions even in the face of the challenge—both domestic and international—of Soviet violations of arms control agreements.
5. Paul Nitze, *The Washington Post*, April 16, 1985.
6. Immediately after March 23, 1983, the President's Science Advisor, George Keyworth, and his National Security Advisor, Robert MacFarlane, convened a panel of senior government Research and Development personnel to define the technical character of what ought to happen as a result of the President's SDI speech. Following Keyworth's and MacFarlane's guidance, the panel defined SDI as a long-term research project that *by definition* excluded using currently available technology to

defend against currently existing Soviet missiles. Rather, it focused on hypothetical defense against hypothetical threats after the year 2000.

7. Ibid.
8. U.S. Department of State, *Special Report No. 151*, August 5, 1986.

Chapter 7

1. *New York Times*, January 16, 1986, p. 1.
2. Ronald Reagan, "Address to the Nation," October 13, 1986.
3. Mikhail Gorbachev, speech on Soviet television, October 23, 1986.
4. Ronald Reagan, Speech to the Nation, October 13, 1986.
5. Ibid.
6. *New York Times*, November 19, 1986.
7. *New York Times*, February 1, 1987.
8. *New York Times*, October 15, 1986.

Chapter 8

1. Albert Carnesale et al., *New York Times*, February 3, 1987. Carnesale et al. received a $180,000 grant from the Arms Control and Disarmament Agency to do a study of "The Lessons of Arms Control." This article is the distillation of that effort.
2. Malcolm Wallop in U.S. Senate, *Congressional Record*, July 1, 1980; May 13, 1982; and July 15, 1983. Also idem, "Opportunities and Imperatives of Ballistic Missile Defense," *Strategic Review*, (Fall 1979). Angelo M. Codevilla, "How SDI Is Being Undone from Within," *Commentary* (May 1986); idem, *While Others Build* York: Free Press, 1987).

The Publication Review Board of the Central Intelligence Agency reviewed this book for security and cleared it for publication on June 24, 1987.

Index

"ABM Capabilities of Modern SAM
Systems," 128–29
ABM launchers, 76
ABM radar, 76–77, 128, 161, 168, 180
Congress on, 94, 203
treaty limits on, 74–78, 95, 128–29,
161, 180
ABM Treaty (1972), 94, 173, 193, 202, 203
anti-missile defense and, 6, 11, 74–78,
113, 118, 127–30, 136, 170–71, 188
SDI and, 161, 162–69
Soviet proposal and, 186, 188, 190,
192–94
violations of, 10–11, 47, 65, 128–30, 157
Absolute Weapon, The (Brodie), 93
Adair, Ross, 34
Adelman, Kenneth, 153
aerospace industry, 160
Afghanistan, 151
Africa, 106
"After Detection—What?" (Iklé), 131–32
Agreed Interpretation D, 6, 11, 130,
162–64, 168, 202–203
Agreement on the Prevention of
Nuclear War, 88
air defense system, 22, 128–29, 163, 183
Air Force, U.S., 102, 105, 141–42
airspace, 24
Allen, Richard, 137
Allied Control Commissions, 17
anti-city terror weapon, 53
anti-missile defense, 12, 51, 117, 203,
205–206
ABM Treaty and, 6, 11, 74–78, 113, 118,
127–30, 136, 170–77, 188
Reagan administration on, 159–60,
168, 176–77, 181, 193, 195–96
Salt negotiations on, 55, 71, 100,
104, 143
SDI and, 170, 175, 192
Soviet proposal and, 169, 182, 185–86,
189–90
in Soviet strategic defense, 7, 10, 65
See also Counterforce missiles
anti-RV mission, 75, 76, 77
armed forces, U.S., 22, 102, 105, 140–42
Armed Services Authorization Act
(1983), 154
Arms Control and Disarmament Act
(1961), 14, 24, 42, 193, 200
Arms Control and Disarmament
Agency (ACDA), 29–30, 36, 101–102,
203
noncompliance and, 63, 128, 153
Arms Control Association, 147
Arms Control Impact Statement, 119
Army, U.S., 105, 161
ASAT program, 146
Ashbrook, William A., 33
Asia, 106, 186
Atlanta Constitution, 29
atmospheric testing, 26
See also Nuclear testing
aviation, in World War II, 18

Backfire bomber, 85, 112
Baldwin, Stanley, 132
ballistic missiles, 36, 75, 130, 180, 189
    Reagan administration and, 148, 177,
        183, 194
ballistic missile submarine, 114, 115
"Ban the Bomb" campaign, 26, 27
Baruch-Lilienthal Plan (1946), 20, 21,
        22, 24
basing modes, 105, 118–19, 120
battle-management radar. 76–77, 113,
        128, 180
    See also Krasnoyarsk, radar at
Bear bomber, 112
Belgrade Conference of Nonaligned
        Nations, 32–33
B-52 bomber, 85, 102, 182
Biden, Joseph, 122–26
biological warfare, 107–108, 151, 153
Biological Warfare Convention (1972),
        107–108, 126, 151
Bismarck, battleship, 18
Bison bomber, 112
Blundering Into Disaster (McNamara), 56
Bolton, Frances, 35
bombers, 141–42
    in balance of power, 112–13, 182
    Salt II and, 80, 85, 102, 123–24
    B-1 bomber, 85, 141–42
Boston Globe, 29
Brezhnev, Leonid, 106
British Committee of the Interior, 41
Brodie, Bernard, 19–20, 93
Broomfield, William S., 31
Brown, Harold, 100, 119, 121, 135
Brzezinski, Zbigniew, 100, 112, 185, 186
Bumpers, Dale, 201
Bundy, McGeorge, 56
Bureau of European Affairs, 136
Bureau of Political Military Affairs,
        137–40
Burt, Richard, 137–40

Cambodia, 153
cameras, high-altitude, 63, 74–75
Carter, Jimmy, 106, 153
    balance of power and, 98, 100, 148
    MX missile and, 120, 141, 142, 182
    Salt II and, 135–36, 199, 201
Carter administration, 38, 39, 93, 98–100,
        106, 147
Central Intelligence Agency (CIA), 37,

        45, 101, 123, 126, 153
Chaffee, John, 201
Chamberlain, Joseph, 41
Champaign-Urbana Courier, 29
chemical weapons, 107–108, 151, 153
Churchill, Winston, 18
compliance, 111–12, 185
    Reagan administration on, 151–52,
        156–57, 168–69, 173, 179, 201
computer software, 77
"Concurrent Testing of ABM and Air
        Defense Components," 128
Congressional Record (September 8,
        1961), 29
conservatives, in America, 10, 123, 157
Conte, Silvio, 32–33
Cooper, Robert, 159
counterforce missiles, 10, 26, 100, 123
    balance of power and, 117, 124, 181,
        183, 204–205
    Reagan administration on, 142, 143,
        147, 160
    Salt I on, 55, 96–98
    Salt II on, 102, 104, 105
    Soviet proposal on, 188, 189, 192
    See also Anti-missile defense
cruise missiles, 102, 112, 114
    in Reagan administration, 136, 142, 148
    Salt II and, 80, 85, 105, 123
cruise warheads, 183
Cuban missile crisis (1962), 43, 44–45, 63

Daniloff, Nicholas, 175, 187
Davis, Bernard, 121–22
defense budget, U.S., 9, 33, 105, 185
    under Eisenhower administration,
        23, 26
    military power and, 51, 116
    under Reagan administration, 137,
        140–44, 146, 155
Democrats, 158, 187
deployment, 68, 145, 147, 182, 185
    ABM Treaty and, 6, 77–78, 188, 203
    in Europe, 148, 149, 179, 189, 191
    Reagan administration on, 119–20, 195
    Salt II and, 83, 126
détente, 105–106
directed-energy weapons, 161, 163
disarmament, 33–36, 107–108, 195
    in Eisenhower administration, 22–23,
        26
    verification and, 20–21, 59–60, 104

Eagleburger, Lawrence, 151
early-warning radar, 77
economy, Soviet, 46–47
Eisenhower, Dwight, 23–27
electro-optical detector, 161
encryption, 68, 69
    treaty compliance and, 80, 82, 83–84,
        103
    treaty violations and, 125, 168, 199
Environmental Impact Statement, 119
"escalation dominance," 44
Eureka College speech (1982), 146, 149
Europe
    American commitment in, 116, 183,
        184, 191
    disarmament in, 128, 186, 187–88, 189,
        195
European governments, 116
    Reagan administration and, 136, 140,
        148–49, 152, 164
    in World War II, 5, 16–18, 19
"extended deterrence," 44

FB-111 bomber, 124
Fedora, 107, 108
"Fencer" bomber, 124
first-strike capacity, 52, 54, 102, 112–13,
    116, 135
Five-Year Defense Program, 140
Flat Twin missile engagement radar, 113,
    128
Fletcher Panel, 170, 185
Ford, Gerald, 99, 106
Ford, Henry, 29
Ford administration, 94, 142
Foreign Affairs, 131
foreign policy, U.S. 19, 42, 136–37
Functionally Related Observable
    Differences (FRODS), 80–81

Garthoff, Raymond, 49–51, 55
Gates, Thomas, 35, 51
Gelb, Leslie, 147
General Advisory Committee (GAC),
    153, 156
Geneva, 152, 186, 187, 193, 194
Geneva Convention (1925), 151
German Social Democrats, 136
Germany, 16, 17–18, 41, 132, 136
Glitman, Maynard, 152
Gneisenau, battleship, 17, 41
Goldwater, Barry, 30, 32

Gorbachev, Mikhail, 46, 184
    at Reykjavic, 60, 116–17, 175–82, 187–88,
        190–96
Gorizia, cruiser, 41
G.P.U., Soviet, 60
gravity bombs, 102

Haig, Alexander, 137–40, 150, 151
Hecker, Guy, 119
Hesburgh, Theodore, 29
Hiroshima, 19
horizontal shelter basing mode, 119
How Much Is Enough? (Smith), 57
Humphrey, Hubert, 29, 30–31, 32,
    150–51

ICBM launchers, 79, 80, 90, 96, 103, 124
ICBM system, 7, 102
    balance of power and, 90, 113–15, 119,
        187–88
    intelligence and, 63, 65
    Interim Agreement and, 71, 72–73
    Salt I limits on, 50, 55–56, 96
    Salt II limits on, 79, 80–81, 98–99, 103,
        104
    Salt II violations and, 122, 123–24, 126,
        127
Iceland, 116–17, 175–82, 187–96
Iklé, Fred, 8, 131–32
imaging satellites, 63, 64–67, 68
intermediate-range nuclear force (INF)
    (1987), 46, 116
intelligence, U.S., 7, 37, 50, 88, 123
    ABM Treaty and, 76, 77–78
    monitoring by, 60–74, 112, 156, 185,
        194, 198
    Salt II and, 79–86
    Soviets and, 46, 127, 180–81, 205
    treaty violations and, 7, 112, 153, 190
    See also Telemetry
intelligence satellites, 24, 63–64, 74
    deception and, 69, 70, 178
    ICBM and, 71–72, 73, 127
    treaty compliance and, 36–37, 118, 179
interceptor missiles, 75, 77, 113, 128
intercontinental missiles, 24, 71, 75,
    136–37
Interim Agreement (1972), 71–74, 88, 90,
    96, 97
interim restraint, 157–59, 171–73, 193, 200,
    201, 202–203

intermediate-range missiles, 71, 116, 148, 187–88, 189, 191
Italy, 41

Jackson, Henry, 94
Japan, 16, 17, 18
Javits, Jacob, 33–34
Johnson, Thomas F., 33
Johnson, Lyndon, 57
Johnson administration, 56
Joint Chiefs of Staff, 38–39, 47, 136

Kahn, Herman, 200
Kampleman, Max, 116, 152
Kennedy, Edward, 94
Kennedy, John F., 27, 29–30, 57, 63
Kennedy administration, 37–38, 43
Keyworth, George A., 159
KGB, 107
KH-11 series, 64
Khrushchev, Nikita, 32, 44
Kissinger, Henry, 112, 120, 137, 153
  on military superiority, 88–91, 92, 93–94, 107
  Salt I and, 38, 95, 143–44, 198–99
Kolyma gold field, 60
Krasnoyarsk, radar at, 10, 128, 154, 168
  intelligence and, 65, 157
  radar quality at, 129, 180

Laos, 151, 153
laser weapons, 160, 161
  ABM Treaty on, 78, 130, 163
  Soviet testing of, 113–14, 180
launchers, 114
  intelligence and, 7, 68, 70
  Interim Agreement on, 71–73, 76–77, 96
  Nixon administration on, 90–91
  Reagan administration on, 147, 148, 177–78
  Salt II on, 79–81, 83, 97–98, 102, 103, 124–25, 127
League of Nations, 17
Leahy, Patrick, 155
Lehman, Herbert, 29
Lessiovski, Victor, 107, 108
liberals, in America, 3, 29–30, 32, 41–42
  in Congress, 44, 123, 144, 157
"limited nuclear options," 97
Lippmann, Walter, 18–19
Locarno Pact, 17
London Naval Agreements, 17–18

London Naval Treaty (1936), 41
long-range missiles, 27, 105, 123, 188
Lubyanka prison, 60
Luce, Henry, 29
Luftwaffe, 41

McClure, James, 122–24, 126, 153
McCone, John, 23
McCormack, John, 36
MacFarlane, Robert, 159
NcNamara, Robert, 51–54, 56–57, 96, 103, 141, 185
"margin of safety," 176
Marines, U.S., 105
Mark-12A warhead, 98, 115, 124
Marshall, George C., 32
Maskirovka, 7
Mathias, Charles McC., 144
medium-range missiles, 186
Mideast, 106
Midgetman missile, 182
military budget, U.S. See Defense budget, U.S.
military program, Soviet, 9, 23, 47, 86, 111, 122, 151
  See also Strategic forces, Soviet
military program, U.S., 5, 23, 105, 140–44, 157, 170
  See also Strategic forces, U.S.
military superiority, 23, 38–39, 131, 151, 196, 204
  in Kennedy administration, 30, 43–45, 63
  Kissinger on, 88–91, 92, 93–94, 107
  political attitude toward, 14, 27, 28, 33–34, 47
  in Reagan administration, 5, 113, 148–49, 176
  Salt II and, 101–102, 143
  U.S. restraint and, 51, 52–53, 56
"Mimimum Deterrence," 200
Minneapolis Star, 29
Minuteman missile, 72, 96, 97, 182
  balance of power and, 53–54, 91, 117, 147
  in Kennedy administration, 28, 43, 51
  in Reagan administration, 120, 142
  Salt II and, 98, 105
Minuteman III missile, 98, 147
MIRVed ICBM system, 80–81, 98, 103, 123–24, 126
MIRVed launchers, 80, 103, 123–24, 142

MIRVed SLBM system, 80, 123, 142
missile guidance system, 76, 77, 97, 123
missile programs, 24, 38, 46, 52–53. *See also specific missiles*
mobile launchers, 105, 118, 127
"mobile missile problem," 127
mobile missiles, 72, 160, 186, 205
  survivability and, 117, 118
  violations and, 123, 127, 128
"Mobility of ABM System Components," 128
Moscow, 37, 94, 113, 175
Moynihan, Daniel P., 154
MRV warheads, 54
Mussolini, Benito, 41
Mutual Assured Destruction (MAD), 100, 103, 125, 200
  U.S. policy and, 57–58, 96–97, 115–16
MX basing options, 118, 120
MX missile, 115, 117–21, 123
  in Carter administration, 98, 100
  in Reagan administration, 141–42, 144, 145, 147, 182
  Salt II and, 103, 105
MX warheads, 120, 142
mycotoxins, 153

Nagasaki, 19
National Geographic, 60
National Security Council, 93, 153, 164–65
National Security Decision Memorandum, 242, 99
national security policy, 11, 12
Navy, U.S., 105
North American continent, 22
North Atlantic Treaty Organization (NATO), 116
Newhouse, John, 55
New York American, The, 60
New York Times, 29, 108, 140–41, 150, 195, 203
Nitze, Paul, 1–11, 152, 157, 193
  Salt I and, 50, 99, 198–99
Nixon, Richard, 56, 88–90, 107
Nixon administration, 88–90, 95
North Dakota, 94
NS-20 guidance system, 97
nuclear testing, 25–27, 32, 53, 124, 146
  ban on, 78, 108, 195
  Soviet proposal and, 188–91, 192
  telemetry and, 82, 83, 125, 179

nuclear war, 29, 198, 206
  military strategy and, 50, 51, 52–53, 55, 73
  Reagan administration on, 143, 150
  Soviets and, 125, 178–79, 184
nuclear weapons, 15, 51, 96, 108
  after World War II, 16, 19–21, 22
  Eisenhower administration and, 23, 26
  Kennedy administration and, 30–31, 44–45
  Reagan administration and, 5, 149–50, 191, 194–95
  Soviet proposals on, 176–77, 178–79, 181–82, 184–86, 188

oil prices, 106
on-site inspections, 60, 179, 180
On the Beach (Nevil Shute), 27
Oppenheimer, J. Robert, 62
optical pointer-tracker, 78, 130
optical radar, 161
optical sensors, 161, 163

Pacific Ocean test range, 73, 80
particle beams, 130
Pawn Shop radar, 128
"peaceful coexistence," 44
peace issue, 5, 17, 36, 41
  military power and, 38, 51
  politicians on, 28–29, 31–33, 105–106, 131, 132
  Soviets and, 180, 184, 189
"peaceniks," 27–28
Pechora-class radar, 129
Pentagon, 57, 102, 119, 160
  in Reagan administration, 140, 142, 143, 155, 162
Pershing II missile, 136, 148
Pershing warheads, 183
Plesetsk, 126
PL-5 missile, 122
Polaris-Poseidon submarine, 28, 51, 171, 172
Politburo, 16, 107
Poseidon missile, 51, 53, 146
Poseidon submarine, 28, 51, 171, 172
Poseidon warhead, 40-KT, 146
Presidential Decision #59 (July 1980), 99–100
Presidential Report to Congress (August 5, 1986), 172
Proxmire, William, 31–31, 33

PSI Soviet silos, 124
Pushkino ABM battle-management
    radar, 128

radar, 22, 65, 73–74, 113
    ABM system and, 76–77, 128, 161,
        168, 180
    noncompliance and, 10, 111–12,
        128–29, 154, 157
    Salt II and, 80, 83
railroad basing, 100, 105, 118
Reagan, Ronald 137, 140–41, 143, 147–82,
        199–200, 202
    balance of power and, 38, 46, 119–20,
        121, 146
    Salt II and, 27, 83, 135–36, 201
    Soviet proposal and, 116–17, 184,
        186–96
    treaty violations and, 9, 10–11
Reagan administration, 5–6, 9–12, 39,
        120–22, 135–96, 200–203
Reagan-Gorbachev meetings (1986),
        175–96
rearmament, 136–37
reconnaissance photos, 63–64, 69, 76,
        80, 85
Regan, Donald, 187
Republicans, 141, 158, 186–87
retargeting systems, 123, 124, 205
Reykjavik, 60, 116–17, 175–82, 187–96
Rogers, William, 48
Rostow, Eugene, 153
Rowen, Henry, 6–7
Rowny, Edward, 152
Russell, Richard, 32, 34–35, 36, 144

Sakharov, Andrei, 184
Salt I Treaty (1969), 22, 49–50, 106,
        120, 137
    balance of power and, 38, 48, 54, 55,
        88–97, 117
    failure of, 143–44, 159–60
    Reagan administration and, 135, 136,
        147, 157, 177
    Salt II and, 100, 101–102, 103, 198–99
    verification of, 58, 73, 79, 81, 83
Salt II Treaty, 191, 196, 201–202
    Carter administration on, 38, 120
    Reagan administration on, 136,
        138–40, 142–43, 157, 171–73, 177, 179
    START and, 147, 148

terms of, 79–86, 97–98, 100–106, 135,
        159–60
    violations of, 27, 122–26, 199
SAMOS photo-reconnaissance satellite,
        63, 64
SAM radar, 128
San Francisco Chronicle, 29
satellites, 24, 27, 46, 63–69, 74
    See also Intelligence satellites
SA-3 missile, 85
SA-12 missile, 76, 113, 128–29
Scharnhorst, battleship, 17, 41
Schlesinger, James, 97
Scoville, Herbert, 147
Scowcroft, Brent, 120
Scowcroft Commission, 120–21, 145
secrecy, Soviet, 24
seismic readings, 78, 108
Senate Intelligence Committee, 154–55
Senators' letter (January 1987), 201
SH-4 interceptor, 113, 128
SH-8 interceptor, 113, 128
Shultz, George, 158, 164, 177, 187
signals intelligence, 63, 67–69, 74
silos, 114, 120, 179
    counterforce and, 51, 100, 112, 124, 142
    intelligence and, 70–71, 72, 73
    Salt II and, 80, 83, 98, 103
    vulnerability of, 53, 118, 204–205
SLBM launchers, 80
SLBM system, 80, 123, 142, 187–88
Smith, Gerard, 37, 96, 121
    Salt I and, 50, 95, 143, 198–99
Smith, Wayne, 57
socialism, 43
Sofaer, Abraham, 163, 164
Sokolovskii, Marshal V. D., 52–53
Soviet arms control proposal (1986), 186,
        187–90
Soviet Communist Party, 47
Soviet Defense Council, 107
Soviet Foreign Ministry, 187
Soviet Military Power(1983), 124
Soviet Military Power (1986), 112
Soviet Military Strategy (Sokolovskii),
        52–53
Soviet Noncompliance (February 1986),
        128–29
space program, 24, 25
Sparkman, John, 32, 35
Sputnik (1957), 23, 24

SR-5 interceptor missile, 128
SS-7 missile, 53, 96
SS-8 missile, 53, 96
SS-9 launcher, 97–98
SS-9 missile, 53–54, 55, 91, 97, 117
SS-11 missile, 96, 112
SS-13 missile, 96, 112
SS-16 missile, 7, 112, 125–26, 127
SS-17 missile, 98, 99, 103, 112, 142
SS-18 missile, 112, 182
    in Reagan administration, 142, 146–47
    Salt II and, 82, 98, 99, 103
SS-19 missile, 98, 99, 103, 105, 112, 142
SS-20 launcher, 7, 127
SS-20 missile, 71, 112, 148, 183
SS-24 missile, 123, 186
SS-25 missile, 123, 126, 127
Standing Consultative Commission
    (1978), 76
Stanford University, 6
START proposal (1982), 147–48, 149,
    178, 187
Stassen, Harold, 23–24
State of the Union address (1980), 100
Stealth bomber, 182
Strategic Air Command, 118
Strategic Arms Reduction proposals
    (1982), 145
Strategic Defense Initiative (SDI), 183,
    185, 203
    military strategy and, 5, 6, 11, 182
    restraints on. 159–62, 163, 166–67
    Soviets and, 146, 175–76, 186, 190,
        192–93, 194–95
Strategic Defense Initiative
    Organization (SDIO), 161, 163
strategic forces, Soviet, 21, 43–44, 49, 62,
    124–25
    balance of power and, 50–53, 112–14,
        120, 204–205
    intelligence and, 7, 66, 123
    Salt II and, 101, 104–105
strategic forces, U.S., 11, 42, 88
    balance of power and, 50, 111–16
    Reagan administration and, 6, 9–10,
        119, 145, 147–48, 200
    restraint on, 51–52, 55, 56–57, 159–61,
        191–92
    Salt II and, 101, 102, 105, 124–27,
        172–73, 202
    See also Anti-missile defense

Strategic Forces Modernization Plan
    (1981), 141–42, 147–48, 158–59
"strategic nuclear superiority," 44
Strontium 90, 25
submarine-launched missiles, 43, 102,
    114, 115
submarine launch tubes, 43, 70–71, 83,
    102, 103
submarines, 102, 112–13, 114
    under Kennedy administration, 28, 51
    under Nixon administration, 90
    under Reagan administration, 147,
        171, 172
surface-to-air missile system, 76, 113,
    128–29, 180
survivability, 95, 102–103, 104–105,
    117–18, 120

technical revolution, 37–38
telemetry, 67–68, 69, 168
    missile tests and, 74, 82, 83–84
    Salt II and, 80, 104, 125, 199
Third Reich, 17
Threshold Test Ban Treaty (1974), 78, 107,
    108
throw-weight, 72–74, 81–82, 105, 122–23
Time, 29
Tirpitz, battleship, 18
Titan missile, 96
Tower, John, 152
toxic weapons, 107–108, 151, 153
Treaty of Versailles, 16, 17, 132
Trident missile, 102, 115, 123
Trident I missile, 123
Trident II missile, 115, 123
Truman, Harry, 21–22, 23, 59
Turner, Stansfield, 65

unilateralism, 157, 186
United Nations, 20, 151
U.N. Security Council, 20
U.S. Congress 16, 58, 187, 199–200
    on ABM Treaty, 193, 203
    on defense budget, 137, 141,
        143–44, 145
    military power and, 29–35, 38, 92,
        119–21, 158–59
    Salt I and, 95, 97
    on Salt II, 172, 201–202
    SDI and, 146, 162, 192
    Soviet proposal and, 176–77, 188, 189

treaty violations and, 37, 122–26,
    153–56, 204
U.S. Consititution, 193, 199–200, 202
U.S. Department of Defense, 9–10,
    112, 193
  in Reagan administration, 136, 137,
    140, 157, 178, 181
  on Salt I, 50, 54, 55
  on Salt II, 101, 124
U.S. Department of State, 11, 101,
    119, 187
  in Reagan administration, 136, 137,
    143, 170, 178
  on treaty violations, 151, 153, 157
U.S. House of Representatives, 146
U.S. Senate
  Reagan administration and, 121, 158,
    187, 188, 193, 199–202
  on SDI, 146, 192
  on treaty violations, 122–26, 153,
    154–55
Utgoff, Victor, 93
utopianism, 19, 20, 149, 190
U-2 reconnaissance plane, 24, 63

Van Cleave, William, 50
Velikhov, Y. P., 7, 193
verification, of arms control agreements,
    21, 130, 132, 152, 184
  Congress and, 34, 37
  Nixon administration and, 88, 107
  Salt II and, 58–64, 84–86, 100, 103, 125
  Soviets and, 25, 48, 118, 179, 185, 191
Verification Panel (1969), 88
Vietnam, 45, 92, 153
violations, of arms control agreements,
    5, 107, 131–32, 204
  intelligence and, 7, 61, 78
  Reagan administration and, 9–10, 11,
    151–58, 179, 184
  Soviets and, 111–12, 115, 127, 189, 190
  Truman administration and, 21, 59

World War II and, 17, 18, 41
  See also specific treaties
Vladivostok Accords (1974), 94

Wallop, Malcolm, 116, 152, 185, 186, 194
warheads, 73–74, 95, 114, 115, 183
  counterforce and, 54, 112–13, 117,
    124, 181
  Interim Agreement and, 71, 96, 97–98
  Reagan administration and, 120, 142,
    146–47, 148, 177–78
  Salt II and, 79–81, 82–84, 102–104
  Soviet proposal and, 186, 187–88
wars of national liberation, 43–44
Washington Naval Agreements, 16
Washington Post, 29, 157
weaponry, 20
  arms control process and, 15, 42, 111,
    117, 131
  intelligence and, 61, 127
  political process and, 16, 28, 57
  Reagan administration and, 10, 160–62
  technology and, 4, 25, 115
  See also Anti-missile defense;
    Bombers; Laser weapons; Nuclear
    weapons; Warheads
Weimar Republic, 17
Weinberger, Caspar, 137, 141, 159
  military predicament and, 10, 113, 181,
    183
Wiesner, Jerome, 25, 27
Wiley, Alexander, 31
"window of vulnerability," 119, 120, 182
World War II, 16–19, 41, 67

Yankee-class submarines, 112
yellow rain, 151, 153
Yom Kippur War (1973), 108

"zero option," 148–49, 178, 187–88, 191
Zorin, Valerian, 60, 84, 179
Zumwalt, Elmo R., 92